THE
GOLDEN BOY

SPORTS
ILLUSTRATED

JUNE 23, 1958

America's National Sports Weekly

25 CENTS
$7.50 A YEAR

JACKIE JENSEN

WHEEL HORSE OF
THE RED SOX

THE GOLDEN BOY

A BIOGRAPHY OF
JACKIE JENSEN

George I. Martin

Foreword by Curt Gowdy

Peter E. Randall Publisher
Portsmouth, New Hampshire
2000

DEDICATION

As Frank Brunk said in his eulogy, "Jack married Katharine, and this single event probably was a major turning point in his life. What a beautiful person, and Jack revered her. She brought out a latent talent in Jack that few people know about. Jack finally found peace and serenity and purpose of life on a farm in Virginia with Katharine."

After years of knowing Katharine, beginning with our common love for the martial arts, and progressing to the publication of Jack's biography, I have come to understand and appreciate what Frank means.

I am most pleased to dedicate this biography of Jack E. Jensen to my friend Katharine Jensen.

Peter E. Randall Publisher
Box 4726
Portsmouth, NH 03820-4726

Distributed by University Press of New England
        Hanover and London

ISBN 0-914339-86-9

FOREWORD

One question I am constantly asked is, "Who is the best all-around athlete you have ever covered in your sports announcing career?"

What a toughie! When you think about broadcasting the exploits of Williams, DiMaggio, Mays, Musial, Spahn, and Kaufax in baseball; O. J. Simpson, Jim Brown, Starr, Namath, Joe Green, Bradshaw, and others in football; Bill Russell, West, Baylor, Oscar Robertson, Cousy, and Bird in basketball: these are all gifted athletes who concentrated on one sport but probably could have played more.

Early last decade, Bo Jackson was the talk of the sports world by taking on two big-league sports, half the season with the L.A. Raiders and a full baseball year with the Kansas City Royals. It is almost an impossible task in these long-season, high-pressurized sports times, but Bo was an athletic wonder.

Jackie Jensen was an athlete of the 1950s who could have duplicated Jackson's two-sports ability. The first time I met him was at the New York Yankees spring training camp in 1950. I was Mel Allen's partner on the Yankee broadcast team, and Jensen's contract had been purchased by the Yankees from the Oakland minor-league team of the Pacific Coast League. One of Jensen's teammates on that Oakland team arrived with Jensen at the Yankee camp—a young second baseman named Billy Martin.

Jack was wearing a blue V-necked sweater—I remember that distinctly—and I was struck by his clean, blond good looks and quiet manner. We started a friendship that lasted until his death.

I wound up as the Red Sox announcer in 1951, while Jackie was traded by the Yankees to the Washington Senators. We were reunited when Jack came to the Red Sox in 1954. He was made for Fenway Park. The Sox had made a very intelligent trade. Jensen was a right-handed pull hitter with power. The left-field wall, "the Green Monster," proved to be an inviting target. Over a five-year period he led the major leagues in runs batted in.

Jack was not just a one-way player. He could run, steal a base, played the big right field, and possessed a strong, accurate arm. He ran hard, threw hard and hit hard. He played hurt—had a terrific work ethic. Jack was team man all the way, and he was named Most Valuable Player in 1958.

We used to talk a lot about football. I knew he had been a star on the California Rose Bowl team and had set numerous Cal records. He gave up his last year of eligibility at Cal to play pro baseball. I talked to his college coach, "Pappy" Waldorf, about Jack's football ability: "He would have been a real star in the NFL," Waldorf told me. "He had everything—power, speed, toughness— and he could come out of the backfield and catch the ball with those good baseball hands of his." Other NFL coaches and scouts never doubted that Jensen would have been a pro great.

When Jensen's Red Sox career was over, he went back West. His fear of flying probably shortened his baseball-playing days. He and his first wife split. He had a solid second marriage, with a gal who stood by him all the way.

When the Red Sox had their first Old-Timer's game in 1982, Jackie was there. He had moved to Virginia and was coaching at Fork Union Military Academy. He was fifty-one years old. Ted Williams was standing by me and pointed to Jensen. "Look at that Jensen," Ted remarked. "What great shape he is in! He looks like he could play fullback in the Rose Bowl tomorrow."

While in Boston for that Old-Timer's game, Jack told me had been elected to the prestigious Bay Area Sports Hall of Fame. He wanted me to come to San Francisco and be his presenter.

"Jack," I said, "you should have one of your old Rose Bowl buddies or California friends be your presenter. It makes more sense."

"No, I want you," Jack said. "You always understood me. I trusted you in Boston."

What a wonderful compliment. I told Jack I would be there in San Francisco the following February. Two months later that summer, Jack died of a heart attack. I could not believe it. To me he was indestructible.

That winter I joined his widow Katharine at that Hall of Fame banquet in San Francisco and made my presentation talk. I remember John Elway sitting in the audience right in front of the podium. I pointed at Elway, who had just wound up his football-baseball career at Stanford, and remarked that he had the same difficult choice that Jensen had thirty years before of which sport to play.

Jack had a shining quality to him. He was a great-looking guy who attracted attention on the field and off. He became one of my favorite friends of all the athletes I had the privilege to broadcast. He just may have been the best all-around athlete I covered.

CURT GOWDY

ACKNOWLEDGMENTS

I express my special appreciation to Katharine Jensen for her invaluable help—providing me with essential narratives and contacts; access to diaries, scrapbooks, photographs, and yearbooks; and, of course, permission to write an authorized biography of Jackie Jensen. A thank you to Dave Beronio for his permission to use his sketch of Jackie.

I am especially grateful to Curt Gowdy for writing the Foreword, and I thank those people who corresponded with me, granted me interviews, or provided help in other ways:

Conrad Aasen
John J. Adams
George Anderson
Paul B. Andrew
Floyd Baker
Anthony M. Barnise
Bill Blair
Milt Bolling
Zoe Ann Branham
Robert W. Brown
B. Frank Brunk, Jr.
Woody Burris
George Bush
Ken Cohen
Stan Cornett
Jim "Truck" Cullom
Jim Darby
Ike Delock
Harry Dracket
Joan Dracket
Glenn Dufour, Jr.
Ray Ehlers
Boots Erb
Dave "Boo" Ferriss

Ron Fimrite
Bob Garsen
Dick Gernert
Sid Gilmore
David Gough
M. Graesch
Jim Herndon
Linda Householder
Sid Hudson
Tom Jable
Bill Jensen
Jan Jensen
Jay Jensen
Jon Jensen
Marge Jensen
Robert Jones
Ralph T. Kerchum
Dick Larner
Paul Laxalt
Tinsley Lockhart
Frank Malzone
Lillian Meglan
Bob Milano
John C. Miller

John S. Najarian
Warren Nelson
Bob O'Dell
Norma Olsen
Bert Padell
Lyle Palmer
Gary Powers
Vic Presco
Phil Rizuto
Roy Sharp
Lloyd Shikany
Guy Shipler
Irving Stone
George Sullivan
Jack D. Swaner
Gregory Thys
Mickey Vernon
Virginia Welch
Mike White
Garff B. Wilson
Kenneth Whitescarver
John Zajc

CONTENTS

INTRODUCTION

"Playing baseball is not so much for fun, but for business." So spoke Jackie Jensen in 1977, as coach for the Cal Berkeley Bears. He himself had stopped playing the sport he loved in 1961, not only because the fun had gone out of baseball, but also because of his fear of flying and family problems. This outstanding athlete was, after all, subject to the same feelings and fears others have.

"Jack's story really began *after* he quit baseball." Jay Jensen was speaking in the living room of his home in Reno, Nevada, just moments after showing off his most prized possession, his father's World Series ring. Jay was the proud son whom reporters had heard say, "This one's for you, Dad," just before he hit a home run in a local championship game the day after he had heard of his father's death.

What makes Jackie Jensen's life intriguing even after he left baseball is his character. He was a modest man. One day, when being complimented by a reporter for hitting a home run out of the ball park, Jackie replied simply that the wind had helped it. He was well respected by his fellow players and fans for the dignity he brought to the game and to his life. As Paul Laxalt remarked in an interview in his Senate office one day, "Jack was a gentleman jock."

Jackie quit professional baseball twice. The first time was in 1959, at the height of his career. He had been named an American League MVP, had appeared on the cover of *Sports Illustrated*, and had led the league three times in RBIs and in stolen bases or stolen base average. After having left the Yankees to play with the Senators, then the Red Sox, Jackie's name appeared twenty-six times in the record books among the top five players in various categories. Jackie returned to baseball in 1961, but despite a

1

respectable .279 batting average, with sixty-six RBIs and thirteen home runs, he quit at season's end.

As an All-American in football and baseball, Jackie Jensen went on to earn the distinction of being the only athlete to have played in baseball All-Star and World Series games, and football Rose Bowl and East-West games. He also had the enviable honor of having played alongside both Joe DiMaggio and Ted Williams.

But the real story of Jackie Jensen lies in how he handled adversity, how he helped others and others aided him, how he lived with difficult—often wrong—decisions, and how his character set him apart from other athletes. This biography follows Jack not only through his professional sports career, but also as he grew up during the Depression in Oakland, twice married and divorced an Olympic diving champion, plummeted from wealth to poverty, and finally found his niche as a tree farmer and a coach at a private school in rural Virginia.

Numerous times after a movie and a book appeared at the end of his baseball career, authors approached him about updating his biography. Jack's response was that his life was not over yet. Now, years after his death, his life can be put into perspective. During this era of bloated player salaries, inflated egos, and news accounts of athletes' illicit activities, it is time for the complete story of "the Golden Boy" to emerge from a bygone era.

PART ONE

1927–1950

In this picture taken around 1860, on the right is Peter Jensen Otte, Jack's great-great-grandfather. He and his son Jens Christian Pedersen (with the pipe) were both ferrymen in Gronsund, Denmark. Standing is Ole Sandvig Jensen, Peter's son, and sitting is Karl (Charlie) Jensen, who became a tugboat captain in San Francisco Bay after emigrating to the U.S. around 1880. Karl is the older man pictured below.

Pictured left to right are Jack's father, Wilfred, Grandfather Karl (Charlie); Jack's nephew Krist; and Jack's brother Bill.

Jack (carrying the ball) playing football in junior high school. Not long after this picture was taken, Ralph Kerchum made the 1942 recording of Jack stating his goals (see text in the appendix). The text was altered for the Dupont Cavalcade Theater film of Jack E. Jensen.

Jack was 16 at the time the photograph was taken by his guidance counselor and mentor Ralph Kerchum. Jensen had a naturally athletic build that was enhanced a few years later when he lifted weights in secret under the super-vision of Jack La Lanne during a time when football players were discouraged from weight training.

Jensen was a football, baseball, basketball, and track standout in Oakland High School, known as the "Pink Palace." Jack also wrote a school newspaper column entitled "Jensen Sez," and became the president of his senior class.

Jensen disappointed professional baseball and football scouts by his decision to join the Navy, following in the footsteps of his brothers and his sea-faring ancestors. He became a radioman, guarded mail runs, and taught German prisoners how to swim when he was not engaged in football, track, basketball, and baseball games.

Teammate Jack Swaner is pictured here with Jack (#36) on the Cal Berkeley field. In his book The Game of Football, *Lynn "Pappy" Waldorf said, "Jack Jensen…could change direction sharply without tipping off his intentions and with little loss of speed." Jack set records for Cal that lasted for decades.*

Zoe Ann Olsen pictured with Jack sporting his All-American sweater. Jack was ranked the best college fullback in the country, and he also became California All-American in baseball. He pitched against Yale and George Bush in the first NCAA championship tournament.

Zoe Ann Olsen was a champion in her own right. Here she is pictured on the left as the winner of the silver medal for springboard diving in the 1948 London Olympics.

Jack and Zoe cutting their seven-tiered wedding cake at the Athens Athletic Club. Over 1,500 people attended the wedding ceremony. The Jensens became known as the Golden Couple, and while some people thought they were the perfect match, others wondered if they could share the spotlight equally. World Wide Photos, Inc.

Area businessmen "weeping" at the loss of Jack Jensen from the Cal football team before a Rose Bowl Game as he decides to enter professional baseball.

Jack joined the Oakland Oaks as part of an agreement with the Yankees, who gave him the largest signing bonus baseball had yet seen.

Jack being congratulated by his fellow players, a team that included Billy Martin, who made fun of Jensen's fear of flying.

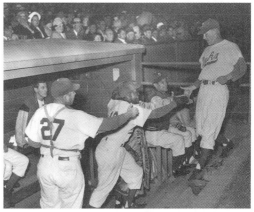

1

YOUTH

The golden-haired boy, just three years old, ambled behind his two older brothers along an inclined street between row houses in San Francisco. Halfway up the hill a lad came out of his home and angrily ordered the brothers to leave his neighborhood, for they had beaten him and his friends the day before in a rubber-gun fight in the brothers' backyard. Before his brothers could object, the three-year-old picked up a rock from the street and hurled it at the boy on the sidewalk, fortunately missing him but not the window of a '29 Chevrolet parked more than 150 feet away. The sound of breaking glass summoned a woman who proceeded to grab the lone boy by the ear and march him toward his parents' home, ignoring his frantic pointing at the little boy who couldn't possibly have thrown a rock that far. Jack Eugene Jensen had just begun to astonish people.

The parents of the boy with the twisted ear paid for the damage, and thirty years later he approached Bill Jensen and asked, "Where's your brother Jack? He owes me a windshield!" Yet he could look back with satisfaction to the time he had witnessed the early evidence of what had become one of the strongest throwing arms in baseball and football.

Jack was born in 1927, the year Babe Ruth set his record of sixty home runs and Lindbergh flew across the Atlantic. Interest in sports was booming. Attendance at baseball and football games soared, the number of golf courses increased threefold from the start of the twenties until their end, and basketball became the new craze. Jack would become a standout in all these sports.

The section of San Francisco in which the Jensens lived was an urban neighborhood of neatly arrayed houses with gingerbread trim, inhabited by blue-collar workers and their families. For a boy growing up in such an environment, opportunities were few and dreams were limited. However, in spite of ordinary circumstances, Jack Jensen had some advantages over many of his neighbors. As one of his close relatives declared, "Jack came from good stock."

Perhaps this explains how he was able to maintain dignity through a life plagued by misfortune and failure. Indeed, Jack had a good start in terms of genes: his grandfather Karl, born in Denmark, had been a robust, hardworking tugboat captain with Viking ancestry; Jack inherited his brawny stature, which would help him excel in sports. Brains complemented the Jensen family brawn; Peter Jensen (1886/1961), Jack's cousin, was the subject of the book *The Great Voice* (Havilah Press, 1975). Peter emigrated to California in 1910 and developed an amplification system that led to the production of the famous Jensen speakers, and he helped change the world of electronic communication, in which Jack would later become involved in the Navy.

Examining the environment into which Jack Jensen was born can help explain how his character was formed. The twenties were in high gear: jazz, cigarettes, movies, speakeasies, and flappers were popular, though frowned on by conservative Americans. However, also at this time museums, public libraries, music and art classes, the phonograph, and radio brought culture to millions. *The Jazz Singer*, the first major film featuring synchronized music and dialogue, appeared; Upton Sinclair published *Oil!*; and Sacco and Vanzetti died in the electric chair.

Much of the time when Jack and his two brothers, Bob and Bill, were growing up during the Great Depression, their father was not at home. Wilfred had grown up in the Bay area and for a while ran his own meat-cutting business on San Pablo Avenue, but after his business failed and a drinking problem later forced him to resign as a policeman, Alice Jensen divorced him just before Jack entered school. Wilfred was the fourth husband to become divorced from

Alice, who worked as a supervisor in a pharmaceutical plant in Oakland and a distillery in San Francisco. Alice was determined not only to support her sons, but also to chart the course of their lives. She worked overtime hours during a period when more than a million and a half people were unemployed. Mrs. Jensen refused charity, and one Christmas threw into the street a turkey that had been given to her by a member of her church.

For a while when their mother was working both jobs, the brothers lived with their father. They moved four times within a few years before their parents reunited; then they stayed with Wilfred again as Alice for several weeks took up residence in Reno to qualify for a divorce; and after this, they lived with her. Jack and his brothers helped put food on the table by fishing and picking fruit from the many trees that lined the streets. The family moved again several times due to financial constraints, the need for increased room as the boys matured, or Mrs. Jensen's desire to be close to work. She and her sons ended up in a house insistently provided by Jack's aunt Lillian Carter, whose fortune was the result of a lucrative lumber business.

Wherever Jack stayed, he readily found kids willing to group in vacant lots to play pickup baseball, at which Jack excelled and found instant popularity. Often Jack would join his brothers and friend Vic Presco for football at a grass lot across from the Grand Lake Theater adjacent to Oakland's Lake Merritt, even though Mrs. Jensen had forbade him to play because he had suffered a rupture in a previous game.

Jack would often say in later years that during the days of his youth he never realized how difficult things were for his parents, for he and his brothers would always find something to eat and games to play. When not playing ball, Vic and the Jensen brothers would fish at Albert's Mill. They got thirty-five cents for each perch they brought to the Chinese fish market, and they would then catch a trolley ride to the triple-feature movie house. Largely responsible for keeping his younger brothers out of trouble, Bill occasionally led them to the Safeway store, where they would ask for a discarded wooden crate to split up for kite sticks, beg wrapping paper from the butcher, steal some string, and make kites to fly high above Lake Merritt.

By the time the draft lottery began in 1940, Alice Jensen had remarried former husband Rex Williams; and Jackie, as he was being called by his buddies, was attending Oakland Junior High School. He became especially well known for his speed; One sportswriter said he ran so fast his feet hardly touched the ground.

By this time Bill had graduated, married, and joined the Navy after trying a year at a junior college, and Bob was a senior in high school. Jackie frequently visited Bill and his wife, Marge, at their apartment, which began a trend of sojourning at friends' and relatives' places over the next several years. Bill had helped to keep the boys and their mother together by working and by acting in part as a surrogate father to Bob and Jackie. However, another man, Ralph Kerchum, began to take a direct interest in Jackie's life. He recognized a boy who needed direction, who should be channeling his energies toward a goal.

At age fourteen Jackie entered the "Pink Palace," Oakland Junior and Senior High School. The imposing Gothic edifice rose four stories above the street, with embossed shields, busts, and wrought-iron lamps adorning the sides of the building as canine-like gargoyles overlooked the three large portals at the top of the huge outdoor stairways. However, Jackie was not to be deterred by the size of the school or the 450 students in his class (which would be divided into "high" and "low" sections, one group graduating in January and another half its size graduating in June). Here was truly a home away from home, a place for Jackie to develop and test his athletic potential.

Jackie signed up for every sport he could; and the baseball coach, a sixth-grade teacher named Charley McEvoy, told his friend Ralph, a principal and coach, 'I want you to meet this kid. He's probably one of the best athletes I've ever seen in my life." While interviewing every girl and boy from four Bay area schools coming into junior high, Ralph immediately recognized Jackie's potential: He was handsome, well liked, athletic, and intelligent. But what singled out Jackie even more were his idealism and his determination to make everything go well for himself. Jackie seemed to believe in a manipulative fate; if he tried hard enough, he could create the kind of world he wanted. People near him liked to identify with that feeling, hoping it would rub off—and usually it did. Those who befriended Jackie said decades later that they had become successful or developed fuller lives in part because Jackie's life had touched theirs.

Convinced Jackie would go a long way, and possibly foreseeing the day when Jackie might have to decide to leave school for professional sports, Ralph invited him to his home in Berkeley, where on March 20, 1942, he recorded an interview with the boy for posterity. The 78 RPM recording (a Recordio) was made on a device called a Phonocord, and the voices on the record still can be heard plainly a half-century later (a transcript is included in appendix A). Two months later Jackie would be given a player's membership card by the Central California Baseball Managers' Association in conjunction with his playing ball for a team sponsored by Maxwell's Hardware, and from that moment on Jackie's name appeared frequently in newspapers. One of many clippings read: "Striking three men out twice with the bases loaded, allowing three hits, fanning nine, and collecting two for three, including a home run with two on, was the work of Jack Jensen, so Milton's Hudsons scored a 5 to 3 win over Stark's Pharmacy. It was a case of too much Jensen..."

An April 17, 1943, newspaper article pictured opponent Bob Cummings tagging up as Jackie threw to first baseman Bill Menken:

> It was a "blooper" that robbed Oakland High School's Jack Jensen of a perfect game yesterday as the Wildcats blanked Tech 3 to 0 in the feature tilt of the four O.A.L. openers. Jensen's chance for a seat in baseball's Hall of Fame was spoiled by Bobby Cummings, Tech third sacker, in the first frame.... The fluke failed to rattle Jensen.... The Oakland

pitcher settled down and played the stingy role to perfection, sending 11 Bulldogs to the bench, via the strikeout route.

Another article read: "Jackie Jensen, the come-through artist of Oakland High, did his fans proud yesterday by whizzing through a one-hitter against McClymonds, sparking his team to a 13 to 0 victory."

Jackie became a sportswriter himself at Oakland High with a column titled "Jensen Sez" in which he commented on football and basketball and gave game run-downs in a "Jr. Hi. Sports" column; yet he continued to be a subject of others' attention, as seen in an article that provided an excellent portrait of Jackie at that time:

> At an election just held, the Junior High Boys' Athletic Council elected Jack Jensen to represent them in the junior school cabinet as commissioner of boys' athletics. Jack has made an excellent athletic record since entering Oakland Junior High two years ago. Every so often a boy comes along who is outstanding in all the four major junior sports—football, basketball, track and baseball. The new commissioner answers this description and is probably one of the best "all-round" athletes in any Oakland junior high school at present.
>
> Jack was born in Oakland [San Francisco] in 1927 and attended McChesney and Cleveland schools before entering Oakland. He is of medium height, weighs 135 pounds, has blue eyes and curly blonde hair. Although he likes all sports, baseball is his favorite. Upon graduating from high school he plans to enter college and then eventually enter the educational ranks as a physical education teacher and coach.

Ralph Kerchum continued to take an interest in Jackie. Ralph's guidance, a trail blazed by his older brothers, and his affable manner enabled Jackie to assimilate easily into the school's culture. Mr. Kerchum, astounded by Jackie's early muscular development, took several photographs of him in various bodybuilding poses with his shirt off on the roof of the high school, where students often would sun themselves. By age sixteen Jackie had developed outstanding proportions, and forty years later West Coast body builder Jack La

Lanne would be heard to say on national television that of all the people he had trained, Jensen had the best natural build. Before Jackie graduated, Ralph Kerchum had joined the Navy, as had Jackie's brothers, and it seemed inevitable Jackie would join, too.

Jack's 1944 yearbook, *The Oaken Bucket*, provided insight into his popularity. He was pictured with a gal in the center of a photograph of a Youth Council dance, and a friend named Ellen had written, "I still can't believe you and Janet aren't going steady." Jack had been elected to the senior-class presidency, and one comment of many was typical: 'You'll make a wonderful President because you are so truly great in character." Another friend had written "To a future all-American," and his note was more prophetic than he had known, as a Christmas card from Bob Ghirardelli found in Jack's 1945 yearbook illustrated:

> Congratulations, Jack, on attaining All American honors. You certainly deserve it and I know this is just the beginning of what the public will hear from you in the future. I'm proud of you, just as much as anyone, Jack, and I hope the New Year will bring you many more honors to which you are worthy. Merry Christmas and good luck.

2

Call to Service

With high school graduation approaching, Jackie had three main options: take advantage of the offers of baseball scouts to begin a career by joining the minors (he had already spent part of a summer pitching for the Cincinnati Red Rookies), enter college, or follow in the footsteps of his brothers and seafaring ancestors by joining the Navy. Like Jack London, who also had attended Oakland High School sixty years before and whom he greatly respected, Jackie followed his desire to sail, so he placed his name on a waiting list to join the Navy. Soon after graduation in January 1945, Jackie received notice from the U.S. Navy Recruiting Station in Oakland to report on Monday, February 26. By the end of March Jackie was in training with Company 106 of the U. S. Training Center in San Diego, and by May 7 was a platoon leader.

Jackie immediately became a focus of attention, not because of his former athletic kudos, but because he excelled in intramural sports as he represented his company. Selected to play in a tournament of seventy-two basketball teams, Jackie saw his team make it through many games to the final one, which, as was chronicled in a scrapbook clipping "...was typical of the intense competition prevailing in the recruit intramural matches."

An article on the championship games continues:

> For 40 minutes, the two teams matched basket for basket and at no time were they more than six points apart. At half time the score was tied up, 14–14.
>
> The second half was just as bitterly fought. A sudden scoring spree by Bill Lonquist and Jack Jensen gave the [defending]

champs a 26–20 edge with two minutes to play...Bill Lonquist and Jack Jensen got 10 apiece for the winners. The All Star team picked by officials found Jensen and Lonquist of [Company 106], at forward...

The final score was 27–26.

Few people know that Jackie, besides being a fast runner, was also interested in track. An early photograph shows him high jumping in junior high school, and those who knew him would not be surprised that Jackie was also on the Navy track team. With three others he shared the honor of setting a new San Diego track record of 55 points, and he tied Ed Cossett of Company 146 with a high jump of 5 feet, 6 inches.

As well as being a fellow football player of Jackie's in high school, John Najarian was the team shotputter. He recalled the time when Jackie walked over from baseball practice to where John was practicing. John was big—6'2" and 225 pounds—compared to Jackie's 5'10" and 175-pound stature. Eyeing the shot John held in his hand, Jackie said, "Show me how you do that."

John gave Jackie a quick lesson, then handed him the shot. Jackie hefted it, spun around, and on the first attempt threw it as far as John ever had! John would later play football with Jackie in college, and remarked that Jackie could have excelled at the decathlon.

Jackie had maintained a relationship with Margie Faunt, and it was rumored that the beautiful girl while a senior in Oakland kept her legs unshaven to discourage additional suitors. Many doubt to this day that Jackie and Margie became engaged, but a June 13, 1945, fading newspaper clipping pasted below a "Margie and Jack" heart alongside a photograph of the smiling couple in one of Jackie's scrapbooks says otherwise:

Miss Faunt Engaged to Jack E. Jensen

Mr. and Mrs. Albert E. Faunt of Oakland announce the engagement of their daughter Margie to Jack E. Jensen, seaman 2c, son of Mrs. Jean Williams of East 27th Street. The future benedict is stationed at Yerba Buena Island Radio School.

Both young people plan to attend the University of California.

The wedding date has not been set.

The engagement was announced to the immediate families on June 13.

In the scrapbook along with a copy of that announcement is an 8x10 engagement photo with Jackie in uniform, and below it reads: "Signed, sealed and approved: Margie Alice Faunt and Jack E. Jensen." However, the wedding was never to take place. Jackie could not get leave often enough, and Margie found it difficult to ignore those who were eager to lavish attention on her. She eventually sent Jackie a "Dear John" letter—something Jackie never wanted to discuss.

After basic training, Jackie had enrolled in radio school, hoping to set out on a communications ship. He continued his training even after the war ended in August, until mid-October, when he became a certified radio operator with a skill level of 20 cipher groups per minute. His rank jumped to RM3c, and Jackie was sent to Bremerton, Washington, to be a radioman on a destroyer, but found his ship to be drydocked. During that time the Navy had been looking over the records of its enlistees because it needed men at Farragut Naval Center for two important activities: guarding prisoners and playing football. As soon as officers realized Jackie's football record, he was offered the opportunity to transfer to Farragut. Jackie's brother Bill had been living at Livermore Naval Air Station, and told Jackie that he had enjoyed the experience of moving to such a station. It would offer all the food he wanted to eat, an Olympic-sized swimming pool, and a warm, indoor climate. So Jackie forsook his chance to travel the waves and transferred to the desolate base in Idaho. One of Jackie's official duties was to guard a mail run, but he also served as a lifeguard and even taught POWs how to swim.

An article in a fall naval bulletin read: "Jack Jensen S1c, slippery half-back, was a top football player in California during his high school days. He is 18, weighs 175 and is five foot 10." Jackie played primarily as halfback, alongside several players with college or semi-pro experience, and Stan Heath, who had been an All-State fullback in Wisconsin. Jackie got used to playing on snow-covered fields, and on Thanksgiving Day helped Farragut defeat Montana 18-13 in Missoula, where Jackie "skirted around left end and down the sidelines 60 yards to score untouched."

The December 1 game against the Fort Lewis Army team was held in Gonzaga Stadium in Spokane. Some profits from ticket sales were earmarked for the Sister Elizabeth Kenny Foundation of Minneapolis to fight polio. The drive was headed by Bing Crosby, who would one day offer Jackie a $75,000 signing deal and become a close friend. Before that last game of the season, Farragut had won six of its seven games, and its coaches had stayed with the team despite being eligible for discharge.

In the spring of 1946 Jackie joined the Farragut baseball team, and by the second game he had established himself as a notable pitcher, as newspaper clippings attest:

> Starting assignment on the mound will likely fall on Jack Jensen's shoulders, considering he is slated to be discharged soon and Coach Jim Leach is endeavoring to win as many contests as possible by using the rugged blond slab artist as often as he can.

Jensen Is Star as Sailors Win

> Pitcher Jack Jensen wasn't the whole ball game—but he was most of it yesterday as the Farragut baseball team defeated the Halliard Boosters 11 to 7 at Farragut. Jensen hurled five-hit ball, hit one homer and one triple to pace his team to victory.

When Jackie was discharged that summer, the local papers were eager to put his name back in print. One reporter wrote: "Jack Jensen, former all city gridder from Oakland, and rated by coaches in the Eastbay as the best prep back in the past 10 years, is out of the Navy and was an interested spectator at the Oakland-Uni clash last Friday."

The prospect of attending college loomed as Jackie thought of taking advantage of the GI Bill.

3

BERKELEY

After discharge from the Navy, Jack considered attending Stanford University, a private, prestigious, powerful school in sports. He knew he would have to depend on the GI Bill, an athletic scholarship, and possibly help from Aunt Lil to pay the high tuition costs; but despite Jack's abilities and opportunities to meet the financial challenge, the fact that he lacked one requisite high school credit and that his grades were only average prevented him from applying to that school unless he first attended a junior college. However, Jack was eager to play big-time college ball, and Stanford's rival, the University of California at Berkeley, accepted him. In 1946 college athletic programs were still under a wartime ruling; so his having played for Farragut did not hinder, but rather helped him make the '46 varsity football squad at Cal as a freshman with eligibility for all four years.

Football at most major universities had suffered during the war years, and the public was eager to be entertained and distracted by sports. Although Stanford abandoned football in late 1942, Cal (which had not had a winning season since 1938) kept playing. The school suffered a 4-6-0 record in 1943 and a 3-6-1 record in 1944. Many doubted the ability of Coach Frank Wickhorst, who had been promoted from assistant coach and had been an All-American at Berkeley fifteen years earlier. However, Cal had as good a chance as any college to produce a winning football team, and Jack was eager to be a part of that effort. Having grown an inch since high school and put on another ten or fifteen pounds while maintaining his muscular build and great speed, Jack was readily accepted onto the varsity team, for which 250 players had tried out. He and his teammates faced a tough season, and they found the fans generally intolerant of losers, as demonstrated by their having torn up wooden bleachers and set them afire after the disappointment of losing a final season game. By mid-September Jack was already catching the attention of sportswriters, who observed him standing out in practice sessions, and they predicted he would give the fans something to cheer about.

Sportswriters predicting Jack's greatness didn't exaggerate his potential. All eyes were focused on Jack as he touched the ball for the first time in Cal's game against Wisconsin. Jack caught a punt return, then ran 56 yards for a touchdown for the Golden Bears' only score in their 7–28 loss to Wisconsin. By the end of the season, despite a dismal 2-7 team record, Jack was being hailed as the finest fullback in the Pacific Coast Conference. He was selected to play in the Shriners' East-West Game—with a special suspension of the rule that only graduating seniors could play.

In his first year at Cal, Jack lived not just at home with his mother and stepfather, but also at his brother Bill's home and at the Alpha Delta Phi fraternity house. One of his football buddies, Boots Erb (whose father had been part of a Cal "Wonder Team") was Jack's friend since fourth grade. The two athletes were destined to develop a long friendship that would provide the basis for many good times, a little misadventure, and an eventual misfortune due to a misunderstanding.

As was the case during his high school days, Jack had things going his way: good looks, popularity, intelligence, and the omnipresent mentor Ralph Kerchum, who often took Jack home for dinner. Furthermore, Aunt Lil had become a guardian angel as she helped finance his education and taught him the social graces. Lil hosted frequent parties, often for the purpose of enabling Jack to mix with "good company" (although it would not be until years later that he would feel at ease in social settings). Lil also provided him with an Oldsmobile sedan, outfitted him with new clothes, and saw to it that he received golf, tennis, and skiing lessons during the odd times he was not involved in college activities. Her home was always open to Jack, who would visit just to relax and play with the cat. Beneath Jack's rugged exterior was a gentle, quietly intellectual person who would one day be late for his own wedding because he was making arrangements for the care of his cat.

Jack adjusted to university life remarkably well, and his feelings about Cal were revealed twenty years after he began attending Cal, when he was asked to give his impressions of the Berkeley campus. In *There Was Light—Autobiography of a University, Berkeley: 1868–1968*, edited by Irving Stone (see Appendix C), Jack had the following to say:

> The University of California is quite impressive to a freshman—at least it was to me. The beauty of the huge eucalyptus trees, Sather Gate, Wheeler Hall and other buildings seemed to loom as an unconquerable menace to my athletic career. But the warmth of its faculty reached me that first year when I needed it most. School had never been hard for me, just the idea that I had to apply myself, and the difficulty was that if I devoted most of the time to study, the many sports would suffer. The University nearly won, but baseball gave it a good fight.
>
> The memories of those years are filled with events that still hold a special place in my life. Not spectacular events, just University life, as it should be. The late night snacks with friends after hours of tough study, the excitement of Big Game week, the proms and double dates, the bull sessions at "Blakes" [a restaurant]—and finals!! These were important years that were peaceful. Everyone had had enough of war and thought it would be the last. No one wanted to fight anything, let alone the "establishment."
>
> I mention my feelings about the turmoil that has engulfed California only because it tends to destroy many of the wonderful images that have remained with me for over 20 years— images that I would wish for every freshman entering the University.

Jack entered Cal in the days when a player would crash

through a brick wall to please a coach, but when Jack himself returned to coach a quarter-century later, he painfully learned that the new generation of players would not hesitate to question a coach's authority, motives, and wisdom.

Jack unexpectedly found himself the object of attention when his image appeared in a series of photos in the October 15, 1946, issue of the *San Francisco Examiner*. A minor controversy involved whether Jack had intentionally grounded a ball while ostensibly throwing an incomplete pass. The linesman did not penalize Jack; subsequently, on the next play Cal scored its first touchdown of the game. A few days later the Golden Bears faced the formidable UCLA Bruins, a team that had beaten Oregon State 50–7, Washington 39–13, and Stanford 26–6! Jack found that evidently people were expecting much from him. On the first page of the *San Francisco Chronicle Sporting Green* he found a large drawing of himself next to Ernie Case of UCLA. When the game was played, Jack helped his team reduce their loss to only 6-13; and for the first time Cal fans realized that their team had some potential for success.

By November 23, 1946, Jack's image had been promoted to the status of a color photograph, when the *San Francisco News* ran a front-page picture of him as a "Frosh halfback, California's top threat," opposite that of Lloyd Merriman, "Touchdown galloper for Stanford." The game between the old-time rivals was the first meeting since 1942, and 80,000 fans were expected to fill the stadium. As expected the Bears lost 6–25. However, by season's end Jack had measured up admirably against veteran players: He also held the 1946 record for both rushing and passing, and he led the team in touchdowns and punt returns.

During all this excitement Jack naturally caught the attention of females, and off and on for about a year he dated Maxine Leach, who worked in Edy's ice-cream parlor in Berkeley, but it was while Jack had been a senior in Oakland High that he had first met his future wife. He had been a lifeguard at the Athens Athletic Club when he saw a fascinating blonde freshman with the physical presence and ability to match his own. Zoe Ann Olsen was a comely girl who had been strenuously training in swimming and diving since a toddler. As a teenager she held numerous swimming and diving records, including the All-American Springboard Diver championship in 1945 and 1946 (she would not only retain the title for the next two years, but also would be voted Outstanding Athlete of the Year for 1946–47). She most likely found in Jack a chance to focus her attention on something other than training, for her domineering stepfather forced her to train continually, which limited her social contacts and free time. In the environment of the swimming pool, Zoe found a pleasant diversion in the companionship of a soft-spoken, reserved collegian, himself an expert swimmer.

Zoe Ann's stepfather was a school principal, and her mother managed the municipal swimming pool in the summer. Although she often missed days at Oakland High School due to practice and meets, Zoe Ann maintained good grades. Jack became friends with Zoe's parents while he was in high school, but didn't really start dating her until he went to Cal. She would come to watch him at football practices, and he would go to her house to offer help with her studies and occasionally meet her in Kerchum's office. Zoe became quite outgoing, but Jack, despite his popularity, remained shy and did not socialize much; his idea of a good time was playing bridge at the fraternity house. Zoe later would say in an interview for *California Today, the San Jose Mercury News Sunday Magazine* (November 20, 1977), that she had been infatuated with Jack. They saw each other occasionally the next couple of years as Zoe Ann trained for the London Olympics, and she set her goals on attending Stanford and getting married. Their romance was to grow and even be encouraged by their parents.

Jack continued his own interest in swimming at Berkeley, and he was an excellent diver, as was attested to by Garff Wilson, professor and director of protocol, who happened to be present one day in the spring of 1947 when the Cal diving coach was giving lessons in the pool of the men's gymnasium. The coach went through different kinds of dives, asking his students to copy him, and "...there was one lad, blond, well built, who duplicated the dive every time almost perfectly." Dr. Wilson asked who the young man was, and was told it was "our football player, Jack Jensen."

That same professor found Jack enrolled in his oral interpretation of literature class in the fall of 1947, and decades later wrote that he had discovered Jack's readings to be "sensitive, controlled, illuminating, although his written papers were sketchy but perceptive." Also, Jack took an advanced class from Wilson, in the company of young actors from the Department of Dramatic Art, who smugly thought the jock would fall on his face. However, Jack surprised them all by an "articulate, sensitive, deeply felt' rendering of the speech Othello gives just before murdering Desdemona. Garff became a lifelong friend of Jack's, and one day it would be *his* turn to do a reading for Jack.

That spring Jack skipped the freshman baseball team and made the varsity squad, and he excelled just as he had in football. Cal led the conference with eleven wins and four losses and beat USC in the championship. Next to a photo of Jack (nicknamed "Marbles") in the '47 Cal yearbook was the caption: "Jack Jensen, fireballer deluxe, warms up to take over the mound chores. When he does the rubber, opposing batsmen quake in their boots and remain loose."

Jack began to make more lifelong friends at Cal through athletics, one of whom was Dick Larner, a roommate on away games (as a pitcher he defeated Santa Barbara State College with thirteen strikeouts). After their regular play in California, the Bears went on to beat Texas in the Western regional championship game, where Jack pitched against another All-American football player, Bobby Lane. They then prepared for the first NCAA intercollegiate baseball championship in Kalamazoo, Michigan, starting on June 27. Cal faced Yale, winners from the East. A little-known player named George Bush played first base. Thirty-five years later the vice-president of the United States would again meet Jackie Jensen, greeting him at the door of the White House and suffering mild chagrin when Jack responded to his question about remembering him from the Yale game, for Jack answered honestly that he could not recall much about Bush's playing during that series. The vice-president, however, did recall how Jack surprised the Yale coach, Ethan Allen, who had told the pitcher to walk the man before John Ramos, whom he saw in the on-deck circle. However, as planned, Coach Evans had Jack smugly walk out to the batter's box in place of Ramos at the last moment, and Jack subsequently drove in three runs with a triple to right center field, ensuring a Cal victory.

In the first of the two-game series, Jack also slammed the ball to drive in two runs and bring the score to a 4-4 tie before Cal finally won. Jack pitched the second day against Yale for five innings until he seemed to have worn himself out, as his team began losing its 7-2 lead. He had driven in a run with a double but had to retire from the mound after Yale started scoring on his pitches. Cal finally won tournament by a score of 8-7 and received the first NCAA baseball title. Jack's overall batting average for the entire season was a remarkable .385.

The Cal team held a victory celebration ceremony in Coach Clint Evans's room, and Jack continued to be the star of the show. His euphoria at having won was evident as he attempted to retrieve a canvas sign suspended from a rope attached outside the coach's room. Jack's teammates had to haul him back into the room as he dangled fifty feet above the ground trying to get the sign. However, his joy lasted only until the next day, when, on returning to campus, he learned some disturbing news. Although students had been permitted to miss final exams to attend the championship game, they were to have done so only with their instructors' permission and plans to make up the exams. Jack had not done that; he failed a course and was declared ineligible from sports until the credit was made up, forcing him to go to summer school.

The academic year ended on a note of optimism, however. The 1947 *Blue and Gold* yearbook featured Jack and his teammates in its football section. The caption next to Jack's photo read: "A shock of butter-colored hair and bright blue eyes could only belong to Jackie Jensen, speedy halfback and sweater boy of the Bears' varsity. East-West star and prize athlete, we look forward to watching him zoom down the field for several years."

While Jack was busy with baseball in the spring of 1947, a great change occurred at Cal. Athletic Director Brutus Hamilton conducted the first search for a football coach since 1931. Berkeley had the reputation for keeping coaches of all sports for extended periods (a tradition that lasted until Dave Maggard fired three coaches the same year in the later 1970s, one of those being Jack), but it was time to find a coach who could put Cal back in the winner's circle. Answering Hamilton's call was a former All-American at Syracuse University, assistant coach at the University of Kansas, Oklahoma A&M, and Kansas State College. A successful coach at Northwestern, Lynn O. Waldorf, affectionately known as Pappy, was selected with the stipulation that he begin a winning tradition.

Working with players in spring training, Pappy was skeptical about the potential of the squad, which had just suffered the worst season in sixty-four years. Little did he know that the missing element in the spring practice sessions was a man who would make history the next season for Cal.

That summer Jack played for Ben's Golden Glows, a local team, and became their star outfielder. Jack's football training seemed to be put to good use in a game against the Moffet Mantecas when he stole third base (with two men out) only because he hit the third baseman so hard that the ball was knocked out of his hands. The collision was deemed unintentional, but onlookers agreed that Jack needed to develop finesse. The Glows won the Oakland Tribune Tournament (where Jack had a home run, a double, a single, and pitched a 6-0 shutout over the Richmond Merchants); and they went on to capture the Northern California and the California semi-pro championship. During that time Pappy was reported as viewing films of the previous season's football games and was devising plans for starting Jack. He could only hope Jack wouldn't consider signing with a pro baseball team, as rival Stanford's Merriman had just done with the Cincinnati Reds.

The 1947 football season opened with a much-needed shot in the arm: Cal beat Santa Clara 33–7, then went on to win four more games. The previous year Cal had lost to USC 0–14—the only game in which they did not score–and perhaps either their overeagerness for revenge or nervousness caused the many errors on Cal's part that led to their defeat 14–39. A 13–7 win over UCLA set things straight again, followed by a trouncing of Montana 60–14.

This led to the biggest game of the season, the traditional contest against Stanford, which unfortunately had lost two players to fatal accidents in the summer and found star Jim Cox (later to play for the 49ers) out due to an ankle injury. The Bears were favored 10–1 over Stanford, and even Jackie made a rare quote, referring to the win over Montana: "We'll do the same thing to Stanford." Here was a chance to defeat the school that wouldn't accept him, one that Zoe Ann admired. In fact, Zoe would even wear Stanford's colors and root for them—which was about the only fault Jack could find in her.

Game day, nearly 85,000 fans packed Stanford Stadium for the fiftieth meeting of the two schools. It was one of the most momentous days of Jack's life. Paul Keckley and Jack's high school buddy "Big Naj," as teammates called Najarian, were unable to play. The lead changed several times before the final play with just seconds left. The Bears were behind 14–18, and it seemed to the Cal fans that they would lose in a huge upset. However, Jack often performed best under pressure, and he wanted to make up for an earlier fumble. Coach Waldorf put in injured Paul Keckley, who pleaded for action. Jack quarterbacked with a pass to Keckley, who went 65 yards for a touchdown, which, followed by another Jim "Truck" Cullom point, secured a 21–18 win. The pass play by Jack was second in terms of a single scoring yardage in Stanford/Cal history only to a 1902 punt return for 105 yards.

The Bears finished with a 10-1 record, and Jack received the Andy Smith Trophy (awarded yearly to the varsity player with the most Big C time). He entered the Cal record books for gaining 434 yards rushing and 271 yards passing for a 705 total, and for having the most interceptions on defense: seven, for 114 yards and a 16.3-yard average. His 80-yard pass play remained for decades the fourth longest in Cal history, and Jack ended up as the conference's third leading offensive player and was voted onto the AP's 2nd All-Coast Team. However, the 1948 season would prove to be even better.

In the first baseball conference game of 1948, the Cal baseball team got off to a great start with a 25–7 victory over St. Mary's, and they went on to place third in the Intercollegiate Baseball Association, with the team's overall batting average of .267 the first in league standing. Jack's best friend, Boots Erb, joined the team, but Jack was conspicuously absent. Cal was most serious about scholarship, and at the beginning of baseball season Jack was placed on academic probation, and could not practice. This made the propositions by some professional baseball and football scouts quite inviting, but the Cal coaches helped keep them at bay while Aunt Lil and Ralph continued to admonish Jack that he'd do better in the long run if he stayed in school. By then Jack had decided that of the two sports, football and baseball, he would like to make his living playing the latter. In spite of Jack's absence, Coach Clint Evans managed to have a pretty good season with twenty-one wins and thirteen losses.

Pappy Waldorf, fortunately, taught Physical Education 313, the Theory and Practice of Football, and he knew Jack was a physical education major (with a minor in speech). Jack had to get his grades up, and it just so happened that he was eligible to take the course, which consisted of not only lectures, but actual contact work as well. So Jack found himself as a "student" back on the outer reaches of the baseball field, but throwing a brown ball instead of a white one (the football team used the same field for practice when the baseball team wasn't around). As a result, Jack did bring up his cumulative average, for he had little difficulty obtaining the grade of A.

While Jack spent the summer digging ditches and cutting down trees to stay in shape, Zoe Ann traveled to London, where she took a silver medal in the Olympics. She was actually disappointed in her springboard diving performance because she had beaten the gold medalist in earlier competition. Contacted in London the day after the event, she reported she would turn down offers to perform professionally so she could compete again in the '52 games. Jack shared a transatlantic telephone call to Zoe with her mother, and Zoe told them both to tell her fans in the Oakland area that she regretted she hadn't won, but that she appreciated their support. Over the next few years Zoe Ann trained incessantly and would attend the '52 Olympics, but such would result in personal sacrifice.

By the fall of 1948 Jack's weight had leveled off to 190 pounds, and he was stronger than ever. About the time Casey Stengel became manager of the team for which Jack had always dreamed of playing, the New York Yankees, Jack was occasionally visiting the home of friend and fraternity brother Bill Laws. Bill's father, Brick, owner of the Oakland Oaks minor-league team, frequently entertained Jack with baseball stories, and naturally he had his eye on Jack: He thought Jack could do at least as well as another talented young man he had signed, Billy Martin.

That autumn Jack gave Zoe Ann his fraternity pin, and on being questioned about their relationship, Zoe responded, "We are only engaged to be engaged." As the season progressed, speculation at Cal abounded: Would Jack and Zoe be married within the year? Would Cal perform well enough to get a Rose Bowl bid? Would Jack make All-American? The pressure on Jack was mounting; he received a telegram September 23 from Robert Sibley, the Alumni Association executive manager, saying: "15,000 pairs of eyes will be watching [the opening game]." Jack didn't let him down—his first run down the field resulted in a 62-yard touchdown. Jack also made two other runs for 64 and 60 yards, respectively, to help Cal win 21–7 with Pappy's new T-formation.

Many across the nation favored Navy over Cal, and the $16,000 the Bears had to pay for the flight cross-country was the most they had yet spent for a contest. Jack was the only man not waving cheerfully as the team stood alongside a chartered plane as Zoe Ann said her goodbyes; this was possibly the first obvious indication that Jack feared air travel. The team won the game in Baltimore and continued a winning streak with great margins of victory until the battle with the defending PCC champions, USC. The largest number of Berkeley fans ever to see an away game helped fill the Los Angeles Coliseum. In the tunnel before coming out onto the field, Jack turned to a fellow player and said, "Well, if I'm ever going to make All-American, today should be the day." Jack had three interceptions on defense and scored both touchdowns, ensuring a 13–7 win!

The final game of the regular season against Stanford was a nerve-wracking win over their rival by one point. Two plays after Jackie ran with the ball from the Indians' 24 to their 7-yard line, Jack Swaner, who was later to become Jackie's lawyer, scored the only touchdown and set a school record of sixty-six points in one season. Reliable Truck Cullom then scored the crucial extra point. Jack himself set a record that day: He rushed for 170 yards in nineteen carries, averaging 9 yards per carry. Furthermore, the '49 Cal yearbook had this to say: "Spearheading the Bear drive was Jack Jensen who displayed inspired running, blocking, and punting. Jensen's fourth and thirty dash was only one of the high spots in the always exciting Big Game."

With the Stanford game over, the Bears realized their first undefeated and untied season since 1922, which enabled them to compete in the Rose Bowl game in Pasadena against Northwestern, the team Coach Waldorf had left only a couple of years before. After the Wildcats scored on a 73-yard touchdown run, Jack responded with his own scoring run of 67 yards by breaking five tackles, but in the third period he slipped on soft ground and pulled a thigh muscle. Northwestern went on to win 20–14, and to this day some argue that Cal would have won had not Jack been sidelined by that injury. Still, Pappy was praised. The 1948 yearbook was dedicated to him, and he and Jack received standing ovations by a welcoming crowd when they entered the men's gymnasium back home to appear in a "University Meeting."

Throughout the season Jack collected page after page of photographs and columns illustrating his exploits on the gridiron. Zoe

Ann was frequently pictured with Jack before and after games, but also with him at a cousin's wedding (Virginia Carter), on his return from the ten-hour plane trip from the Navy game (when she was given a symbolic game ball), at her mother's house where Jack gave Mrs. Olsen a Pomeranian as a Christmas gift, and at the Central Police League's Christmas party for Cal players at the Filbert Street Boys Club. Zoe also joined Jack for an interview on the San Lorenzo Sports Parade broadcast on radio station KLX at Pland's Villa.

However, Jack and Zoe had their separate times in the limelight, too. Next to an advertisement for the Swimsuit Manufacturers of America, which featured Janis Paige, Betty Grable, Esther Williams, and Virginia Mayo, Zoe Ann also appeared in a swimsuit. Just before she was to give a diving exhibition at the Elks Temple in Oakland, Zoe Ann was pictured about to be thrown into the pool by several of Jack's teammates prior to the Rose Bowl. Similarly, Jack was pictured with three young Northwestern women in swimsuits, and he also was photographed with four Cal coeds in one article and with Rose Bowl Queen Virginia Bower with her court of five comely females in another article.

Although many would have hoped otherwise, the Rose Bowl game was to be Jack's last football game until an alumni game in 1959, but some of the records Jack set—including rushing, punt returns, and kickoff returns—remained unbroken until 1975 (and his overall career rushing total average of 6.0 yards continued unbeaten beyond that). Also, Jack was featured in the October *National Police Gazetteer* and the November *Sport* magazine, was mentioned in *Collier's* and *Look* and was voted by Oregon State players to be the best all-around fullback they had ever played against or even seen. Jack also was ranked first in the PCC for total offense and rushing and second in the United States for rushing, and he was voted Top College Back by the Touchdown Club. Finally, some considered the greatest honor Jack's selection as the only fullback on the Players' All-American team, the choice having been made by 1,955 fellow players' votes. It was Jack's overall versatility that won him so many accolades: He was terrific at running, blocking, and passing.

Jackie the football player was still vividly remembered by teammates who met in August 1986 in Frank Brunk's office in Oakland, where Truck Cullom, Paul Andrew, and Dick Erickson joined Frank for a bull session inspired by the prospect of Jack's biography. Their words painted a picture of a dedicated, spirited player with a single intention: to do the best he could. Some of their comments attest to their admiration of Jackie: "He was the only guy I've seen who could fake at full speed. He was everything on defense as well as offense—he was the complete athlete as far as a football player's concerned"; "He was my best booster, though. He'd come off the field, and, hell, I'd fumbled three times in a spring practice that sealed my doom as far as Pappy was concerned. And it was an uphill battle after that to try to get to play, and Jack would come in off the field and say, 'Why don't you get Brunk out there?'"; "[He was] the best-looking—that's what bothered me. I enjoyed going around with him because I got the crumbs, which weren't all that bad."

Pressured by columnists throughout the fall and winter for any tidbits about Jack's and her intentions, Zoe Ann finally gave a reporter something substantial enough to warrant an announcement. In early February came the first verification that a wedding was indeed forthcoming: The *Chronicle* ran a photo of Jack with his arm around Zoe as they held a paper of some kind, and she was quoted as saying: "Jackie and I definitely are not yet engaged, but we intend to marry. I don't believe in high school girls becoming engaged. We will, in the near future, however, announce our engagement, and then set a date for the wedding. I'd like to be a June bride."

Zoe Ann further stated that she'd prefer to see Jack play major-league baseball rather than professional football. Her words were somewhat prophetic, for just a couple of weeks later it was reported that the injury Jack had received in the Rose Bowl game was not healing properly and would most likely keep him out of football in the fall. As soon as football season ended, Jack began asking his fraternity brothers to pitch ball to him so he could get ready for baseball season. Just as he had opened the football season with a great performance, so too he opened the baseball season—pitching ten strikeouts to give the team a 7–3 victory as big-league scouts watched from the stands. By mid-March the *Tribune* sports editor, Alan Ward, was right on target with his prediction (after talking to scouts) that Jack would be offered at least $25,000 to sign with a pro team, and that Jack wouldn't necessarily be a pitcher: "He's a natural hitter and has a strong arm. He seems to have everything a good outfielder needs."

A month later Jack was declared "Cal's No. 1 box office attraction" at a time when Pacific Coast Conference Commissioner Victor O. Schmidt visited Berkeley, declaring that organized baseball should not sign boys until after they completed their education. Coach Evans admitted he would be disturbed if Jack left the team, and a UC official went so far as to say that Cal football would suffer a $100,000 loss in profits if Jackie left.

A week later, in a *San Francisco Examiner* column, Prescott Sullivan wrote, "Jackie Jensen, one of the greatest all-around athletes in the University of California's history, has had offers from six different big-league clubs as well as two Pacific Coast League outfits–the Seals and the Oaks. There is little doubt that Jensen will accept the choicest of these within a month or so, almost certainly before another football season rolls around."

Highlights of the season for Jack included a home run against USC and a 3–0 game he pitched against UCLA, although the Bears lost two of three games against Stanford (the last one 1-3, though Jack walked only one man). He ended up with over a .300 batting average for the season. Jack's reputation as a slugger was greatly enhanced when he hit a ball at Cal that traveled to the street where someone had written on a wall there "535 ft." Many other wallops by Jack that would have been homers in the Seals stadium were caught by opponents who played on fields that did not have a home-run wall behind them. Coach Evans described Jack as having incredibly fast reflexes and the ability to adjust well to any kind of pitch. Although Jack exhibited a great intensity, he appeared almost mechanical when he played, and many in the crowd tried to interrupt his stoicism by heckling him. The more he ignored them, the greater their joy at trying to rile him, and they'd yell out "Golden Boy" and "All-American" to distract him. He didn't mind that too much, but he did admit it was difficult to handle those who shouted out things about Zoe Ann: for example, calling Jack "Mr. Olsen." The heckling would never stop entirely; and years later the day came when Jack climbed into the stands after somebody yelling something about Zoe.

As the spring season ended, salary figures were being thrown around like so many baseballs in a practice session. Jack had already been offered $20,000 to join the Seals, but reportedly just laughed at it. Several clubs were said to be reluctantly considering sums as high as $35,000, and Alan Ward said Jack was holding out for no less than fifty grand. Jack held all the cards, for he had several reasons not to sign: support for his college teams, a desire to complete his education, and another year to gain experience and attention through more playing time. The fact that Jack was named All-American in baseball, though, made the major-league teams—who depend on the box office—consider more seriously Jack's holdout offer.

4

Minors and Marriage

Near the end of Cal's baseball season things happened rapidly, virtually on a day-to-day basis. The *Tribune* reported that "seasoned scouts" regarded Jackie as the "finest diamond prospect in the country," and on May 22 the Pirates General Manager, J. Roy Mahey, called Jack with an offer difficult to refuse: a three-year contract in the amount of $75,000 (when most players were lucky to earn $15,000 a year) and the promise to match any other bid. Bing Crosby, the Pirates' vice president, had also called Jack and was rumored to have offered Zoe a movie contract to sweeten the deal. Perhaps, though, the Pirates did not want to risk arousing anyone's ire by snatching Jack away from college, or maybe they wanted him to gain a year's experience in the minors, for they stipulated he couldn't begin to play until the 1950 season.

While the media focused on Jack's abilities and opportunities, they hadn't considered something that was largely a private concern: Jack's family, or more particularly, his mother. Jack was worried about her lack of financial stability, since his brother Bill, who had been giving Mrs. Jensen a portion of his earnings as well as guidance, was married and had his own family to support. Also, Jack had been going steady with Zoe Ann for more than a year and was seriously considering marriage within the next few months — something that required money.

Still, there was the thought of staying at Cal another year; a college education would be something to fall back on in the event a professional ball career fell through, and Aunt Lil *had* advised against quitting school. But what was the purpose of college if not to prepare one for the working world or to broaden one's horizons and provide a general base from which various options could arise? In these respects Jack had already received most of what he needed from school, and he had put as much or more into Cal than he had taken out. As if to put off the decision temporarily, Jack accepted Brick Laws's offer to work out with the Oakland Oaks. However, the pressure was on, as the Pirates demanded an immediate decision.

Of course another option was pro football. A player might come close to earning $20,000 a year, but Jack was still carrying a goose egg on his right shoulder tackling a player in the Oregon State game long before. Furthermore, the leg injury he suffered in the Rose Bowl was a constant reminder of the fact that no matter how strong and in how good condition Jack might be, he could still be put out of commission easily. Most people knew baseball was Jack's favorite sport, and it seemed by its nature to cause fewer injuries; but had Jack been able to look ahead, he would have seen that his favorite team, the Yankees, would have seventy-one separate injuries in one season; and Jack himself was to be sidelined with an ankle injury in the not-too-distant future.

With so many options swirling around, it was time to ask for help, and Ralph Kerchum was only too glad to offer advice: Sit tight and continue to work with Laws, who wanted Jackie on his team as much as anyone else did. Sure enough, within a week a scout from the Yankees called Jack —a dream come true. They offered $40,000 for the first year of play, but, like the Pirates, didn't want Jack to start until the next season. Returning to Laws, Jack heard the owner explain that all major-league teams would require that he spend a year in the minors, and Brick proceeded to offer him something unprecedented by any minor-league team—a $50,000 bonus. The Yankees then made a similar bid, but Laws also agreed to forgive a $1,000 college loan Jack owed him.

However, one more inducement helped sway Jackie's decision. Considering that Jack was still a young man, it's understandable that he was influenced by an additional offer from Laws. An editorial from *Baseball Magazine* thirty-five years earlier sought to give advice to new ballplayers, but it's doubtful Jack had read it or would have been influenced by it: "It is, as a rule, a man's own business how he spends his money. But nevertheless we wish to call attention to the fact that many men do so in a very unwise manner. A glaring instance of this among baseball players is the recent evil tendency to purchase and maintain automobiles."

Well, Jack didn't have to purchase an automobile, just maintain one, for Brick Laws additionally offered Jack his choice of any car; and some believe this is what finally convinced him to leave college. Accepting the Oaks offer, Jack selected a new gold Cadillac convertible, although his brother Bill advised against it, saying, "Don't get a convertible; as soon as you get to New York, someone will cut open the top." His prediction would prove correct.

A convertible had its advantages, though—especially to a young man who didn't mind being seen with a pretty girl. Zoe Ann still had three weeks of school before graduation, and Jack knew just where to park on MacArthur near Park Boulevard to meet her for lunch. The young couple couldn't help but show off a little, as a good portion of the school would turn out in an attempt to catch them smooching.

Probably the first to know (after his family) that he had decided to leave Cal was his close friend and teammate Dick Larner. Jack asked him to accompany him to a jewelry store in Berkeley where he was picking up an engagement ring. Dick asked, "How in the world are you going to pay for this?"

Jack replied, "I'm going to sign a pro contract in the next few days; so I'll have plenty of money."

Indeed, in a couple of days Jack publicly stated that he decided to join the Oaks simply because he couldn't wait another year to play ball, and two days later the team (likely as a publicity stunt) announced it had insured his life for $75,000 with Lloyds of London.

The day of Jack's first game found him eager to please, yet very nervous; while friends from Cal looked on in the stands, Jack over-

threw a ball to the third baseman and it landed in the street. After
the game Jack was consoled by Truck, who agreed to ride with him
in Jack's Caddy. It wasn't long before flashing lights signaled Jack
to pull over. Walking to the car, the Oakland police officer recognized Truck and said to Jack, "I've been hearing about this new car
of yours, but didn't know it could go so fast." They shot the breeze
for a while, then went their separate ways. Jack was relieved he
didn't get a ticket.

At the demand of Coach Chuck Dressen, Jack sat on the bench
for a few games to get to know how the team functioned together,
but he was suddenly called out to replace an injured player near
the end of a game against Seattle. Although no balls were hit to
him, Jack saw plenty of action at the plate: He had three hits and
three runs in the twelve-inning game. However, Jack went into a
slump the next few days and became quite discouraged. The nadir
of the season was a game June 3 that found Zoe's father, Jack's
brothers, Ralph Kerchum, Brick Laws, and several friends in the
stands. Jack wasn't able to get a hit for the entire game, and in the
outfield for the last inning with the game scoreless, he waited for
the final out as the Seals were batting with a man on second. He
temporarily lost the fly ball in the lights, then was pleased to have
the ball land in his glove—only to drop it!

A smattering of boos added to Jack's utter disappointment in
himself as he trudged off the field, and only with the encouragement of fellow players and friends was Jack able to get himself up
for the next day's game, feeling fortunate that Dressen kept him in
the lineup. The next day made up for everything. Zoe Ann and
Jack's other loyal followers traveled to San Francisco to watch him
play against the Seals, and he didn't disappoint them: His first time
at bat he hit a home run, and he went on to have another homer
and a single to help the Oaks win 8–7. Later in the day he "officially" proposed to Zoe at an open-house party given by her parents on their twentieth wedding anniversary. In front of two
hundred guests he gave her a star sapphire mounted in diamonds.
The date of the wedding was set for the fall, largely because both

athletes would be so busy during the summer. Jack was faced with many games, while Zoe Ann planned on graduating from high school within the next two weeks, then leaving for a European exhibition and competitive tour sponsored by the Amateur Athletic Association. Zoe Ann also anticipated defending her national title in August at Tyler, Texas.

Years later Zoe revealed that immediately after the 1948 Olympics, her parents resumed their demands that she practice hours every day to the point of exhaustion (she even collapsed once in the middle of a dive), and finally she reached the breaking point. Wanting to gain some freedom from their control, she felt a way out would be to marry Jack. One night, after an argument with her mother and father, she telephoned Jack. He picked her up and they started their wedding plans. Additionally, Zoe faced one more decision: Stanford had offered her a scholarship, but, understandably, Jack wasn't too pleased with the prospect of his future wife attending the college that had turned him down and was traditionally Cal's rival.

Both athletes had much in common: good looks, intelligence, popularity, and a drive to excel. This last trait would be largely responsible for future problems, but to the eyes of the public, their engagement portended nothing but marital bliss. Dubbed "the Golden Boy" of the Golden Bears, Jack was the epitome of manhood; and Zoe Ann, who had beauty and brains, was the envy of every teenage girl. Accordingly, she became known as "the Golden Girl," and their marriage would become one of the greatest spectacles yet seen on the West Coast.

In June, Jack was named to the All-Coast baseball team by the National Collegiate Athletic Association, and a month later was named as a third-team All-American. Although it was known that Jack wasn't planning on graduating from Cal, he was still considered to be in the class of 1950, and on June 29, 1949, he was awarded a Certificate of Merit by the Big 10 Club of Southern California. The wording of the certificate explained Jack's selection:

The Big 10 Club of Southern California, composed of alumni of the Universities of Chicago, Illinois, Indiana, Iowa, Michigan, Minnesota, Northwestern, Ohio State, Purdue and Wisconsin, hereby awards its Athletic Certificate of Merit to Jackie Jensen of the University of California—Class of 1950.

In recognition of his splendid sportsmanship, athletic ability and unselfish devotion to the ideals of his Alma Mater. He shall henceforth be an honorary member of our Club and entitled to all of the privileges of membership as long as he continues to demonstrate loyalty to the traditions of the University.

It was rare indeed that such an honor go to a player not a member of any of those institutions! However, Jack rapidly found that he couldn't live off his laurels as he began his baseball career. He had to approach practice and games differently, for mistakes he made might well determine his future more than great plays or pitching strike-outs. Jack needed the pressure to play intensely, but too much pressure would burn him out. It became evident as time went on that what Jack lacked was consistency.

By mid-season of baseball Jack had signed with the Music Corporation of America to handle all of his business dealings outside of baseball, which started rumors that he and Zoe Ann would make a motion picture together. Another rumor was that Jack would write a football column, but, unlike during his high school days, Jack had little time or the desire to pursue that idea—he had to concentrate on his game. His batting average slipped to near .200, but with advice and encouragement from Coach Chuck Dressen, Jack learned how to handle the tough pitching he was getting. He raised his percentage past .250 and ended the season with nine home runs and seventy-seven RBI's, which helped compensate for the sixteen errors he had accumulated. Most important, Jack learned to live with his mistakes and to look ahead.

Jack received an early wedding gift when Brick Laws informed him that he and Billy Martin had been sold to the Yankees. Reactions to Jack's transfer to the big leagues were mixed. An article by Joe Wilmot referred to Jack as "the blond belter by way of the University of California who has been tabbed 'as fine a looking baseball prospect as there is in the country.'" However, another article was more realistic: "Out in Oakland in the Pacific Coast League this year he was not particularly sensational," but it went on to say, "Weiss [the Yankees' general manager], who is the Luther Burbank of baseball and knows how to accomplish things down on his farms, enlisted Jensen for the 1950 competition."

Meanwhile, preparations were under way for a wedding extravaganza as the sports pages took on the role of newspaper social sections. One writer was quick to note that Jack and Zoe Ann had picked up the thirteenth license on the thirteenth of October, and even the words of the license clerk were noted as she asked Jack for his name and occupation. Clerk Marian Edwards, as she handed Zoe the customary cookbook Almeda County gave out with certificates, said, "If you start married life with this, it's a cinch your husband will be the best fed ball player in the big leagues."

The wedding of the "Golden Couple" took place at the First Presbyterian Church on 26th and Broadway, Oakland, at 4 p.m., with Boots Erb as Jack's best man. The ceremony was performed on a Sunday, a rarity at that time. Zoe Ann at first wanted a small wedding, for she felt she had been getting too much attention lately. Ever since she was eighteen she had been featured in many magazines and even in *Who's Who*. By her wedding day she had won fourteen national diving championships and 150 medals and awards. Her constant practicing and ongoing appearances taxed her energy, so she envisioned a modest wedding. However, the public demanded more, and while Zoe was in Europe on an exhibition tour, Mrs. Olsen made elaborate plans. As Zoe Ann later explained: "When I finally got back home, I was exhausted. Most of the wedding was planned. Mother had chosen five sets of silver which she thought were nice and I picked one to be ours. The whole thing was like that. Jack and I had little to do with it. Most brides and grooms spend months deciding what they want. Not us. Everyone was so excited about our wedding that they took over, and we just kind of got swept along in the current. The wedding was entirely out of our hands. Everybody took care of it. It was meant to be. The fairy-tale romance. I had to move with the flow of the tide. It was out of my hands. I was moved along."

The media had a field day. Columnists offered gifts if they could get an exclusive story, and hotels offered to finance the honeymoon if Jack and Zoe would only wed in their city. UPS deliverymen said they had never before seen so many presents as the number delivered to the Olsens' home, and one policeman was assigned guard duty at the house while two squad cars were sent to escort Zoe Ann and her bridesmaids to the church.

It was unheard of in the late '40s to have photographs taken in church, but this wedding was the exception. Television cameramen jockeyed for the best positions, and the police had their hands full keeping order. Zoe Ann's close friend from grade school, Carol Froning, was her maid of honor, and other friends and a daughter of Aunt Lil served as bridesmaids. Jack's former teammates and fraternity brothers were groomsmen. His football buddies had just survived a grueling game the day before and came to the wedding with cuts and bruises; Frank Brunk had just run a 104-yard kick-off return to win against USC. Hundreds of people showed up for the wedding, spilling out of the Presbyterian church (which seated 1,500) and onto the street trying to get a glimpse of the Golden Boy and Zoe Ann, who looked stunning in her flowing white gown. After the ceremony, a police motorcycle escort, sirens screaming, led a procession of fourteen cars and the newlyweds in their convertible down the left side of the road to the reception at Athens Athletic Club, where, three hours later, they finally gave up trying to greet all the guests (400 were invited, but 1,500 came). The *Oakland Tribune* gave this account of the reception: "At the club, Zoe Ann and Jack received hundreds of friends standing before a large fireplace banked with magnolia leaves, greens and white chrysanthemums. Champagne punch was ladled out at one long table near the windows, hor d'oeuvres disappeared from a broad table centered with a swan sculpted from ice and filled with red red roses, and the wedding cake stood seven tiers high, on a third table flanked with a many branched gold candelabra."

Zoe Ann and Jack left the Bay area behind on their honeymoon, driving three thousand miles in ten days through Lake Tahoe, Reno, British Columbia, and Yellowstone. Two months later Zoe learned she was pregnant, and Jack wondered if he'd be able to be with her when she gave birth; he would be based in New York by then, and could be anywhere in the country when the time came. This was perhaps the first of many harsh realizations Jack would face as a professional baseball player. However, he took some comfort in knowing that Zoe's parents, Norma and Art, volunteered to be with her when the child was due. Zoe, on the other hand, faced the prospect of giving up her diving career. She had already forgone attending Stanford, but she had her heart set on finally getting a gold medal, in the 1952 Olympics.

Before Jack embarked on his major-league career, however, his college achievements were recognized by the San Francisco Touchdown Club, which gathered football greats from both Cal and Stanford. In a group photograph were Stanford players Ernie Nevers (class of '26), Bobby Grayson (class of '36), Jim Coffis (class of '38), and George Quist (class of '47). From Cal were pictured "Brick" Muller (class of '23), Arleigh Williams (class of '35), Sam Chapman (class of '38), and Jackie Jensen (class of '50). Sam Chapman had himself come out of Cal as a football hero before entering major-league baseball. Hired on the recommendation of Ty Cobb, he floundered for three seasons with the Philadelphia Athletics until he became skilled enough to become an asset to the team. Regulations then were that players such as he could not be sent to the minors for improvement. Jack, however, was under a new "bonus" ruling. It stated that any player who received at least a $6,000 bonus could be sent back to the minors from the majors, but would later be up for grabs from any club willing to offer $10,000 for the right to buy.

In a July 8, 1950, edition of *Collier's*, Chapman said, "If I had a kid brother, I wouldn't advise him to learn baseball in the big leagues." Hearing this, Jack responded, "If I had my choice, I'd like to come up through the minors. At least, I'd like another year at

Oakland. Well, maybe not Oakland, because it's awful tough in your hometown where they expect so much of you..."

Jack had his work cut out for him as a new husband, professional ball player, and soon-to-be father.

5

TRIED AND TRUE

Jack left the Oaks with only a fair batting average, and he had not performed as well as he had hoped in the field; so he feared the Yankees might send him back to the minors if he did not impress them. However, Casey Stengel had faith in Jack's potential and gave him a chance to prove himself. Furthermore, those with a good memory recalled that Joe DiMaggio hadn't been a star in right field playing for the Seals—it took the move to center field to bring out his talent. In the Phoenix, Arizona, winter camp, Stengel made the following pronouncement:

> I got a good look at Jensen, whom I had not seen in the Coast League. Jensen has tremendous possibilities. The boy showed me plenty at Phoenix. He can run. I mean RUN. He can throw. He looks like a hitter, even though his Oakland average for 125 games was only .261. He drove in 77 runs. Yes sir, you'll be very much interested in Jensen when you see him in Florida shortly. Perhaps the fact that the bonus rule was not killed, forcing us to keep Jensen, will work to our advantage in this case. I must receive him in camp as a fixture on our squad and handle him as a contender for a job. I'm delighted to do that.
>
> In short, I like Jensen.

Additionally, Stengel noted that Jack had a lot to learn: turning his back on long fly balls while running back for them from the shortstop position, practicing hitting of curve balls, and catching grounders. Perhaps the most notable thing Stengel said was, "All he needs is the experience," for this certainly proved to be true.

After the Yankees began working out in St. Petersburg, Florida, the *Oakland Post Enquirer* pictured Jack with a broad grin as he knelt alongside Joe DiMaggio and Billy Martin. At last Jack was finding himself in the company of Joe, a man whom he had idolized since he first saw him play in 1936 when Jack was just nine years old. However, on the other side of the continent, the *New York Daily News* pictured Jack swinging a bat, with the caption: "Jackie Jensen, Yank rookie outfielder and a bonus baby, sent in his signed contract yesterday. The ex-California U. All-American fullback probably will receive $25,000 for just warming the bench this year."

Thus having caught the readers' attention, the article went on to give additional figures: "Jensen had a $100,000 price tag on him when the Yankees outbid a half dozen other big league clubs and shook him loose from Oakland. The Oaks went overboard on Jensen when they outbid the majors last year and took Jackie away from his classroom. Oakland gave Jackie a $50,000 bonus, payable in three years. When the Yanks made the Jensen-Martin deal, which involved $175,000 in cash and four players, they agreed to assume part of the original deal for the powerful Cal gridder."

Some were quick to find fault with Jack, but didn't count on others making rebuttals. When critics sniped that Jack and Dick Wakefield drove Cadillacs into the training camp while DiMaggio shared a rented Ford with Joe Page, Art Rosenbaum responded, "We'd like to reassure the Messrs. Leiser and King that DiMaggio, for one, isn't out of automotive tailfins. His Cadillac sits on blocks in the garage at his Beach Street home, ready to roar to the golf courses next winter."

What many didn't expect was that Joe would become very supportive of Jack and a good friend despite the fact that the young Jensen was a little overeager during one of their first games together. Wimpy Jones, who was to become Jack's neighbor that year, later recalled one of Jack's favorite stories: "Here I am a rookie back there and Joe DiMaggio's playing center field and there was a real stiff wind coming over from right center, and the fly ball goes to right center, and here I am yelling to one of the greatest fielders in the history of baseball to 'Watch the wind! Watch the wind, Joe, watch it!'"

Meanwhile, Zoe Ann was not forgotten. Having moved to Florida with Jack, in a March interview she reaffirmed she was through with competition, and she expressed her first public sign of discontent as a professional ball player's wife:

> "I like being the wife of a big league baseball player, especially since the husband is Jack," she said, "except for one thing. It's terribly lonely. I find I have to be by myself so much. But the wives of the other players are kind and have taken me into their group. As a matter of fact, there are four others in the group expecting babies, so we have a bit in common."

In the same article, Jack answered a few questions, too, but he was described as not in good humor (possibly because he had just had to make a tax return amendment to give up more of his bonus to the IRS). Jack said that the players and Stengel treated him fine even though resentment could exist because of the bonus he was receiving. Two weeks later, across the country, Mrs. Olsen confirmed the news that because of Zoe's pregnancy, the Jensens would cancel plans to visit relatives in Denmark that fall. Plans were for Zoe Ann to stay in New York until after the baby was born, then fly West, but these plans were to change.

A former Rutgers coach who was scouting for another professional team later said that Jackie was ruined by football—was too tight in the shoulders. He further stated that football and basketball were incompatible with baseball; however, he realized that few colleges gave baseball scholarships, so many baseball players had to play those other sports. Yet the positive articles about Jack outnumbered the pessimistic ones. Titled "They're Saying Nice Things About Jensen," an article quoted James P. Dawson, a *New York Times* veteran as saying, "All surface indications now point to the probability that the graying skipper of the Yankees [Stengel] will find some outfield strength in the rugged activities of husky Jackie Jensen, all 'round ex-collegian in whom the club has an investment of $75,000."

Casey himself was quoted as saying the following: "I'm not fixing to ship Jackie Jensen to the Oaks, Seals or anywhere else. I'm taking him to camp and—sure as you're standing here—will wind up with a great player. Do you know he has the second best curve on the club? Only Reynolds has a better one. Jackie also has a slider and a fast ball, he can field his position well and might win his own game on hitting or base running. Jackie is our best base runner after DiMaggio, Rizzuto, Collins, and Berra. Yes, sir—tremendous possibilities."

Most people thought Jack would audition only for an outfield position, since he hadn't done much pitching for the Oaks, but Stengel recognized that at some point he might try Jackie on the mound or even in the infield. Managers like Stengel were experienced enough to know a new ball player didn't just step into a given position simply because he had performed well there before. Playing with different teammates against different opponents could alter how one might perform, but a man with good basic skills would eventually find his slot on the team. Jack himself still feared that after his requisite bonus year with the Yankees, Stengel might eventually farm him out to a minor-league team for additional experience rather than let him gain it with the team, which was risky for any manager who could be reasonably assured of wins with experienced players.

Jack's game debut with the Yankees consisted of a practice contest where he flied out as a pinch hitter; however, he fared better in his first "official" major-league game (an exhibition match in St. Petersburg against the St. Louis Cardinals) when he got to replace DiMaggio in center field and had one single in three times at bat. By March 22, Jack led the team in home runs by hitting his third homer during a loss to the Senators. However, Jack's overall batting average dropped, and he started to get discouraged, especially after he tore a tendon in his ankle during a March 27 practice, the same day he was asked by a reporter how he felt about being a bonus player. Perhaps, in spite of what he was quoted as saying— that he sensed no resentment from teammates–Jack was sensitive about the other players' feelings. Most of them were making less than $10,000 annually, after having spent several years in the minors. So Jack responded that he would have preferred working his way up through the Pacific Coast League somewhere other than in the Bay area, where fans expected so much of him. He had, in fact, batted over .300 when on the road for the Oaks, but the fact was moot, since Jack would play with the Yankees for a full year, anyway.

The day after that interview, Jack pinch-hit unsuccessfully in the fifth inning, and soon afterward received his first lesson in how important it is for a public figure to be careful of what he says. A player could be blamed but so much for a poor performance if he tried his best, but his words were a matter of choice. Reporters were constantly hanging around the camps looking for an interesting story, and Jack inadvertently gave them one that was soon to bring despair to himself and others. He insinuated that he hadn't been coached as well in high school, college, or the Coast League as he was being trained in the Yankee camp—that nobody had suggested he was striding too long and leaning into the ball too much, so couldn't handle an inside pitch (although teammate Billy Martin said Jack didn't realize what he was saying—that he must have learned *something*).

Jack's impetuous words were immediately regurgitated by Red Smith, a New York sports columnist, and West Coast reporters took them up, seeking out Jack's previous coach, Chuck Dressen of the Oaks, who had the following response:

> So, the boy never was told a thing when he played for the Oaks, eh? I guess it wasn't Dressen but somebody else who spent many hours of his own time at the park giving Jackie pointers in hitting and fielding. I guess it was two other fellows, not Coaches Cookie Lavagetto and George Kelly, who spent a great deal of their own time instructing Jensen. I hired pitchers to throw special batting practice to Jackie afternoons when he could get away from his studies at California. He mentioned a long stride, which caused him to get his shoulders in the way of the ball. Well, sir, after a dozen or so private lessons a major

league scout called me aside and said: "I notice Jensen has reduced his stride. Looks as if your instruction is doing him some good."

I seem to remember afternoons when I could have been taking it easy at home, but I went to the ball park to show Jensen the proper way to field a grounder into his territory.

Dressen went on to say that there were times he had kept Jack in the lineup only because he had promised Brick Laws he would use Jackie, but Dressen thought carefully before answering the question about whether the Oaks had lost their pennant race because they had to play Jack too much, and he tactfully refused to answer the question outright. Laws himself was also asked what he thought of Jack's remarks, and responded: "Funny, but I always thought Jensen was happy with his treatment here. I specifically asked him if he'd sign with Oakland if he had it all to do over again. He said he would."

Of course, Jack's remarks were not in any way directed against Laws. Jack had been a family friend for some time, so it would seem unlikely that the old friendship would dissolve due to a few careless remarks. However, Dressen didn't want to take anything for granted, so he wrote both Jack and Red Smith. Jack might have expected Dressen's letters, for the coach had always been a forthright yet fair person; and Jack knew something had to be done to smooth the ruffled feathers. He immediately wrote a special delivery letter, which was the best thing he could have done. Parts of his letter were made public:

Dear Charlie:

First, I'd like to apologize for any inconvenience or embarrassment which the article may have caused you all. I told Red that I had had lots of help but none of it corrected my fault at the plate. Perhaps when you worked with me you overlooked the one thing that would improve me most—I think and hope.

Ever since Lou Macke (high school coach), Clint Evans of Cal and you three guys (including Brick Laws in there) I've had more help than I warranted, and I appreciate every minute of it.

You all helped me as much as you could, but nothing actually took effect until Bill D. tried something different. That is what I told Red, and after that he concluded what you probably thought was a slam at you, Cookie and George Kelly.

I hope you understand what I mean and will straighten out my embarrassing predicament.

Dressen seemed satisfied with Jack's letter, reasoning that if Jack considered himself above those of his past, he wouldn't have responded at all. If nothing else, the fact that Jack answered the letter quickly showed that he was concerned with the feelings of those back home who had helped him and encouraged him and enabled him to get where he was. Besides, a player in Jack's position could never be sure when he might be traded down for a year and find himself again under the mentorship of a minor-league coach.

Fortunately, Jack started climbing his way out of the depression he had slipped into: He helped his team beat the Cardinals in the beginning of April when he was substituted in a late inning and had a double and a run; and the following day (a scrapbook clipping attested) he "was the whole show for the Yankees and even forced the Reds to go into a modified Ted Williams shift to retire him," as he had a homer, a triple, and a single. After the game Stengel said: "He's seeing big-league pitching for the first time. The boy himself knows he's not ready to step into a regular job on a pennant contender. But he hasn't been physically overpowered. He's been fooled and that's normal."

At this time Jack made a statement that would prove to be all too true: "The best thing that could happen to me is to play regularly, and I don't figure to do that with the Yankees this year."

Casey Stengel seemed pleased with Jack's performance to date. "I wouldn't carry a bonus player if I didn't think plenty of him," he said. "He has been hitting curve balls and I know he can help me. I know Jensen is green, but he's a definite prospect. You're going to like him the more you see him."

Jack was to learn how literally those words of Stengel were to be taken—the words "he can help me," for that was what managing a ball club was all about. Throughout his life Jack trusted people and gave them the benefit of the doubt that they were interested in doing things for him, and whereas Casey probably was pleased to see Jack doing well, he wasn't about to risk the standing of his club just to have Jack playing as often as he would like.

Arriving in New Jersey, Jack found a telegram sent from Zoe's parents. It read: "good luck God bless you and blast that ball we are all pulling for you. Grandma Grandpa Great Grandma Rita Ingrid six kittens and Buff love=Art and Norma="

Jack didn't disappoint them, hitting a home run in a 17-6 win over the St. Louis Browns.

Before driving to New Jersey, Zoe had had an agent scout ahead for an apartment in Newark, but they ended up in Belleville instead (about a half-hour drive to New York City). The newspapers of the East were as eager as the California ones to feature Zoe, who later was dubbed by *Collier's* "the delectable little blonde." In a full-page *Star-Ledger* feature, Zoe appeared in a series of shots. She posed in a swimsuit for three photos at the Jewish Community Center Pool where she had begun to swim for leisure. Two other photos were taken at her apartment where she romantically gazed at kittens and "cheerfully" washed dishes while a superimposed image of Jack hovered above the sink.

But not all of the article was so sentimental, for Zoe declared she was still upset over missing a gold medal in the Olympics by just half a point to a woman she had recently defeated by eighteen points. Furthermore, she reflected on the life she had to give up because of her training and said she didn't think she'd go into competitive diving again, although she was looking forward to touring abroad for an exhibition since Jack was invited to go with her. She seemed to have adjusted well to the move from Oakland; after all it was not much different from journeying across the country and overseas for swimming and diving, and the baseball wives formed their own social clique. However, other players' wives were not celebrities in their own rights, used to primary, not secondary attention; and Zoe was not accustomed to spending so much time in relative obscurity. Also, Jack lost the wedding ring Zoe had given him, and she felt hurt that he evidently didn't share the loss as deeply as she. Later she would look back on the incident and wonder if it was the first indication of marital discord.

By the end of April 1950 Jackie was again showing good promise and was featured with Billy Martin in a *St. Louis Sporting News* front-page story favorable to them both. Stengel put Jack in the starting lineup for a Washington game that was rained out the last day of April. The next day Stengel was asked if Jack would be on his final twenty-five-man roster, which needed to be finalized by the eighteenth, to which he only replied, "I know he can run and throw, but whether he'll hit is something else again. After all, this is only his second year in organized baseball."

Jack, when asked, candidly responded, "I don't know whether I'll make it or not."

PART TWO

1950–1959

Jensen as a Yankee with a bat boy. Jack and Zoe Ann took Bert, a bat boy, into their home and enrolled him in a junior college; Bert later became a lawyer and an agent for celebrities. He said, "Jack took care of me like a younger brother."

Zoe Ann, Jan, and Jack Jensen appeared on the June 21, 1952 edition of Collier's. *They were depicted as the "All-American Family." Zoe was featured training for the 1952 Helsinki Olympics and she said she didn't want Jan to become a champion because "It's too much work."*

Jack was traded to the Washington Senators, and here is pictured with Zoe Ann, who would often go to his games. The accompanying article stated, "Jackie hopes to prove he is star material this year." In a letter to the author, Zoe stated that Jack hated living out of suitcases, yet "he loved the VIP first-class treatment."

Jack led the Senators in hits and RBIs in 1952 and had 165 hits and 10 homers in 144 games. In 1953 he batted .266, hit 32 doubles and drove in 84 runs. Years later Casey Stengal said that trading Jack for Irv Noren was the worst trade he had ever made.

The Jensens frequently skied during Jack's off season. Here Zoe and Jack are pictured at Squaw Valley seated next to Stein Ericson, a 1954 Gold Medal skiing champion.
Bill Crouch photograph.

Newspapers ran a drawing made from this photo. Jack's 5' 11" muscular frame remained constant at 190 pounds during his professional career. Red Sox Trainer Fadden wrote, "Jack plays with bruises, pulled muscles, and tendons that would keep out other players for days or weeks."

The Saturday Evening

POST

March 2, 1957 · 15¢

THE SIXTH FLEET
Watchdog of the World'
Most Troubled Area

Jackie (center) was featured on the March 29, 1957, cover of The Saturday Evening Post. *Jensen later admitted he and his fellow players were reluctant to pose for Norman Rockwell! Many years later he and Katharine searched in vain for the original painting by the famous illustrator. Curtis Publishing, Inc.*

An obviously proud Jackie with his first son, Jon (five years old in this picture) at Red Sox Father-Son Day in Fenway Park. One article featuring the game ran the subtitle "Photographer nearly Beaned by Young Jensen Warmup." The fathers graciously lost to the sons by a score of 5–0.

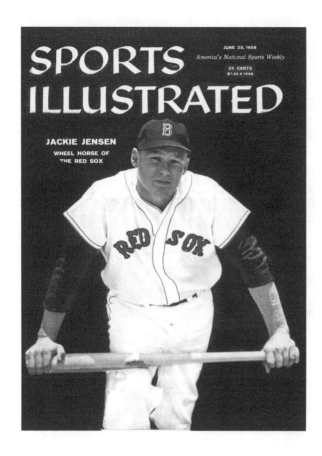

Jackie was extremely pleased to be featured on the cover of the June 23, 1958, edition of Sports Illustrated, *which identified him as "Wheel Horse of the Red Sox." A caption read, "One of the most underrated players is steady, dependable Jackie Jensen of the Red Sox, an athlete who has a longing for home instead of the headlines." Sports Illustrated, Inc.*

The photo caption read "Baseball Commissioner Ford Frick appeared at the Red Sox spring training camp at Scottsdale, Ariz., to offer his congratulations to Jackie Jensen, who was chosen Most Valuable Player of the American League for 1958." He led the league in RBIs.

6

MAJOR MOVE

Although in the spring of 1950 he was to learn that his mother had been sued for divorce by her second husband, Karl Wendt, Jack was pleased to learn he would be a father in the fall and was thrilled to be on the final Yankee roster. In the opening game against the Red Sox he was called in as a pinch runner for a pinch hitter in the eighth inning and scored to help put the Yankees ahead 13–10 (they had been trailing 4–10 the previous inning). When it came time for Jack to bat, he eyed the left-field fence only 315 feet away. However, Stengel shocked him by having Delsing bat for him, and Jack missed his opportunity to belt the ball. When he did get a chance to pinch hit, he flied out, but a week later at least he had a single, and then he started and played for six innings in left field next to DiMaggio. The next day saw his first full game, in which he singled but made an error. It would take time to adjust to major-league playing.

Jackie didn't get to play much for the next several weeks but found himself the topic of an article entitled "Reluctant Yankee," written by Red Smith for *Collier's*. The story opened with a color close-up of Stengel looking over the shoulder of Jack, who was smiling. It gave a rundown of Jack's fabulous high school and college days, then went on to show how he had unfortunately messed up while playing in the Pacific Coast League. The bonus rule was criticized, and Jack was again compared to Sam Chapman, who "floundered for three seasons."

Zoe, adorned with a gold football pendant Jack had given her, was pictured looking lovingly at Jack in his paisley shirt, but Smith devoted only three paragraphs to her.

However, the June *Mademoiselle* featured a photo of Zoe Ann speaking to Jack from the baseball stands. The gist of the article was supposedly stated by an astute West Coast newspaper columnist who called Smith a "brilliant New York observer," who "probably thinks something is about due, or he would not have timed the *Collier's* piece for just now. There isn't much sense in a long yarn about an up to now obscure bench warmer, unless something has a chance to happen."

Jack appeared in the August issue of *Sport* magazine in a fashion article that opened with him posing outdoors as the well-dressed collegian. The first page read, "The young rookie outfielder of the world champion New York Yankees, a former University of California grid star, steps out in a smart, styled-for-youth wardrobe of practical clothes designed for informal wear this fall." In one photo (with a couple of shapely coeds placed subtly in the background), Jack struck a jaunty stance in a McGregor sports jacket while holding a fedora. Cal students might have felt slighted by another ad picturing Jack: He assumed a pensive look while wearing a sleeveless Peruvian alpaca wool sweater and gabardine sports shirt as he cradled books under his arm. The text stated that the combination was "...a 'must' from Dartmouth to Stanford."

On September 19, 1950, Jack's first child, Jan Kai, was born, and the newspapers showed the baby in the arms of a beaming mother—looking refreshed in makeup and styled hair. Just as popular was the next day's photo of Jack, cigar in mouth, gazing admiringly at wife and daughter in a "Soundphoto" that had been passed hand-to-hand to him in the dugout of Comiskey Park, Chicago, where he was playing the White Sox. He had learned of the birth the night before via telegram and was eager to hand out cigars.

The Yankees went on to beat the Phillies in four straight games, but Jack didn't get to play except to pinch run in the third game, and his spirit was further dampened when Casey announced that Jack would pitch the next year; after all, he had performed in only forty or forty-five games and averaged .171, and there were plenty of other outfielders. Casey told reporters in Philadelphia: "I saw him throw from third base to first the other day, and my eyes bulged out. The ball didn't get five feet off the ground and was screaming when it got to Mize. A boy with that kind of an arm just has to be a pitcher."

Jack objected some, preferring to play outfield, but the next week his attention was elsewhere. He returned to Oakland to see his daughter for the first time. Jack brought home with him a six-teen-year-old Yankee batboy named Bert Padell, who stayed with the Jensens while he looked over schools in California. As a young boy, Bert's dream had been to be a New York batboy. He had stubbornly written letter after letter to the Giants, Dodgers, and Yankees and finally got a job as visiting batboy for the Giants in 1948. He later transferred to the Yankees, where he occasionally caught some pitches during practice and then met Jack. Thirty-six years later Bert would recall their trip West:

> We drove from the Concourse Plaza Hotel to Bemis [Street] and met Zoe in Oakland, California. Jackie was very anxious to see his wife and new baby daughter. I stayed with Jackie almost four months. He took care of me like a younger brother. When I went out there I weighed 135 pounds and when I came home to see my family I weighed almost 200 pounds. I matured and my body became muscular through the help of Jackie's friend Norman Marks [Mr. California]. In February 1951 Jackie helped get me into school. I met his mother and brothers who were always nice to me. Jackie's wife, Zoe Ann, was super. She always made sure I would eat; which I hated, did my exercises, ran, etc. Zoe Ann's parents were also very kind to me.

Perhaps inspired by Jack's rise to success, Padell earned degrees from Santa Rosa Junior College, Long Island University, and Brooklyn Law School; and he came to Jack's aid in a future legal dispute. He later headed a New York accounting firm employing eight partners, twenty CPAs, twenty-five bookkeepers, and twelve secretaries. In *The New Yorker, Manhattan Inc.,* and *Newsday* articles, Bert mentioned the need to be appreciative of his beginnings and how he cherished his memory of Jackie.

Within a couple of weeks Jack was pitching for the E. Bercovich & Sons Furniture team in the Alameda Winter League and admitted that his pitching was much improved: "In college ball I just threw hard, but now I've steadied down a great deal."

On October 29, 1950, Jackie played in the 23rd Annual Alameda Elks All-Star game between the Majors and the Minors to a crowd of 3,500 in inclement weather. He pitched two scoreless innings for the Majors in their first win (10–3) over the Minors in five years, then switched between pitching and playing right field. At the plate he hit a home run, a triple (which might have been another homer had it not hit the center-field loudspeaker), and a double. Of those four hits he also drove in three runs. After the game, the Yankee catcher who handled Jack's pitches said he considered Jack a good pitching prospect; Stengel, watching from the stands, dodged questions about using Jack on the mound the next season.

November 1950 was homecoming for Jack, who was invited to participate in honors bestowed on two of his former coaches. On the sixth Jack posed with other former Cal players—Bob Hogeboom, Mel Duezabou, Jack Albright—and Hugh Luby, chairman of the evening, as Coach Clint Evans was awarded a Certificate of Merit by Oakland Aerie No. 7 of the Eagles for his contributions to the young men he had coached. Three days later Jack and others were pictured with Pappy Waldorf and his staff, who were honored at the Commercial Club luncheon sponsored jointly by the California Alumni Association and the Commercial Club.

A couple of columnists criticized Jackie for leaving Berkeley a year early and contended that he was no longer a hometown boy, but Win Currier of the *Alameda Times-Star* came to his defense in a November 17, 1950, column when he spoke of Jack's dedication to a team that other major-league ball players might have thought not important. "The AA games were scheduled [E. Bercovich & Son vs. Ashland in San Leandro], but the wet grounds and threat of more rain left considerable doubt as to whether they would be played." (Told that the game had been called off due to wet grounds, Jack went out to play golf. The game was reinstated and manager Kirby Spranger called Zoe, who was told what clothes and equipment to put into Jack's bag. She then quickly chased him down and rushed him to the ball park.) Mr. Currier explained:

> What is impressive is the way he is playing all out in every game. So many of these big timers who come to play winter ball just go through the motions and don't actually put out. Not so Jensen. And it's strange, too, with all the vitriolic remarks that have been made about the ex-California athlete. Maybe not this year, maybe even not next, but before many seasons, we're looking forward to seeing Jensen as one of the tops in the big leagues. And then won't it be interesting to see the fair weather friends change their boos to cheers.

Jack had been taking courses at Berkeley in the fall of 1950 and hoped to get a degree by January 1952, but it would be many years and in a different location that he would finally realize that wish. He played ball every Sunday until nearly Christmas, then prepared once again for spring training. He was surprised, however, by a statement of Stengel's that Jack was no outfielder. When Jack started spring training in Phoenix, he began pitching training again under Coach Jim Turner but still lacked the control needed to be a good professional. Although Turner said Jack had "the second best curve on the club," and Jack realized that he could probably make more money pitching than playing outfield, he preferred the latter, and did not live up to expectations in pitching practice. It was reported that he had Phil Rizzuto "skipping rope" with his powerful yet uncontrolled pitches, so Stengel gave up on the pitching idea by the final week in March, moving him into left field.

That same month it was reported that Jack started to use a thinner bat, which might have helped him gain runs in a win over Cleveland, 16–14. It was reported: "The Yankee outfielder, whose slight hitting in the past almost forced Manager Casey Stengel to shift him to the pitching corps, electrified a record crowd of 5,431 by flailing away for two homers, a triple and double, knocking in eight runs and scoring four himself."

Sent to his address at Country Club Apartments, Phoenix, Arizona, a telegram arrived the next day (March 14, 1951) from Hollywood songwriter Jimmy McHugh: "nothing less than sensational am proud of you and love see you Friday." This surely boosted Jackie's spirits. However, Jackie went into a slump for the next several games, and many wondered if he'd be traded to the Seals. Stengel decided to keep him on the Yankee roster, for the time being, at least. After an April 3 game against the Braves in St. Petersburg, Jack admitted he had problems adjusting a new batting style to major league pitching, and two days later lost to Detroit 6–4. Stengel thought of sending Jack to the farm camp at Kansas City but instead decided to give him one last try in the outfield. When the team moved back to New York to play the Dodgers, Jack started in left field and hit a homer and a double; and shortly thereafter, in the start of the regular season against the Red Sox, Jack again had a home run and a double, but found himself benched when a right-handed pitcher was hurling. He learned that Stengel was a great believer in platooning, and Jack's enthusiasm to play every possible moment made it difficult to accept Casey's style of coaching.

The Yankees finished their preseason series with a game against the Dodgers on April 26, by which time Jack led the team with a .429 batting average. When asked how he explained his success, he responded, "I quit trying to copy Joe DiMaggio. I figured that Joe had the idea with his upright stance and thought it would work for me. It didn't. So I decided to crouch at the plate. Now I can see better and unload on the ball."

Zoe Ann and Jan had moved East with Jack, and Zoe found herself being interviewed by *The Fair Lawn and East Paterson Shopper* on May 10, which ran a photo of her responding to a question about urbanization of the area; she said she was against the idea of more industrialized firms locating there—that she and Jack had moved to Fair Lawn to find peace and quiet. They had given up living in Bellevue because of heavy traffic conditions, and it took half the time (twenty minutes) to reach the stadium from

their new home. Jack would often car pool with other neighborhood Yankees: Henrich, Woodling, and Houk. The Jensens considered themselves fortunate to be able to lease on a month-to-month
basis (something Stengel suggested new players do, if possible), for
Jack never knew when he might be transferred.

In another article Zoe commented that the couple were maintaining their own home in Oakland, which they had built on Bemis
street on what their future neighbor, Wimpy Jones, an old friend
and confidant, would call Fat Man's Hill. The street was named
after a man who had made his fortune from a chain of White Log
Cabin Restaurants and had invested in much property on a hill
overlooking the Bay area. To induce people to build there, he gave
Jack a good price on the best lot—from which five bridges over the
Bay could be seen—because he knew others would be impressed
by the fact the famous sports figure would be living there. The
home was a contemporary showcase with custom-made tables,
monogrammed bedroom night stands, a polished-copper fireplace
rising to the ceiling, and a shining, ultramodern kitchen. The article ended with Zoe saying she might go back to exhibition diving,
try golf, or even modeling; and baby Jan was described as loving
the water: "All of which indicates there may be another athletic
luminary in the family Jensen in the not-too-distant future."

Turning away from his disappointments with his performance
on the Yankee team, Jack entered the 1951 Mayor's Trophy Game,
one designed to help finance "sandlot baseball which teaches and
exemplifies good citizenship and clean American sportsmanship,"
as stated on a Certificate of Civic Merit awarded to Jack by Walter
T. Shirley, chairman of the 1951 committee and signed by Mayor
Vincent R. Impellitteri on June 25. This would prove to be the
beginning of several years' devotion to charity by Jack throughout
his professional baseball career.

As the season progressed, Jack was finding himself no longer
being compared to Billy Martin and Joe DiMaggio, but to Mickey
Mantle, a slugger who had the advantage of being a switch-hitter,
batting against all pitchers. Unlike Jack, who had been in the lime-

light since junior high, Mantle was a virtual unknown from the Midwest. Each found himself alternating from bench to field according to Stengel's apparent whims; but Jack did get a lot of playing time against the southpaws, starting with a game against Washington (his second appearance that season), when he had a single, a double, and a home run, stole a base, and batted in two runs. Stengel was especially impressed with Jack's speed, and he often attempted to steal bases–but not always successfully.

Recalling those games twenty-five years later, in a *Sacramento Bee* article by Ben Sweney, Jackie would relate the following story about DiMaggio: "I remember we played a doubleheader in Washington and it was hot and humid. For some reason Joe was scheduled to play in both games. He was playing center and I was playing left. Around the fifth or sixth inning in the second game Joe called me over to center. He told me, 'Jackie, see this area,' and he made a circle about 20 feet in diameter. 'If any ball is hit out of this area, she's all yours, baby.'"

In the Washington games Mantle fielded poorly and didn't hit at all, so Casey switched Jack to Mickey's position for the games against the Red Sox. Jack failed to hit against their right-hander in the first game, but got the hang of his pitching and did well for the following games. With the team starting out west on the road, Jack received a great surprise–Stengel was starting him in center field, DiMaggio's position (Joe had a sore neck); and in the first game against St. Louis Jackie had a home run, a triple, and a double. This was the day when Casey would remark to Jack that it had been a mistake to try to make a pitcher out of him. In the last game against the Browns, Jack had the best day of his Yankee career, hitting a home run, two doubles, and a single. He continued to perform well in a series against the Detroit Tigers, getting his fifth home run of the young season in the fifth inning of the last game, which went into extra innings. With one out in the eleventh and Yogi Berra on first, Stengel pulled Bauer (who had hit two homers that game) and Jack from their scheduled at-bats, and the team lost. Jack was incredulous that Stengel would do such a stupid thing. Utterly frustrated, Jack let the situation get the better of him, and his .316 average rapidly declined as he thereafter failed to hit time after time. Mantle, whom Jackie had termed "a dangerous boy with a bat," hadn't been doing too well, either, and was sent to the Yankee's minor-league club in Kansas City. Jack started a comeback with a homer at Fenway, and by mid-July had brought his average up to .297 with eight home runs and twenty-five RBIs, but he was soon to suffer the same fate as Mantle.

7

TURNING POINTS

Although Jack was doing well with the Yankees in July with a .298 batting average, they wanted players who could do even better, so they decided to trade him. The Oaks and the Seals immediately hoped to get Jack out West again as the Yankees owed Oakland an option player on another deal, and the New York team had a working agreement with the Seals. Room was needed on the Yankees roster for two men in particular, outfielder Bob Cerv (batting .349) and southpaw Bob Weisley. A Yankee spokesman explained that Jackie was "being optioned to Kansas City so that he could play every day and gain needed experience." Additionally, Jack was expected to help the minor league-team win its own pennant in the American Association—small consolation for Jack, who impetuously thought about quitting. He even considered joining pro football, for he realized he was in his last bonus year and could count only on $7,000 the next year with the Yankees.

However, Jack could be called up at any time, and if he rejoined the team by September 1, he could play in the World Series. Jack had once said in spring training camp: "I'm willing to try anything if it will give me a chance to stay up there with them"; so, realizing he'd get his wish of playing on a regular basis, he reluctantly made his move to Middle America. Apparently Jack didn't let his discouragement influence his playing, as a news article of August 27, 1951, attested:

> Minneapolis baseball enthusiasts were most favorably
> impressed with the all around ability of Jackie Jensen, former
> California University football star, who showed with Kansas

City here last week. The way the former collegian handled himself in his lone appearance against the Millers made many wonder why he still isn't in the major leagues. Blessed with a powerful physique Jackie seemed to be able to do about everything on a baseball diamond. Jensen didn't say as much when he was in the Twin Cities, but he left the impression that he thought he was being kicked around a bit by his Yankee owners.

The September 1 deadline passed and Jack hadn't yet been called back to the Yankees. With just two weeks left in the major-league season, Jack left Kansas City with a .262 batting average and nine home runs for the Blues; but before he left the Midwest, he met in Minneapolis with Tony Morabito, owner of the San Francisco Forty-Niners. Both were reported to agree it might be difficult for him to get back into the game, as it had been close to three years since he had last played; and with football still lacking the popularity of the national pastime, Jack was offered only $5,000, which decided the issue for him.

He returned to New York with just two weeks left in the major-league season, ineligible for the World Series, even though he played well during that short time. The last day of the season Joe DiMaggio told Jack that the Series would be the final games of his career, but that Jack would go a long ways. Joe would later give him the bat he used to hit his last home run.

Jack and Zoe drove back West while the Series was on, not caring to watch because he "felt so badly about the treatment [he] received from [them]" and because he wanted to enroll in the fall courses at the University of California (he signed up for twelve of the twenty-seven credits he needed to graduate). Reporters were waiting for the Golden Couple, eager for anything interesting. Jack had learned to choose his words with care, but sure enough, he was misquoted as saying he was better than Mantle, when he actually had stated he thought he could beat him out for an outfield position because of Mickey's bad leg and the fact that Joe was quitting. But that news was nothing compared to what came out in the papers a few days later. At the Bow and Bell, a restaurant that later would figure prominently in his life, Jack had openly stated that he was discouraged with the Yankees' practice of platooning and wouldn't mind being traded. Jack also expressed his views in an October 12 article:

> "I do not feel that the Yankees were justified in sending me to the minor leagues. When I was shipped to Kansas City I was doing as good a job as any Yankee outfielder and better than some of them. I was hitting .296, which was 10 points better than Hank Bauer and 30 points better than Joe DiMaggio, Gene Woodling, and Mickey Mantle. Yet Casey Stengel didn't give me the chance I felt I deserved."

Upon hearing of Jack's discontent, George Weiss called Jack and chewed him out, saying that Jack would not be the one to determine whether he would be traded. Despite Jackie's run-in with Weiss, he was entitled to a full share of the World Series pot ($6,446.09), as determined by the baseball commissioner. Asked to comment, Jackie said, "I guess the players might have thought I was helping the club, even if the front office didn't. The Yankees have always been generous with their World Series money, and I appreciate it."

In the beginning of November, attention shifted to Zoe, who was the subject of a report of an October 29 performance when she gave a diving exhibition at the Hearst gymnasium:

> Mrs. Jensen completely won her audience, first by her warm sense of humor and, as the sun continued to fall, by braving water so cold that vapor could be seen rising from it—accompanied by father Art who explained the finer points of diving. Among the dives Mrs. Jensen demonstrated were the jack knife, the swan and the back dives, the half twist and full twist and the half gainer. To top these off she did a complicated combination of a half gainer with a half twist and a somersault.
>
> Despite the fact that it has been two years since she has done any serious diving, Mrs. Jensen gave a performance that won the applause of her audience after every dive.

Jack refrained from playing winter-league ball because he had pulled a tendon in his shoulder in his final week with Kansas City, but he was not forgotten. He was invited in early November to join twenty-four all-time football greats honored by 350 guests at San Francisco's Touchdown Club. They celebrated the 82nd anniversary of the first game between college teams held in 1869 (Rutgers vs. Princeton). A couple of days later Jack was photographed with Sam Chapman and Vic Bottari at the San Francisco Commercial Club luncheon honoring Lynn Waldorf at the Merchants Exchange.

Bygones were bygones. George Weiss sent Jack a telegram Christmas Eve reading: "a very Merry Christmas and Happy New Year to you and yours which of course includes another world championship in 1952." Yet, not so joyous news was to follow. Jack learned Stengel would not be as forgiving as Weiss had been of Jack's remarks of the autumn before.

The new year saw Eisenhower and Nixon return the Republicans to the White House for the first time in twenty years, and surely Jack had voted for them. Aunt Lillian was a staunch Republican and had little tolerance for those who didn't share her political beliefs. Later in the year the first hydrogen bomb was exploded, and Americans began to build back-yard bomb shelters. On a smaller scale, local attention again turned to the Jensens: One headline read "1952 May Be Big Year on Sports Scene for Jackie, Zoe Ann Jensen." The columnist hoped Jackie would take DiMaggio's place and Zoe would take the gold medal in the Olympics. However, it was to be a year of continued uncertainty for Jack and disappointment for both him and Zoe. Hank Greenberg, the Cleveland Indians general manager, was negotiating for a Yankee outfielder. Jack's name had come up, but the trade never occurred. By the end of January, however, Jack did sign on for another term with the Yankees and was pleased his salary hadn't been cut (although he would take home less money because his three-year bonus had run out).

Shortly after the contract signing, Jackie attended a baseball session at the Oaks' park and was again asked if he could take away the center-field job from Mantle. He simply replied, "Uh-huh," but his short answer, overheard by a sports editor, required an explanation. When pressed, Jack nonchalantly gave his reasons, saying that although Mickey was a fine ballplayer, Jack himself could hit, throw, and run the bases better—which was true. Mickey himself just responded to Jack's statements by saying, "I don't know what to think about that guy," that he (Mantle) was just more interested in playing baseball than in any particular position. Jack's honesty was interpreted by some to be boasting, but *Tribune* sports editor Alan Ward supported Jackie by quoting a former ballplayer (who asked to remain anonymous). The baseball alumnus commended Jackie, saying he couldn't miss with his natural ability, self-assurance, and a desire to improve . "The year isn't far away when Jensen will be a great ball-player. Remember I said GREAT!" (To be sure that neither Mantle nor Weiss misconstrued his remarks, Jack wrote them letters.)

About this time Zoe Ann also became optimistic for success; in a few months the Helsinki Olympics would be held—perhaps her last chance to make her years of training pay off. As she explained three decades later: "It just started eating on me. I looked around and nobody was really that good. So we talked it over and I decided to make an effort." Although the decision to compete had been made for her in the '48 Olympics, this time the situation was quite different. Now she was not only a wife, but also a mother; and her parents, who encouraged her to try again, held little power over her. The decision to compete would be almost entirely hers; Jack wouldn't have any basis to object, even if he were not supportive of Zoe's quest, for he and Zoe had long since realized that a baseball family had to give up thoughts of a normal life—a nine-to-five, weekends-free schedule. More so than her marriage, Zoe's decision to participate in the Games marked a turning point in her life, for marriage had simply meant a perpetuation of responsibility to others—from her parents to her husband.

Jack, on the other hand, had not yet reached such a decisive point. His choices seemed to have been determined throughout his life not so much by himself but by others; he had been carried along by a tide of optimism and his natural abilities. Whereas Jack was the idealist, Zoe was the realist. She carefully chose her courses of action and decided that if she were ever to try for a gold medal, it had to be the summer of '52, although she would have to leave her baby daughter behind. Even though her husband was arguably the sole breadwinner, for years Zoe Ann (and her parents) had looked forward to the day when she could perform aquatics professionally and reap the benefits of advertising promotions. She considered either finding a babysitter for sixteen-month-old Jan or else taking her along to training sessions, which could be as much as three hours' long, every day, for five months. This problem was solved with the decision to leave Jan in the care of her grandmother Norma, as Art traveled East with Zoe Ann to help her train. Another challenge would be finding a pool with an expensive championship diving board; she had been unable to locate one in New York, but hoped to find one in Florida when Jack went there for spring training. Tryouts for the Games were scheduled for early July in Indianapolis, and Zoe decided that even though she had only practiced about a dozen times since 1949, she didn't need to compete anywhere before July, for she had thirteen years of competition as experience. Some believed Zoe had become pregnant again, but the press mercifully avoided any conclusions when she ultimately decided to pursue her quest and appeared to be in perfect form.

Jack seemed to be still on Stengel's bad side for his remarks in the fall; he was directed to participate in a pre-training course in Phoenix held for rookies and others with special need for attention. After Jack reported and saw Stengel, the latter briefly greeted him, then ignored him for a week until he chewed Jack out about his comments about his superiority to Mantle. When the team opened its preseason games against Philadelphia, Jackie, still smarting from Casey's reprimand, failed to hit in nine times at bat and was benched in the opener against Washington, but they had right-handed pitchers. Allowed to hit against the Athletics' southpaw, Jackie finally broke his slump by hitting a triple one day and a two-run double the next, and he ended spring training with a .353 average.

Jack had hoped he might be on the road to making amends with Stengel, but thought otherwise when, in a game against a Boston lefty, he was not told to play. Sure enough, by only the third week of February there was talk of trading both Jackie and Billy Martin to the Senators, and by March the Indians were seeking Jackie, too. Up to the last moment before the Yankees' exhibition game against the Dodgers, it was a toss-up whether Jack or Mickey would take DiMaggio's place in center field. Jack was given the honor but fully realized that Stengel might replace him at any time. Although Jack preferred left or right field, he liked the center-fielder position because it was more of a challenge, and he was determined to do his best to hold onto it.

It had taken a few years, but Jackie learned to be somewhat more realistic about professional baseball, understanding that most positions were tenuous. When word came May 3 that Jack was traded to the Senators, he asserted that "the Yankees made the wrong move in trading me." His words would prove to be accurate, as Stengel himself would verify years later. In the short two weeks he started with the Yanks, he made no errors in the field and had several assists, but was batting just .105; and the team, Jackie himself conceded, needed consistent batters. Although the Senators moved from second to fifth place early in the summer, Jack personally had a good season, including a hitting streak of twenty consecutive games. Many felt the Senators' problem was lack of confidence—that they felt they could never really win a pennant. Confidence seemed to be something Jack was building, however, despite occasional slumps. He was becoming known as a slugger even though Griffith Stadium, in Washington, D.C., had not been designed with home runs in mind. Only the right-field wall was in range of most of his long hits. It measured 328 feet from home plate, and the center field wall was 420 feet distant. So Jack often watched in disappointment as many long drives that would have been home runs in other stadiums were caught by outfielders hanging back. Another thing that bothered Jack was the heat: He had been used to cooler temperatures in New York and Oakland. He did find the managers and fans to be fair; however, he was particularly pleased to do just as well at home games as away, unlike in his earlier years. His abilities were not going unnoticed, for he received a pleasant surprise.

Although many, if not most, players didn't often agree with Stengel's tactics, he did seem to be a fair man, one who placed the interest of the team before that of the individuals. Casey became responsible for selecting American League players for the All-Star game against the National League in July; and he called on Jackie, who by then was hitting .318 as a right fielder for the Senators. Perhaps Jack felt his old manager had a soft spot in his heart after all, for Jack commented: "Many things have happened to me since I broke into the majors but my being picked to play in the All-Star game is the best of them all. I never expected to be named." (In later years he asked not to be named to All-Star games so that he could spend the time with his family instead.)

If some Americans hadn't heard of the Jensens by June 21, 1952, they did when *Collier's* hit the newsstands. They were on the cover, referred to as "Jackie Jensen's All-American Family." The feature article described Jack's trade as a "high spot" with the notion that by playing regularly he could prove himself; and Zoe Ann, pool side in a swimsuit and in the baseball stands smartly dressed, was actually pictured twice as much as her husband. Attention was drawn to her perfect form in diving and the fact that she would go on a road trip of her own if she didn't make the Olympic tryouts. Little Jan was pictured often: relaxing on her daddy's lap, being held by her mother, sitting in the stands, and playing in the sand; but by the time the story ran, she was with the Olsens in California. Zoe herself was said to have adjusted to Jack's being away so often, but it was Jan who suffered the most, from not having both parents around much, according to her letters written years later to Ralph Kerchum.

Zoe Ann managed to get two full weeks of training in New York before traveling to Indianapolis, where she placed second and qualified for the Summer Games. The day of her springboard event in Helsinki was to become perhaps unique in the competition's annals—she performed three times for just one score. After her first dive, the judges decided a technical fault existed in the fulcrum of the board, so they asked her to perform again. Zoe just walked out onto the board, concentrated; and executed her dive, but on exiting the water, she learned that she should have waited for a whistle: Some of the judges had not watched her; so again she had to dive. Unnerved by the circumstances, she wasn't able to make her best dive, and she left the pool and headed straight for the showers, sure she hadn't won anything. However, word came to her that in fact she had won the bronze medal by just two tenths of a point.

Fully realizing how difficult and impractical it would be to set her sights again on a gold medal, Zoe ensured that she wouldn't develop false hopes for the '56 Games by signing advertising contracts immediately on her return (for Ovaltine, orange juice, and even cigarettes—though she didn't smoke at the time). She would continue to perform sporadically, eventually amassing a record of 230 public and service exhibitions in addition to her previous national women's diving championships, and the distinction of having been "the youngest diver to annex both high and low boards." On turning professional, Zoe Ann shed the last remnants of parental control over her and turned her thoughts to the Jensen family. By the end of the summer, she was pregnant again.

Throughout Zoe's absence, Jackie was gaining the much needed experience he and others had hoped he would get playing for the Senators. He went to bat 589 times, more than any previous year or any of the eight seasons yet to come. He recorded a .286 batting average, with ten home runs and eighty-two RBIs in 144 games. After the season Jack enjoyed a well-deserved rest, but kept active playing golf and skiing with the family at Lake Tahoe.

In early 1953 Zoe and Jan traveled with Jack to Clearwater, Florida, for the Senators' spring training. They were housed in a motel with just one and a half rooms, a two-burner portable stove that functioned as their kitchen, and cracked linoleum floors that permitted easy access for the inch-long red ants that made themselves at home. The March 24, 1953, edition of the *Washington Times Herald* reported that the Senators refused an offer by the Cleveland Indians to trade Jack for Larry Doby (who led the American League the season before with thirty-two homers). Manager Bucky Harris succinctly explained why he didn't want to trade Jackie: "I don't blame them for wanting Jensen, but I wouldn't trade him for Doby or anybody else at this moment. He's going to be our solid man and the way he's been going he looks like the best outfielder in the league." At that time Jack was hitting .417 and had four home runs in exhibition games. In April Jack was excited at being present as President Eisenhower threw out the first ball of the season. Another memorable moment for Jack was being on the field when Mickey Mantle hit his record fly ball 565 feet.

In the middle of May, Jack's son Jon was born in Georgetown Hospital, and he would receive much press attention over the next few years.

Throughout the season the team had to struggle just to maintain its fifth place position, but Jack continued to prove himself a worthy player: at season's end Jack had hit 10 home runs, made 84 RBIs, and had a .280 batting average. Looking back at his trade from the Yankees and his two years with Washington, Jack said:

> "Washington was a second division ball club. Once in a while, we'd come in maybe fourth place. But, because of the economic structure of the Griffith family and the Washington franchise, they just weren't able to compete with the top-flight division leaders such as Cleveland, Detroit, the Yankees, the Red Sox. They just didn't have that kind of an organization. It was a little disappointing to go to spring training because you knew you weren't going to win the pennant, and that would be disquieting to any Major Leaguer, not to feel you had a chance."

Jack's words accurately described the position of the Senators and prophetically hinted at their future. He was ready for a change and needed a chance to develop his potential. He had gained valuable experience with the team but felt restricted, for he couldn't adequately progress if the club had no hope of going anywhere. At least he got in a lot of play during an All-Star tour to the Orient, although he felt uncomfortable about flying. During the flight, Jack took some tranquilizers to help him get to sleep but was rudely awakened by his old Oakland buddy Billy Martin, who stood over him wearing a life vest saying, "I just thought you might want to know. We're going to crash." Jack didn't take kindly to the joke but kept his temper.

During the fall Jack enrolled in a couple of courses at Cal to keep working toward a degree, and during that time learned that nearly every American League manager wanted him. By early December his was the first big trade of the winter baseball season bargaining rounds. Lou Boudreau, manager of the Boston Red Sox, astonished Jack with news of his trade for left-handed pitcher Maurice McDermott and outfielder Tom Umphlett. Boudreau explained that he needed a strong hitter behind Ted Williams, so pitchers would be less tempted to walk the star slugger. Jack was euphoric—the Red Sox were a powerful, wealthy team owned by Tom Yawkey, and they had a much better chance of winning the pennant than did Washington. Also, as Cookie Lavagetto, former coach of the Brooklyn Dodgers, remarked—Jackie would do well in home games: "Many of his fly-ball outs at Washington will go for base hits at Fenway Park. This is a great move for Jensen." Furthermore, he would play with Ted Williams, a man he idolized as much as he did DiMaggio.

Many thought the Senators got the better deal, and thus believed New York benefitted the most as the Red Sox had been closer to the Yankees in the standings than Washington. They were mistaken, though. Jackie was quoted as saying the year would be his "greatest season in the big leagues with a pennant-winning ball club." In one sense he would be correct; in another wrong—it would be his best to date, but better years lay ahead.

Jack left the Senators on very good terms and with a dozen baseballs autographed by his teammates—to be given away at the Oakland Junior Chamber of Commerce Christmas tree lot, which was donated by J. D. Rhoads, manager of the East Oakland Chevrolet Company. Jackie, Andy Carey, and others helped open the lot and offered the autographed balls to the first twelve children of parents buying trees. Not only would this volunteer work begin a lifelong commitment to charity by Jack, but twenty-five years later, selling Christmas trees would become his primary way of making a living. Outside his own home, Jack surprised Zoe Ann with a palomino named Kristi (Christmas), which he arranged to be kept in the stable of a neighbor who had ten acres adjoining them.

Also during Christmas vacation, Jack was contacted by his former public speaking instructor Garff Wilson, who asked if he'd join a few other athletes for a beer blast. This seemed unusual, but the offer was not to be turned down, for the guest of honor was Robert Frost, who had received an honorary degree from Cal in 1947. The famous poet had asked Garff if he knew any athletes, since he'd become tired of visiting so many literary people, so Jack's presence was much appreciated. Frost's interest in sports would become increasingly well known (as noted, for instance, in *Newsweek* (2-8-60) regarding football: "Some people say it doesn't matter whether you win. I call these people liberals. They always feel sorry when they beat somebody." Regarding his philosophy on sports, Frost stated simply: "Spike them as you go around the bases.")

During the party in Garff's house Frost recited poems from memory, then sat down and got to know Jack, who promised to invite him to a Red Sox game—a promise that was fulfilled. One other event occurred before the New Year, one that would result in years of satisfaction and the cementing of an old friendship, but would end in misunderstanding, accusations, and regrets. Boots Erb, who had gone to school with Jack in the fourth grade and at Cal, had moved back to Oakland earlier in the year, after spending time in Los Angeles learning the restaurant trade and working at the Redwood House and Smokey Joe's Barbeque. Having suffered a bad romance and the loss of his father, Boots needed moral support, so Jack and Zoe suggested he temporarily move in with them. Boots's enthusiasm about starting a restaurant in the Bay area stimulated Jack to ask if he'd like a partner. This was Jack's first firm investment idea; and it was decided that he would lend his name and fame to a restaurant, invest 51 percent, and in the off-season help Boots. They bought the Bow and Bell in Jack London Square on the Oakland Estuary not far from the Berkeley campus and began business in January 1954, catering especially to families. Their first major event was a going-away party Boots threw for Jack before spring training. An idea novel for the area included a children's menu shaped like a baseball glove, and a gift for each child who finished his or her meal (one year the reward was a miniature Jackie Jensen bat made especially by the Louisville Slugger Company).

Over the years celebrities of all kinds would visit the Bow and Bell, including practically all the Yankees and Red Sox and such luminaries as Willie Mays, Mickey Mantle, Joe DiMaggio, Kareem Abdul-Jabbar, Jerry West, Rick Barry, Jack Nicklaus, Joe Namath, Vince Lombardi, Ronald Reagan, Pat Brown, George McGovern, Erskine Caldwell, and Robert Frost (to name just a few). One special event Boots recalls is the night Betty Grable had "a little feud" with Harry James and dumped a bowl of soup over his head. The restaurant was a sideline for Jack for many years; a decade later it would figure prominently in his life.

Boots and Jack made investments in batting cages, the *Villa de la Paix* fishing boat (which ended up at the bottom of Lake Tahoe), and two houses at Tahoe, both built by Jack and his uncle. For the next several years Jackie would correspond weekly with Boots about the goings-on of the Red Sox, and these letters were drawing cards for customers and friends, as Boots shared them with all who entered the restaurant—including eagerly awaiting reporters and columnists. Jack was destined to succeed with the Red Sox and would continue to be remembered in Oakland as he won awards with the Boston team and contributed photographs and trophies to the walls of the Bow and Bell.

8

ONWARD AND UPWARD

Spring training with the Red Sox was considerably better for the Jensens than it had been with the Senators. The accommodations in Sarasota were much nicer than they had been in Orlando and Clearwater, and Zoe was pleased at the improvement. Jack was thrilled at playing alongside Williams, but he and his teammates were truly worried when Ted broke a collarbone in practice, sidelining him for over a month. Jack learned that the Red Sox had relatively slow runners; so his speed truly stood out, and he would become the team's and the league's champion base stealer. What concerned Jack, though, was his tendency to hit into double plays because of other runners' slowness and his proclivity to take such strong swings that he would be late leaving the batter's box. Thus he concentrated on trying to hit home runs. Opposing pitchers were quick to size up the situation and pitch low to him, forcing him to hit many grounders. However, Jack was to establish himself as an excellent fielder, playing center at home games and right field on the road.

Eager to prove himself, Jack did just that his first two games—hitting a single and a home run against the Athletics in a doubleheader and breaking a 3–3 tie in the ninth inning of the second game with another homer. Soon Jack found himself in a pattern of peaks and valleys as he faced pitchers from varying teams. He brought a spring batting slump up to .405 by April and hovered around .350 for a month until he was plagued by the double-play hits. He found the Red Sox fans unmerciful in their booing, but at least Williams was back in action by late spring and well enough and nice enough to take Jack aside one day to give him a batting tip that boosted both his morale and his percentage as Jack started an upward climb with a home run against Detroit.

Throughout May and June, Jack continued his ups and downs but often was thrilled to help bring victory to the team through his skills. Perhaps Jack couldn't have helped but gloat just a little when he hit a home run against the team that traded him down to the Senators—the Yankees. He also had a thrilling two-run triple against the White Sox to win the game. When the Red Sox made its second trip West, Jack again fell into a slump and asked to be benched for a while, which he was. Quite possibly the thought of leaving behind his wife and children nagged him, but travel with the kids would have been most impractical. Zoe Ann had been forced to adjust to marriage to a man who had to spend weeks at a time away from home, but in a newspaper feature entitled "Zoe Olsen Content to Leave Glory to Hubby Jackie of Sox," she said that she enjoyed attending home games in Boston. "Up to now," Zoe Ann said, "in New York, Kansas City, and Washington I've seldom attended more than 10 games a season. The sample I got here during the first week of the Boston season convinces me I'm ready for more frequent visits."

Asked about her own sports career, Zoe responded that she would not want to live through all the pressure again, despite her medals in the '48 and '52 Olympics, saying, "There are too many political angles in amateur sports nowadays." Referring to Jack's new position, Zoe replied with guarded optimism and enthusiasm:

> There's no way of forecasting what lies ahead for any ball player. You just try to produce your best and hope it is good enough. I know the Big Moments I have enjoyed while watching Jackie were at Yankee Stadium. Jackie hit his first New York home run in 1950—the only one that year—and his homer in the 14th inning against the Yankees at Fenway Park last Patriots' Day evening at 7:45 o'clock. That ended seven hours of watching and was worth every minute of the wait.

Despite a slump of a few weeks, Jack was again selected by

organizer Casey Stengel to play in an All-Star series, where he hit .250 and had ten home runs and forty-six RBIs—but he thought those figures mediocre. After that, things really picked up as Jack gained six RBIs against Philadelphia, helped beat the White Sox with three home runs, and had a single, double, and home run against Cleveland. A typical headline was this one from the August 12, 1954, *Boston Daily Globe:* "Jensen's Tremendous Homer Has Fans Buzzing," subtitled, "Jackie Looms as Sox Power Hitter of Future." Even those who didn't favor baseball could not help but be impressed by the account of Jack's hit: "More than one was buzzing about the titanic home run Jackie Jensen smote off the light tower in left field. Seldom has a ball been hit with more authority in any ball park. Conservatively, had not the ball struck two-thirds up on the light stanchion it would have landed on the Boston & Albany Railroad tracks."

By this date Jack led the American League in stolen bases with seventeen, and was fourth with eighty-four RBIs and fifth in home runs: nineteen. A news article quoted Jack's reason for success— confidence: "This is the first season I've really felt I could hit. I finally feel that I can go to the plate and do as well as the next guy."

Some found fault not only with Jack's tendency to hit into double plays, but with his fluctuating batting average as well. To the rescue came outspoken Dave Egan in a column entitled "Jensen Proves Hod-Carrier on Sox." He compared Jack's .268 average with Williams's .364 and said that he could prove "that Jensen has won more than a dozen games with his bat alone, while whole posses of citizens could scour the records without ever finding a solitary game which the bat of Williams has won." Of course, Jack and Ted were good friends, but one might wonder how Williams reacted to Egan's words. The column made an interesting observation about Jack's temperament and dedication to trying his best: "Jensen does not study the *Wall Street Journal* after a losing game, nor will he be found singing in the bathtub. He kicks the clubhouse down after a defeat, and this is good. Tom Yawkey can build a new clubhouse every day, but he cannot come upon a competitor like Jackie Jensen every day."

At season's end, Jack was rewarded for his overall performance by receiving the Ted Williams Award, which brought with it a new Nash Rambler automobile. Although Boston finished fourth in the league, Jack had hit .276 (the best among right-handed batters), had 117 RBIs, belted twenty-five homers, and led the American League with twenty-two steals (although he also held the dubious distinction of having hit into the most double plays). His final reward was a notable increase in salary for 1955—to nearly $25,000 [equivalent to $150,000 today].

That fall two misfortunes occurred that bode worse times to come. During postseason play Jack again joined an All-Star team for a tour of the Orient, where he experienced an incident that would alter the rest of his life. Zoe had traveled with him as far as Honolulu, having left the children with her parents, and Jack flew on to Japan. During the descent Jack looked out the window to witness a near-collision with another plane. From that moment on Jack greatly feared air travel. Also, a state tax lien was filed against the Jensens for nearly $900 for unpaid taxes and penalties based on an incorrectly filed 1950 return. Whereas this was not too much, considering Jack's income at the time, a decade later he would face something similar in an amount ten times as much.

Having learned to take taxes more seriously, the Jensens moved to the Nevada side of Lake Tahoe, "the Jewel of Nevada," where they established residency and were relieved of the confiscatory California taxes. Their home at Crystal Bay was near Incline Village, which nestled in an 11,000-acre glacial amphitheater populated by tall firs and overlooking the most beautiful part of the lake, with its intensely blue water dotted with a few tiny islands. Skiing, a favorite sport of both Jack and Zoe, became convenient with Squaw Valley nearby; a few golf courses, the fairways often visited by deer, offered Jack the opportunity to hone his skills for tournaments; and the casinos catered to the Jensens' occasional whims to go out on the town.

The publicity of the tax lien had been embarrassment enough for Jack, but the next month he was to endure more chagrin, although some speculated publicity was the *cause,* not the *result,* of an incident involving Boots Erb. On November 17 a statue of Jack London near the Bow and Bell was dedicated in the square previously named in his honor, and that same night a reunion of Cal football players took place at the nearby restaurant. Three nights later the statue was defaced with red paint, just after a publicity agent named Hendrickson tipped off the city hall pressroom about an impending Stanford raid on the area around the Cal alumni's business. Police Captain Jack Brierly was naturally skeptical, so after the vandalism he called in Boots, Jackie, and Hendrickson for questioning; on the advice of his attorney, Boots refused to take a lie-detector test, whereas Jack was asked only to help out in the investigation. Jack wanted the situation cleared up quickly and saw the police captain two days later to offer suggestions. The police proceeded to track down a car with a license plate number recorded in part by a witness to the foul deed, while other members of the force sought to trace the source of the paint. A week after the incident, Boots admitted he and a group of friends had devised the raid but had intended to have the young men posing as Stanford students only paint a few red "S"s on the sidewalk—and Boots furthermore said that Hendrickson originated the idea as a publicity stunt, but the latter denied it. Along with the resolution of the problem was Captain Brierly's statement that Jackie had not been involved with the prank. Perhaps it was much ado about nothing, but the Bow and Bell restaurant certainly got publicity as a result.

The year ended on a great note for Jack. On December 28 he was voted one of the outstanding young men of the year by the California Junior Chamber of Commerce, which noted that Jackie was "the only person ever to have played in both a New Year's Day Rose Bowl game and the World Series." Jack—the only athlete represented—was one of five men selected from sixty-two nominees, "the winners chosen because of their extraordinary talent and initiative and contributions to their professions and to the general welfare of the people."

Jack was the first Red Sox player to sign a contract in January 1955, and in the spring the family again moved to Sarasota. Mike Higgins, the new manager, started Jack in right field. The Red Sox were off to a blazing start in their preseason schedule as they won six of their first seven games. Jack got a hit in each of the first six games and led his team to a doubleheader victory against the Orioles with a total of three singles, one double, a home run, and four RBIs. The whole team then went into a slump until Jack hit two home runs against the Athletics, a grand slam against the Tigers, and another homer against the Yankees. Jack again played on an All-Star team and did well into the summer. Although he suffered an arm injury in August, he surprised everyone by playing in a game the next day. He established a reputation for "playing hurt," never using an injury as an excuse to miss practice or a game.

As trainer Jack Fadden declared: "Jensen never makes a project out of an injury and I know he's played many a ball game, and played it up to the hilt, even when he was hurting good. He always minimizes an injury and is always available." Jack was likely constantly reminded of the injury he suffered in the Rose Bowl several years before, which might have cost his team the game, so he was not about to let down his teammates. The men had readily come to like Jack, and a couple of players became good friends with him. Milt Bolling recalled the following episode:

> I guess the closest people to him would be Sammy White, whom he roomed with on the road a lot of times, and Frank Sullivan, another close friend of Jackie's. I guess I'm the only one who found out—when they were on the road, I went to eat with them a few times, just those three—as soon as they finished eating they'd hurry back to the hotel and go up to their room, and I'd say, "What's going on with you guys?"
>
> This goes on for about a week, and they said, "We'd let you in on it if you promise not to tell anybody."
>
> Everybody does some crazy things every once in a while, some nutty things, so I said, "I won't tell."

So I went up to the room with them, and they had brought all these toy soldiers and these toy cannons, and they were playing war up there. After every ball game they would just play war. If we had a night game, the next day they'd be up to three or four o'clock on the floor in there shooting these little toy cannons at toy soldiers. They'd just do it all night long, but they didn't want anybody to know about it. You could imagine if the press got hold of that! But they did that for one whole year they traveled. Every town they'd go to they'd find some new soldiers and new cannons.

What impressed people about Jack was his gentlemanly conduct and his conservative nature. Even when he wished to smoke (a habit he began when emulating Joe DiMaggio), usually between innings, he'd go off by himself where few people could see him. Rarely did he do anything to draw attention to himself, and what was daring for him was considered ordinary for many others. For example, a couple of times during a road trip Jack wore Bermuda shorts and long socks to dinner, but gave up that attire after a few guys on the team teased him about it.

Jack was still following Ted Williams in the batting lineup, and once before an August game in Yankee Stadium, packed with 61,628 fans, Jack stood outside a batting cage from which Ted hit balls high into the right-field stands. As he left the area, the crowd gave Ted a standing ovation, which continued as Jackie got up to take his place. Amid the ongoing applause, Jackie turned to *New York Times* columnist Arthur Daly and said, "See, Arthur, they still remember me."

Inevitably, the pressures of moving around the country and the extended separations took their toll on the Jensens. The first signs of discontent made public were revealed in the August 7, 1955, feature article in the *Worcester Sunday Telegram's Feature Parade*. The cover sported a color photograph of the smiling Jensen family nestled together, and inside Jack was humorously pictured sitting on a wall in front of their West Newton home, supervising lawn mowing by Zoe and Jan. The story itself was more realistic and

actually centered on Zoe, who admitted to nervousness and con-
fessed to suffering for Jack, in that she could empathize with his
pressures as an athlete. It is interesting to note how a word was
taken out of context for a subtitle at the top of the page, which read:
"Baseball Wife: Zoe Ann Jensen, wife of Red Sox Slugger, Follows
Game Closely, 'Suffers,' Is Former Olympic Diving Star."

From her slim frame Zoe claimed she had lost eighteen pounds
since leaving competition—ostensibly because she had to run after
the children; but perhaps it was restlessness, anxiety, or unhappi-
ness as she saw Jack becoming ever more popular while she was
turning into a domestic. In contrast to a statement made more than
a year before that she intended to watch many Boston games, now
that the family was more settled into the area, Zoe admitted she
attended only about a dozen games a year. However, their home
seemed their best one yet, apart from the house they still maintained in California. The article continued: "The Jensen residence is
a two-story middle-class stucco dwelling on a West Newton side
street, a few blocks from the shopping center. The Jensens are renting it furnished for the baseball season, and are much happier with
the space than they have been other years in cramped apartments.
In the driveway is usually parked their 1955 station wagon. On the
rear panel is painted 'The Bow and Bell,' Jack's Oakland, Calif.,
restaurant which he hopes will support his post-baseball years."

Little did Jack realize that those hopes would be dashed—his
marriage would turn sour, his partnership with Boots dissolve, and
his two children turn away from him.

By the end of the summer Jack was still gaining popularity to
the point of equaling that of Ted Williams. Coach Dressen said, "He
has done a terrific job. Anyone who bats behind Williams and drives in as many runs as Jensen must do a good job. [The pitchers]
pass Williams so much to get to the next guy that it is a real pressure job. Yet Jensen comes through under pressure."

By mid-September the Boston fans were expecting perfection
from Jack and let him know it whenever he disappointed them.
Although they were traditionally known to be considerate specta-

tors, they criticized Jack relentlessly. The visiting White Sox manager, Marty Marion, said: "It's the first time I ever saw Boston fans get on a local player." Many would unmercifully boo Jack if he failed to get a hit or made a rare, bad play in the field, but some sportswriters, such as Ed Rumill of the *Christian Science Monitor,* supported Jack in columns like the one entitled "Jackie Does Not Rate Booing He Gets."

Perhaps the man who Dressen said performed well under pressure was handling it well externally, but not internally. Whereas Jack had said, "I really don't blame them for getting 'on' me. I made a bad play the other day," sportswriter Rumill commented, "You know he feels it deeply and is now trying so hard he has trouble doing anything right."

Jack might have been suffering a recurrence of problems he had while playing for the Oakland Oaks, when he did well on the road but poorly at home.

He, like Mickey Vernon, did play well away from Boston. At one point Jack had an average of .361 with three homers, three triples, and ten RBIs in ten games. In spite of his failure to measure up to his own expectations, Jack was always optimistic about the Red Sox's chances for success, and he gave credit to his fellow players, stressing their team effort. While Jack and many newspapers praised the efforts of Ted Williams, Billy Klaus, Jim Piersal, Sammy White, and Norm Zauchin, others centered their attentions on Jack, whose own modesty often betrayed his confidence and ability. An article by Walter Judge exemplified the belief some people had in Jackie: "As a matter of fact, the club's best player is Jackie Jensen. Jackie can do it all. Possibly not since Jackie Robinson's prime has there been a base runner who caused the pitcher so much trouble once he reached first base. He bluffs beautifully."

This is the same article which recognized that Ted Williams was on the downslide, and it looked as if Jack might be the man to take Ted's position as the foremost Red Sox player. Recalling Judge's words that Jack "bluffs beautifully," one might wonder if that statement had broader implications—Jack apparently concentrated on his game, but worried about not seeing the family enough.

While Rita Hayworth and Columbia Pictures were suing each other, and Rock Hudson was denying rumors that he and Phyllis Gates were getting married after the filming of *Giant,* Jackie entered the movies in his own small way. He signed a contract in August to play himself in a Four Star Production of his life story. Two actors played Jack in his younger days: as a young lad who had a chip on his shoulder and as a high schooler who barely resisted the temptations of a baseball scout to drop out of school and play professional ball. The movie ended with Jack's playing for the Red Sox, but it didn't mention his wife or his children. Jack's part involved several lines at the end of the movie as he revisited Ralph Kerchum, who was featured as much as Jack throughout the television special.

Near season's end Jack was tied in a league RBI race with Ray Boone of Detroit, and it was later reported that with a 3–1 count during the September 28 second game with New York, the umpire asked Jack, "What do you want on the next call?"—Jack purportedly replied, "A strike, no matter where it is, if I don't swing" (so he could have yet another chance to drive in a run). A strike was called on what some deemed to be a wide pitch, but Jack was walked on the next pitch anyway. Umpire Paparella angrily denied the accusations, and when Jack was asked if he'd talked to the umpire, he uncharacteristically responded with a curt, "Hell, no!" He went on to explain that Tom Sturdivant's pitches had been wild, and so Jackie said to nobody in particular, "Boy, it's time he got one across." Things got distorted from there.

Although Jackie had gained eight pounds to weigh a solid two hundred by the end of the season—the result of a high-protein diet—he didn't seem worried about putting on any flab, which was especially easy to do after the season when attending the high-calorie dinners that accompanied speaking engagements. One such event was the Boston Sportswriters' banquet, where Jack received the Gene Mack Memorial Award (for most valuable member of the club), and he was also awarded the Ted Williams trophy. He had closed out the year with a .275 batting average, twenty-six home runs, and 116 RBIs—tying Boone for the league record.

Around that time, a group of Bay area businessmen approached Jack about sponsoring an annual golf tournament for charity near San Francisco. Jack liked the idea, but wanted to help perpetuate, in his own way, the Jimmy Fund (initiated by the Boston Braves to support cancer research in Boston Children's Hospital). Jack lent his name to the first annual tournament and facetiously referred to it as "The Poor Man's Bing Crosby Tournament." Taking place at the Diablo Country Club, in Danville, California, the First Annual Jackie Jensen Pro-Amateur Invitational Golf Tournament was held on February 17, 1956. The entry fee was only twenty dollars, which included a dinner ticket from Jack. He himself received one of the postcards announcing tee-off time; his was 11:46 a.m. The committee was composed of Frank Brunk, Boots Erb, Bob Hannon, Jackie Jensen, and Alex Stewart. It went well, and Jack received praise from both the participants and the media. An article by Bob Goethals read, in part:

> After seeing the way some local golf tournaments get botched
> up, the recent Jackie Jensen invitational was a model of effi-
> ciency in comparison. Probably most of the credit should go to
> Alex Stewart of Hayward, who acted as tournament director.
> He did a thorough job. For example, every player in the field
> of more than 100 received three individual letters [a postcard
> with players' starting times, a thank-you letter from Jack and
> Boots Erb, and finally a letter from Mrs. William Howard Oliver
> of the Children's Hospital of the East Bay, which received
> $1210 from the tournament].

The day after his tournament, Jack registered as a member of the Loyal Order of Moose, having been "created" a Baby Moose on May 22, 1953, and he still kept other ties with California, as witnessed by his 1956 membership card for the University of California's Big C Society. A couple of weeks before the tournament (February 2, 1956), Jack was nominated to the

Independent Order of Foresters in Oakland ("one of the oldest and wealthiest Fraternal Orders in existence, its records going back almost eight hundred years"), and three days later he participated in the Tenth Annual Polio Benefit Baseball Game in El Cerrito, California.

Jackie visited the Reno YMCA's Father and Son Banquet in early 1956, following which the director, Dick Taylor, wrote Jack a letter expressing his thanks and the fact that the mayor had a key to the city for Zoe Ann and her mother's swimming group if they could help dedicate the new pool. However, Jack received the letter in an unusual and sad way. Addressed to the Bow and Bell Restaurant, a second letter accompanied the original, whereby Mr. Taylor's secretary, Marjorie J. Willott, explained why she had to sign Dick's name. He had been killed in an automobile accident before he could send the letter.

The rest of the winter was uneventful, but early in 1956 Jack wasn't as eager or naive as the season before to turn in his contract; instead he asked for a $4,000 raise over the $18,000 he had received previously. He returned two contracts, making it known he could play for a team other than the Red Sox, before he settled on his terms. He then went on to the Red Sox camp in Sarasota, where West Coast reporters who had visited the Seals training camp in De Land, Florida, stopped by for some newsworthy tidbits. They quoted Ted Williams's objections to the Army inducting Brooklyn Dodgers pitcher Johnny Padres; and Billy Martin, while visiting the training site, agreed with Williams. Then Billy turned the conversation to Jack, saying: "Look, there's Gorgeous George, a great guy that Jackie. We went up to the Yankees together at the end of the 1949 season and I still can't understand why our club let him get away from us."

Spring training in 1956 was a little different for Jack in that Zoe Ann did not accompany him East, for she didn't want to take Jan out of school, and, as she would later admit, she honestly wasn't a baseball fan. However, she did move to Boston with the children in June and stayed until late August. It had been a long time since

Jack had either put his foot in his mouth (regarding his college and minor-league pitching coaches) or had his words twisted. This time Jack was quoted as saying he felt he was making good money in baseball and probably couldn't make as much doing anything else; this was construed by some to mean that he played baseball only for the money. Once again the "fans" at Fenway found something to boo about, and they let Jack have it when he came onto the field, but he generally ignored them.

May opened with newspaper cartoons announcing the fact that Jack was in "a new Starring Role"; one caption read: "the spotlight on one of America's great and versatile athletes focuses on a new endeavor as the Red Sox outfielder turns TV star for the DuPont Cavalcade Theater." The movie in which Jack had acted was finally shown to the public, and it received much hype. In its final version it primarily sought to illustrate how a young lad from the Great Depression could make it to hero status through athletic ability and the guidance of a concerned mentor. Several parts were exaggerated, such as Jack's hanging around with adolescent thugs and being physically rescued by Ralph, but the theme of the movie was admirable. Schools across the country watched the film in auditoriums or on television sets. Especially altered was the wording of the record Ralph Kerchum had made fifteen years before in his living room, asking Jack to state his goals in life. (Transcripts comparing both are in appendix A and appendix B.)

The new season started out great for Jackie. Headlines of the *Boston Globe* said, "Jensen's Miracle Throw Saves, Homer Wins Game" and "Sox Outfielder Records Greatest Day of Career." The article seemed to be influenced by the recent movie:

> May 21—The sports career of Jackie Jensen already had reached fantastic heights. From a backyard in Oakland, where a tow-headed kid threw rocks at tomato cans, it has gone on to the Rose Bowl and the World Series. Yet yesterday, before 23,500 at Comiskey Park, Jensen—at the age of 29—had the greatest day of his professional career. From his position in right field.
>
> Jensen made a play that few men in the majors ever made.

Racing to a long hit ball by Luis Aparicio, Jack snatched it up with a one-handed backhand pickup, wheeled around, and fired a perfect throw to the chest of catcher Sam White, who tagged out Ron Jackson racing from third base for what would have been a winning run.

Earlier in the day Jack had hit a home run off Dick Donovan for the first score in the doubleheader; but in the ninth inning of the second game he hit another about 400 feet into the stands against Bob Keegan, who had held batters to only one earned run in thirty innings of pitching. Sportswriters continued to support Jackie, and his performance seemed to improve along with their praise. Dave Egan, in "The Colonel," began his column with "Jensen Rates Better Deal" (*Boston Daily Record* Tuesday, May 22, 1956). Referring to Jackie's hecklers, Egan wrote: "It only goes to prove that each city has a minority of gawky clodhoppers who deal out anonymous abuse to men of the character of Jensen and [Al Rosen] and have their keepers write anonymous letters to sports columnists. They are the flotsam, the jetsam, the riffraff, and the lunkheads that can be found in any big city, and I ask Jackie Jensen not to measure and judge Boston by its foolish few."

A couple of days later, on returning from a western trip (where he had three triples and as many home runs in twelve games), Jackie, in response to remarks about his .381 hitting clip, compared to .214 while at Boston in the spring, shrugged off the compliments while looking to the challenges ahead. "It takes nine players to make a winning team," he said, "not one. I just hope I can keep it up. The fans back home? Oh, I don't know. They may not change toward me. All I know is that I'll do my best and hope that I can help the team."

Despite the praise by columnists and assurances that the Boston hecklers were merely a vocal minority, Jack, always eager to have things go right, couldn't help but be affected by them. He bore up as well as might be expected until one day in early August, when a spectator particularly angered him. Pitcher Mel Parnell and Coach Paul Schreiber had to restrain Jack as he tried to climb up into the stands after a "boo-bird." Upon looking back at the incident, Jack said: "I guess I was a little edgy that day. I thought he got too personal in things he was saying about my wife."

This was the same day another frustrated player was fined for spitting at fans and assessed a penalty that gave him the dubious distinction of tying Babe Ruth for the largest fine in the history of baseball—$5,000. Ted Williams was also becoming famous for throwing his bat, and with Jack and Jimmy Piersall, a trio of sensitive players was becoming notorious.   ·

At season's end, Jack's batting average was the highest of his career, .315, while he hit twenty home runs and earned ninety-seven RBIs, but he accumulated twelve errors—also the highest he would ever have. At that time Al Rosen, the thirty-one-year-old Cleveland Indians player often compared with Jackie because of being booed by fans, announced his retirement from baseball. This event was probably the first that really got Jack thinking about quitting, for he was realizing more and more that he was missing a home life. His marriage was starting to fail; in fact, an incident recalled by Garff Wilson illustrates how unfortunate the situation had become. That winter the Jensens made Lake Tahoe their principal residence when they sold their home in Oakland. Garff (by that time a good friend), accompanied by Jim Cherry, a football buddy of Jack's, was met by Jack at the airport and driven to the Jensens' home. When they approached the front door, Jan came running out, yelling "Welcome!" Zoe Ann, behind her, said apologetically, "Jan is a bit too demonstrative." When they left, Jack's son Jon, sobbing, clung to the visitors and said, "I want to go with you."

During that visit Jack had a heart-to-heart talk with his former teacher and told him that his marriage was falling apart. The gist of it was that Zoe blamed him for depriving her of a college education and the experiences associated with it. Furthermore, Jack had tied her down to a family, so felt he had to be a father not just to the kids but also to his wife. In a rare instance of expressing his feelings, Jack said he needed a partner and helpmate and a shoulder to cry on, but instead he had to be strong and comfort himself.

Meanwhile, some of the more romantic newspaper writers sought to perpetuate the Golden Couple's image as happy parents. In Sec Taylor's column "Sitting in with the Athletes," an article entitled "From Pool to Snow" pictured Zoe Ann (who loved skiing as much as swimming) with Jack and Jan as the six-year-old girl tried on a ski. Jack was also photographed with some of his old college buddies that winter; just as he had been privileged to welcome Pappy Waldorf at the start of his illustrious coaching stint at Cal ten years before, so was he to able to express his fond farewells at a dignified Bow and Bell party held in Pappy's honor.

Shortly thereafter, Jack received a call from Zoe in Lake Tahoe, saying she had received a telegram informing Jack he was to train with the Seals (a farm club of the Red Sox) in Fullerton, California. Jack knew the accommodations there were fantastic, since the team stayed in the Disneyland Hotel, and he thought at once how his family could enjoy the theme park. Although Jack hadn't talked to anyone about his fear of flying, obviously the team manager or owner knew Jack would appreciate not having to travel to Sarasota just to train for a few weeks, then return to California for an exhibition series with the Seals the third week of March. Although Jackie hadn't been consulted in the matter, he was nonetheless grateful for a chance to be at home more and avoid flying.

However, not everyone was pleased with the prospect of Jack's training with the Seals: Charley Graham, vice-president of the Sacramento Salons, complained that Jack was being pampered, that the Pacific Coast League would be hurt by the arrangement because sportswriters would ignore the minor league-players and focus their attention on Jack. Regardless of whether Jackie's fear of flying was the reason for the change, both the Red Sox and the Seals benefitted: Several days that Jackie would have spent riding the train were instead spent on training, and Jackie assisted manager Joe Gordon in handling the Seals' outfielders.

Just before that training began, in February 1957 Jack joined

Boots in starting another eatery in Alameda, naming it the Red Sox Restaurant. It was modeled after Smokey Joe's, from which Boots imported as a partner Dave Rosien, the man who had all the recipes and management skills. Specializing in barbecued ribs and hamburgers, the restaurant did a brisk lunch trade. Its supper business never did meet expectations, however, and it closed in 1960 (without a loss).

Jack accepted 105 of 320 people who wished to play in his second annual golf tournament. But golf and the Bow and Bell seemed to keep Jack away from the family nearly as much as baseball. Not long after the photo of the Jensens on skis was run, Zoe broke her leg on the slopes, soon after Jack had left for spring training. In a phone call, however, she informed him that it wasn't necessary for him to come back home; she didn't mention the break was serious enough to require a cast for several months. Jack wouldn't see her again until August.

Jack also suffered an injury. At the end of spring training he developed a cold in his back, and the malady worsened as the team moved north. This was especially rough for him, as he hated not playing (as noted earlier). So Jack missed the first week of the regular season but, fortunately for the team, Williams was back in style, hitting over .400 game after game. Jack, on the other hand, had a rough time getting back into the swing of things; it wasn't until Memorial Day that he started on a roll—hitting a home run against Baltimore with the score tied 6-6 in the tenth inning. After Jack finished the season with a .281 average and 103 RBIs to tie Frank Malzone for the league record, he was able to spend some time at his Lake Tahoe home, where the whole family enjoyed the winter sports. Zoe wouldn't let her accident from the year before keep her from skiing again; and Jan herself was fast becoming an excellent skier, swimmer, and diver. Jon, four years old, seemed to be a clone of his father. Jack undoubtedly wondered if his children would follow in his and Zoe's footsteps. Professional sports indeed paid well; he signed a contract for the 1958 season for $27,500.

Occasionally Jack would drive back to the Bay area to check on the restaurants and to golf, but most of his time was spent at home; and as spring training approached, Jack and his family had to readjust their thinking once again to accept his anticipated long absence. However, this year would be very different, for while it would mark the high point of his career, it would also be the turning point in his marriage.

9

GOLDEN GLORY

In 1958 Americans looked to the stars, for Sputnik had just gone into orbit, but a down-to-earth luminary was rapidly coming into view: Jackie Jensen would receive the recognition many said was long overdue. The public's attention began to turn to Jack as he turned his attention to others. Having done more than his fair share already in contributing to the Jimmy Fund through his golf tournament, Jack found another opportunity to raise money without much difficulty. The *Record-American-Advertiser* announced it would donate $50 to the Jimmy Fund for each of the first ten home runs hit by individual players, $75 for homers eleven to twenty, and $100 for all such hits over the twentieth. The season started out with a bang for Jack; he hit a two-run homer, followed by three more in the next four days.

Still, Jack wanted the best of both worlds—a happy family life combined with a successful baseball career. For one day he was able to come close to realizing just that as five-year-old Jon followed him onto the field at Fenway Park, dressed in a miniature Jensen uniform. The Father's Day contest was played between the double-header Red Sox games against the Kansas City Athletics. One newspaper article was subtitled, "Photographer Nearly Beaned by Young Jensen in Warm-up," and when Jon first came up to swing at the tennis ball, he took a left-handed stance until he was picked up and moved to the other side of the plate by Sammy White. The fathers cheerfully lost to the sons 0-5.

On June 23, 1958, nearly five years to the day that Jack had appeared on the cover of *Collier's,* he achieved the ultimate in magazine fame—the cover of *Sports Illustrated.* Next to the picture of Jack clutching a bat at both ends across his thighs was the title "Jackie Jensen, Wheel Horse of the Red Sox," and the inside cover's caption read, "One of the most underrated players in the major leagues is steady, dependable Jackie Jensen of the Red Sox, an athlete who has a longing for home instead of headlines."

The feature article, entitled "All-Star Who Can Do without Glory" by Roy Terrell, was subtitled, "Jackie Jensen, unsung hero of the Red Sox, doesn't mind if others get headlines. He's had them—and would rather go home." The Jackie of bonus days was compared with the current one, a "friendly, pleasant, gentlemanly sort of guy, a devoted family man and a real hard-working, steady ballplayer who does just about as good a job as anyone could ask, whether it be to run or field or hit or throw."

Attributing his success simply to experience, Jackie seemed to turn the conversation to his domestic life: "In baseball you get to the point where you don't think you have a family. It just looks like I'm not built for this life like some ballplayers. You are always away from home and you're lonesome, and as soon as I can, I intend to get out."

When asked how he felt about Stengel, Jack, who had been quite offended by the manager when traded, put things into perspective and said he understood why Casey had to trade him—he just wasn't doing the job for the Yankees. In fact, he said, "Casey is a wonderful, sweet old guy. I think he is the smartest manager in baseball. I know he taught me more in two years than anybody before or since."

Jackie admitted he was worried about how to field a ball hit in front of him (Jack was one of the best in going back for a fly ball), and went on to lavish praise on Ted Williams. Jack himself was praised for his honesty by Joe McKenney, the Red Sox publicity manager, who related how after Jack had dropped a ball and was questioned by reporters, he answered simply that he had misjudged it, although all kinds of excuses could have been made. The last section of the article, consisting largely of quotations, was written by Guy Shipler, a stringer for *Sports Illustrated* who had moved to Nevada two years earlier after working in New York for *Newsweek, Time,* and *Business Week.* An independent man, Guy had sought to escape the rat race by moving West, and he thoroughly enjoyed freelance work. However, while interviewing Jackie, he felt uncomfortable. Harry Spencer (an entrepreneur who worked for Charley Mapes, a hotel owner), a friend of Jack's, had arranged for the interview with the Jensens over dinner at a restaurant; and Guy, knowing how affable Jack was, expected everything would go smoothly: "He was about to leave for spring training, and he was very upset. In fact, the interview was not too good; it was very unlike Jackie in terms of his outgoing attitude and warmth, you know. He was glad that they were doing the story, but he sure as hell didn't want some reporter there bothering him. He and Zoe Ann were holding hands, and he was going to have to leave her."

Without alluding to the fact that once again Jack had mixed feelings about leaving Zoe behind, the article concluded by mentioning that the star player would frequently drive his Thunderbird to the Bow and Bell, which was averaging three hundred lunches a day (compared to forty some five years before); and it concluded with lamentations by Zoe Ann about her separations from Jackie, although, she admitted, "We're building security and I'm grateful for that." Unfortunately, that security was never to be realized.

A few days later the *Boston Evening American* reported Jack had "earned" $1,175 for the Jimmy Fund with nineteen home runs, followed by Gernert ($650 for twelve), and Williams ($400 for eight). At that time Jack was tied with Bob Cerv for the most home runs in the American League, and the race between them would continue throughout the season. Sportscasters and players alike were focusing on Jackie as never before: Roy Sievers, 1957 American League leader in home runs and RBIs, who at the beginning of July was third behind Jack and Bob Cerv, said, "I can imagine how Jackie feels. Jackie's strong and he's got the power." People were also starting to take notice of Jack's other statistics. Despite his frequent slumps, it was noted that "during the years he has worn a Red Sox uniform he has driven in more runs than any [other] American League player over the same stretch."

By Independence Day the loyalty of Boston fans for Jack was finally evident. For the first season ever in Boston, he was not booed when he hit into double plays; in fact, one paper reported "Even Gamblers Like Jensen." It explained that even those who lost bets on Jensen wouldn't think of criticizing him if he slipped up, for it had become apparent that Jackie was always trying his best. Jack enjoyed cheers when he went out onto the field or came up to bat, and he admitted he was receiving the most fan mail ever. By the time he was elected by fellow players to participate in the All-Star game, Jackie led the league in homers and RBIs and was batting .315; furthermore, he had hit safely in the last fifteen games.

Since the end of June, when Jack and Ted both hit three homers to come from behind and defeat the White Sox, Jack earned a place alongside his idol and would go on to surpass him in popularity. For instance, a July 11 article reported that Jack received a standing ovation as he took the field after hitting his twenty-fifth home run—a grand slam. Incredibly, Jack's response to his marvelous hit was quite modest: "That home run I hit tonight was a matter of hitting the ball as hard as I could and, of course, I got some help from the wind." He further explained his success: "I'm not the master batsman who can say that I did this or that to get rid of a hitch. I just know that I'm meeting that ball now and everything is swell as long as it continues."

The next day, one paper headlined, "Jensen Replaces Ted as Mr. Big," as it reported his batting average at .319 and that he was leading the league in home runs and RBIs. Still, the legendary Williams was the big drawing card, and nobody was more disappointed than he when he failed to live up to the fans' expectations. In one game the discouraged star flipped his bat, almost hitting the first-base coach walking toward the Red Sox dugout, but Jackie was there to lift the team's spirits when he hit a two-run homer. White Sox catcher Earl Battey said, "Jim Wilson pitched a good ball game, but what're you gonna do against a guy goin' like Jensen?"

Jack's humble response was, "I'm not up with Wilson, even with the home run. He's been awful tough on me, good stuff, and a smart, smart pitcher." He continued that the home run "didn't feel real good. I wasn't sure it was a homer when I hit it—you can tell with most of them—my bat vibrated and I thought I'd broken it. But, a home run is a home run." In spite of his modesty, even Jack was finally recognizing his superiority as a player; he was quoted as saying: "It has always been my ambition to be named the top right fielder in our league. Somehow, I hardly thought I'd ever make it."

As Jackie's fame soared, so did attention to his family. Zoe joined the wives of Joe McKinney (public relations director), Ted Lepcio, and Dick Gervert for a fashion show at the Hotel Somerset. Whereas the other women wore dresses, Zoe, still shapely, modeled a swimsuit. She also appeared at poolside in a feature article centered on her daughter; it was entitled "Jan Jensen Doesn't Play House—She Climbs Trees" (*The Boston Sunday Globe,* July 13, 1958). Seven-year-old Jan, who had been swimming since she was eight months old, was described as a natural athlete, and Jon was pictured as a copycat. Zoe was quick to point out that she and Jack didn't push the children to engage in sports, for Zoe vividly recalled the pressures on her during her youth. She did say, "Our family revolves around sports; it's my love and Jackie's business." They had also enjoyed horseback riding but had to give it up when they moved East. Referring to the recent Father-Son game, Zoe said she never took the children to a ball park. Jon was showing the same early development as his father did when very young. In fact, it was reported that Jon had to be fished out of the pool three times.

By the end of August even General Manager Cronin said, "Jackie has become the strong man of the troupe." At that point Jack had his eye on Al Rosen's record of 145 RBIs as Jack led the league with 110, with thirty-five homers and a .312 batting average, making him third and fifth best in the league, respectively. Near season's end, Jack received two surprises: a kiss from Miss Hawaii, who was in Atlanta City for the Miss America pageant, and an appearance in the September issue of *Sport* magazine, where Al Hirshberg asked the question: "What Do They Want from Jackie Jensen?" Hirshberg said that Jackie had taken the blame for the Red Sox slump at the beginning of the season. He recalled the strikes Jackie had against him: his glamor-boy image, his double-play syndrome, his slumps, and his candid remark about baseball being a business.

Coming to his defense, Hirshberg enumerated Jack's home run and RBI statistics, his honesty, and his playing while hurt. The problem lay in that people took his successes for granted. Manager Mike Higgins asked: "Why do they boo that guy? He's got power, and he hits with men on bases. He can powder the hell out of the ball. When he gets hold of one, he'll hit it as far as anybody else. Aside from his power, he can do more things well than anyone else on our club."

Thirty years later, ex-teammate Milt Bowling, a Red Sox scout, compared Jackie to the prospects he currently saw, and he said something similar: "[today] he'd be a million-dollar player. I scout—and he does the five things you look for, average or above average; you can't find those today: good-average arm or perhaps above-average arm, above-average speed, average hitter with above-average power, and he was above-average outfielder; and he could steal a base, too."

Jack himself recognized the difficulty of hitting fourth or fifth in the lineup, and he made simple statements of fact normally over-looked by many: that even a .300 hitter misses seven times out of ten, and that if people cheer him when he succeeds, they have a right to boo him when he fails. He spoke deprecatingly of his own performances, saying: "I'm not a good enough hitter to be batting fourth or fifth," and that he hated hitting into double plays more than anyone, but truthfully Williams and other batters who pre-ceded him were slow runners. While he was voicing his opinions, Jack suggested that records should be established for a man who moved others along the bases, even if he didn't get them home, for such a person would be just as responsible for an RBI as a hitter who followed him. Jack concluded the article by saying he liked Boston in spite of the booing ("one boo can carry a long way"), and that although he believed luck had a lot to do with his early success, he had learned that a professional ball player needs more than that to succeed. Jack replied negatively to Hirshberg's last question, which would turn out to be ironic considering what was about to occur: "Do you resent not being appreciated?"

After the end of the Red Sox season, Jack took the train West and was met by Zoe and the children in Reno. Soon afterward, the *Sporting News* selected Jack as player-of-the-year: "Nobody on any club in baseball meant more to his team than Jensen did to the Red Sox this year."

The title "Golden Boy" was brought to life again on November 21, 1958, when the media announced Jack had won the American League Most Valuable Player Award (selected by the Baseball Writers' Association). One particularly flattering sketch was drawn by Bob Coyne, accompanied by the caption "Jackie Jensen. The Golden Boy has a golden crown." The write-ups were indeed glorious—stating that he was the season's top RBI man (122), was third in home runs (35), and ended up with a .286 batting average—even after a September slump blamed by many on the fact that he burned himself out by trying so hard during the months before. He was described as the best right fielder in the league, credited with only six errors in 154 games, and his name appeared on twenty-three of the twenty-four cast ballots. Jackie had finally joined his teammates, past and present, at the pinnacle of baseball fame—for Mantle had received MVP the previous two seasons, Yogi Berra the two before those, and Ted Williams in 1949.

Jack was contacted at his home in Lake Tahoe and said simply, "You have no idea how happy this makes me," and he admitted he had thought the award would go to the Yanks' Bob Turley, who was the winningest pitcher in the league.

Jack basked in the spotlight a little longer. He attended banquets in his honor and received the Washington Touchdown Club's baseball player trophy. He also was named the year's outstanding professional athlete by the Athens Athletic Club (in attendance was Lefty O'Doul, who, when Jack was a youth, had given him his autograph). Furthermore, he was named "Athlete of the Year for the Sierra Nevada Region" by the Sierra Nevada Sportswriters and Broadcasters, and received a sixteen-foot motorboat as a gift from two hundred friends who honored him at a dinner. Jackie reflected on his baseball career to date, saying, "When a fellow becomes a pro baseball player, it [the MVP award] seems so far out of reach, yet he hopes he can obtain it."

Where was Jack to go from there? He himself said the MVP award meant he was at the top of his profession, and he had always striven to be the best at whatever he did. He recognized that one goal ahead of him was simply a happy family, yet realized that he couldn't continue playing all around the country while giving Zoe and the children the attention he felt they deserved. Jack was in a compromising situation—he couldn't devote himself fully to the family *and* to baseball, so he began more seriously wondering how long to stay in professional baseball.

As if to have the decision made for him if he demanded a huge pay hike, Jack uncharacteristically became tougher when it came time to discuss the next season's salary. He had three reasons to seek a large raise for the 1959 season: He had negotiated successfully the year before; he had been named the league MVP (which other players said was worth at least a $10,000 raise in itself); and he thought that if he had to quit baseball, he could make a living close to home and achieve the goal of being with the family more. Jackie did realize that the more money he could earn before his inevitable retirement, the better off his future would be, so he asked for $40,000 to return to the Red Sox. This he thought was not unreasonable; after all, ex-teammate Mantle was asking twice that amount. "I'm not going to bicker or bargain," Jackie said. "I feel my services are worth so much and I am not going to change my thoughts. If I don't get [the price I quote], I'll have more time to spend with my family."

Encouraged by friend Dom DiMaggio, who said, "Don't let them get you cheap," Jack sent back two separate contracts of $32,500 and $35,000. Representing Boston, Bucky Harris said the publicity involving Ted Williams receiving $125,000 was what was prompting Jackie to ask for so much; but here was a player many others dared to say was better than Williams, yet he was asking for only one third the salary. Finally Jackie signed on his own terms (actually with a slight compromise; he settled for $39,500—equivalent to over a quarter million dollars today) after a five-minute conference with Harris in Scottsdale, Arizona.

Jack's desire to leave baseball soon was taken more seriously when the April issue of the *Saturday Evening Post* hit the newsstands. In an article entitled "My Ambition Is to Quit," by Al Hirshberg, Jack referred indirectly to his recent contract: "The more money I get, the sooner I can quit." To explain this puzzling statement, Jack went on to say that he hated the day-to-day existence, shifting from games at night to those during the day, and of course flying. In the article Jack was pictured kissing Zoe good-bye on the steps as he held a suitcase. Jon was standing close to his father, his hand outstretched to the chest above him, and Jan was behind her brother, casting a disdainful look. The caption was a touching one: "'I spend less than half my time with the people I love most,' laments Jensen."

The salary squabble over, Jack focused on the future. It was only the money, he explained, that was keeping him on the team: He felt guilty that he had been away from home when both children were born, when Zoe broke an ankle and was ill with pneumonia twice, and when Jon was bitten in the head by a dog. Another reason he was concerned so much with being with the family, he said, was because of his poor situation in early childhood—he didn't want to see the same scenario repeated. Finally, Jack stated that he had left the decision of when to retire up to Zoe Ann, who replied, "I'll never ask you to quit." When fear of flying was mentioned, Jack admitted that when forced to fly, he could, but only with the help of sleeping pills and tranquilizers.

Several weeks later Jack was again featured in a major magazine. The *Look* article (5-26-59) took a different slant from that of the *Post*. In fact, it optimistically suggested Jack would not retire soon: "He should contend for the [MVP] award from now on, because, at 32, the muscled slugger appears to have reached his true level as a player." Whereas some fans might have had the impression that Jack missed many games because of his problems, it was pointed out that he had played 755 of 770 games. Trainer Fadden reminded readers, "He plays with bruises, pulled muscles and tendons that would keep out other players for days or weeks. One night he played with a 103-degree temperature."

Photographs of Jack with friends Bing Crosby and Tony Martin were next to an explanation that Jack had invested "wisely," which was partially true. The Bow and Bell was reported to be grossing $250,000 a year, and Jack had invested $20,000 in land at Lake Tahoe, where he planned to build homes, but purported investments in a racehorse and an oil well lost money. Back home Zoe would often host the *Bonanza* television crew who filmed in the area, and apparently Jack was jealous of her associating with certain members of the cast. Jack, as teammate Frank Malzone related later, was never one to seek female companionship on the road, and it often seemed as though something was troubling him. Jack started wondering openly if he could hold the family together; Al Rosen's quitting unexpectedly a year before remained in the back of his mind. He would later be quoted as saying, "What's left in the game for me to prove anyway?" He considered getting involved with radio or TV announcing in addition to his restaurant and real estate interests.

As the '59 season began, Jack increasingly refused to fly with the team. At times it seemed as if he had conquered his fear, and Jack would assure the traveling secretary, Tom Dowd, that he'd be at an airport, but he would not show. Instead, Jack drove, his luggage making the trip ahead of him by plane. This wouldn't present a problem except that Jack did not tell anyone of his change of plans. In one instance, when public relations director Bill Crowley, in Boston, called Zoe Ann, she simply explained, "We planned to go to the airport, but then Jackie said he'd rather drive. He's accustomed to long drives. He knows all the fast highways from Boston to Detroit."

Jack appeared to be frustrated with baseball entirely, despite his recent glory, for he said, "I'll get out of baseball—and I mean totally out. I don't want to be a manager, scout, coach, farm director, general manager, traveling secretary, league president, commissioner, or batboy." However, in the years ahead Jack would indeed take on more than one of those jobs. Referring to Rosen's early retirement, Jack said that until Al's announcement to quit, he thought nobody else had felt the way he himself did; and when asked about his wife's advice on the matter, he replied, "Zoe won't say so in so many words, but I know she wants me to give up baseball. I used to dream of the day when I'd have a family of my own and a place I could really call home. Now that the dream has come true, I think it's understandable that I want more time to enjoy it."

Of course Jack had stated publicly a couple of months before that Zoe Ann wouldn't ask him to quit—evidently she didn't want to make the decision for him, but later he said: "We were both tired of living out of the suitcase."

By August Jack was again in contention for the RBI title, but he had become increasingly unhappy. When the *Boston Globe* quoted an "informant" as saying Jackie would retire at the end of the season, across the country the *Oakland Tribune* simultaneously quoted Zoe Ann as saying that Jackie was more serious than ever before about quitting. The next day a rumor surfaced (8-3-59) that Jack might be traded to the Giants, where he could play at least half the season closer to home so he wouldn't have to end his career, Manager Bill Rigney said he'd welcome Jack to the team; but Jack wouldn't give reporters verification of his decision—simply because it hadn't been made. He was determined to wait until after the season and was sorry a story had broken so soon about one of his considerations.

Throughout the season (in which the Red Sox finished a disappointing fifth place), Jack was again the one to catch for the RBI title, even though he played in the fewest games since he left the

Yankees in 1952. Retirement weighed heavily on his mind, for his performance—though better than 90 percent of all other ballplayers'—was slipping. He ended the season in glory, however: In his final contest against the Senators, he tied the score in the ninth inning by doubling home two runs, then went on to win the game with a homer (his twenty-eighth) in the eleventh inning. However, his number of runs batted in had dropped by ten, his home runs by seven, and his batting average to just .277. In fact, the RBI title didn't seem to mean anything to him, as he declined to play in a second game against the Senators at a time when Rocky Colavito of the Cleveland Indians trailed Jackie by only a few RBIs but went hitless in four at-bats later that day against the Athletics.

Jack had been eager to get home the last day of the season, September 27, so he obtained permission to skip that final game so to catch the two o'clock train. When asked about his future, Jackie replied, "I plan to decide on my future in three or four weeks. I want to let Mr. Yawkey know in case it affects any trades he might have in mind for the winter. In October Jack began to look seriously into becoming a home-building contractor in Lake Tahoe and starting a second Bow and Bell at the south end of the city to take advantage of the forthcoming Olympics. By early the next month came word from Bucky Harris that "Jensen won't be traded." Speculation about Jackie's retirement continued through the rest of the year until the last week of January 1960, when Jack told the Associated Press in Los Angeles that he had turned down a generous offer by the Red Sox to return.

Ironically, Jackie was one of nineteen sluggers from fifteen major league teams to participate in the *Home Run Derby* (see appendix L) between seasons, becoming the third-highest winner. Despite five homers in a row, he lost to Mickey Mantle 10–13 in one game and 2–9 in another. However, he beat Rocky Colavito 3–2, and, in what was described later by David Gough as the most exciting game of the series, beat Ernie Banks, his National League MVP counterpart, 14–11.

PART THREE

1960–1973

The caption with this news photo in Ron Fimrite's article in Sports Illustrated read: "JENSEN COMFORTS WIFE—Jackie Jensen comforted his sobbing wife early today after returning to Reno, Nev. He quit the Boston Red Sox 'because I couldn't play any more in the major leagues.' His wife, former diving star Zoe Ann Olsen, wept as he approached her car at the train depot." Zoe was hop-

ing he would continue his baseball career, and Jack did return to the Red Sox for one year, then quit for good. World Wide Photos, Inc.

Jack and his friend Ray Ehlers study plans for one of their spec houses. One house they built at in Incline Village was named "The House That Jack Built." Jack would later put the building skills he learned to good use in Virginia.

Jackie Jensen 8th Annual Invitational — Diablo C.C. — 1962

Jackie Jensen's 8th Annual Invitational Golf Tournament held at the Diablo Country Club in 1962. For many years Jack and Boots Erb ran the BOOTJACK Golf Tournament. Shortly before he died Jack won the Kingsmill-Michelob Celebrity Golf Classic in Williamsburg, Virginia.

Singer Gordon MacRae between Jack and Boots Erb, Jack's partner in the Bow & Bell Restaurant.

Jack and Katharine Cortesi first got to know each other on a trip to California to interview O.J. Simpson. They were married in a Piute Indian ceremony on a dude ranch. Here they are pictured with a limit of chukar partridge on a hunting trip in Nevada.

Dining in Reno at Vario's with Joan and Harry Drackert, proprietors of the Donner Trail Ranch, where the Jensens lived in the game-keeper's cottage.

A Nevada promotional film featured Jack with a cougar. Nevada Fish & Game Commission photograph.

Jack served as a color man for ABC sports and is seen here with announcer Keith Jackson covering an NCAA game. He also hosted a ten-minute pre-game Jackie Jensen Show *on Channel 2 TV in Oakland, became sports director for KTVN-TV in Reno, and was Director of the Board of the Reno Rodeo Association. Also, he was a star in promotional clips for Holiday Lodge, and even announced demolition derbies.*

Jack became the head varsity baseball coach for the University of Nevada, Reno, where he also enrolled in courses to complete a degree in public speaking. When not coaching, Jack gave speeches and enjoyed outings with Katharine into the Nevada desert to collect artifacts such as arrowheads.

Jack and Katharine at the stadium in Jamestown, New York, where he coached the Red Sox Minor League team.

Katharine and Jack bound for Rapallo, Italy, aboard the SS Raffaello, *to visit Katharine's aunt, the Baronness Raffalovich (they are pic-*

tured on the right together in a 1943 portrait by Greta Kempton). Although he fully recuperated from his heart attack, Jack was dismayed to learn while in Italy that ABC would not renew his contract.

10

TY COBB'S ADVICE

Less than two years after receiving the American League MVP award and numerous RBI, homerun, and stolen bases honors (in addition to appearances on the covers of *Collier's* and *Sports Illustrated*), the Golden Boy was ready to enjoy a well-deserved rest at home. Such was the conclusion of Al Hirshberg's *The Jackie Jensen Story* (Mesner Press, 1960). However, as one of Jackie's sons said more than twenty-five years later, "Jack's story really began where that book left off."

Hirshberg couldn't possibly have foreseen the turbulent life that awaited his hero. Like the DuPont Cavalcade movie produced two years earlier, Hirshberg's book inspired young men to make the best of their talents while adhering to high moral standards. Hirshberg had mentioned Jack's early life during the Great Depression with a single parent and the role his high school guidance counselor had played in shaping Jack's character. Furthermore, Jack's fear of flying had been justifiably listed as a cause for his quitting the sport he loved, while his marriage problems had been glossed over. Hirshberg's references to such famous teammates of Jack's as Billy Martin, Joe DiMaggio, Mickey Mantle, and Ted Williams must have piqued readers' interest.

When Jackie announced that he would not start the 1960 season with the Red Sox, despite a respectable .277 batting average the year before, with 112 RBIs and twenty-eight home-runs, and sixty-seven stolen bases, most of his fans and many sportscasters did not believe him. However, one person took him most seriously. Writing from a hospital bed, Ty Cobb, the seventy-three-year-old

"Georgia Peach," apologized in his February 6 letter for giving Jackie unasked-for advice. He felt strongly that Jackie was making a mistake in quitting, and he related his own experience to Jackie's:

> I was a ballplayer. I know so well your feelings per being away from your family.
>
> I have been through it, with 5 children their growth and developments and my having to be away. The salary amount as quoted is too much to toss aside. Your family future is in the picture much. Remember you are not going to drop out of baseball for a year or two and come back in your present stride.
>
> You are a hell of a fine ball player Jackie, you *are* the top man on that club, the figures show. I go on record to you, I say you *should not* quit, you *should* lay your true cards on the table....you represent a lot of money to them also you represent a material amount per salary for your families future. You hav[e] a short period to earn & save, don't kick such aside, unless you really mean it. If its your desire to quit Jackie that's your business only but always remember this letter.
>
> *Get the money sure,* how much that's also your business. I stress to you, keep this confidential. *No* one. I do not need publicity, I only felt an urge to write you & shed the light of my experience.

Evidently Jackie did not deem Cobb's advice valuable enough to change his mind, for he stuck to his decision not to return to the Red Sox. However, Cobb's letter did prove to have extrinsic value: Two decades later it was sold at auction to Malcolm Forbes for several hundred dollars.

Jackie's decision not to play perplexed his fans. He had driven in more runs in the past six years than any other player in the majors. When a reporter asked Jackie if he felt he was leaving a hole in the Red Sox outfield, he simply stated that the team wouldn't have much trouble replacing him (Ted Williams, whom Jackie had replaced, was returning despite an injured neck). Jackie stressed that Zoe Ann had not influenced his decision—if anything, she thought it was too early for him to quit.

While looking for new avenues of employment, Jackie was intent on avoiding idleness. When Nevada Governor Grant Sawyer asked Jackie to serve as the state's March of Dimes chairman, he readily accepted. Unfortunately, Jackie and Boots Erb were unable to construct a Lake Tahoe restaurant in time for the 1960 Olympics. This was regrettable, for the Olympic events in nearby Squaw Valley attracted an average of more than 30,000 spectators, setting attendance records. However, the Jensen family—Jackie, Zoe Ann, sons Jon and Jay, and daughter Jan—were all avid skiers, and got to see most of the events.

Jackie visited his Oakland restaurant only occasionally to promote publicity, and he faded from public view during the spring and summer as he looked into how he might make a living in local enterprises. Throughout the year Jackie engaged in occasional house building with friend Ray Ehlers, from whom he had bought his most recent home, and he thought about speculating in homes in Tahoe City with Boots, but a market survey revealed that the area was already overbuilt. Options seemed to be running out, so Jackie started thinking about playing baseball again. Soon reporters were vying with each other to get the scoop on his possible return. Jackie's statement in a telephone interview, "I'm still in retirement but nothing says things can't change," was taken by many as proof enough that he would soon be on the playing field again. This assumption was supported by the report that Jackie was invited to Boston to attend the opening of the Brighton Bowling Alleys, run by Sammy White, a former catcher on the Red Sox with Jackie.

Before finally making up his mind, Jackie had a long talk with Dick Larner, a close friend of many years since their baseball days at Cal Berkeley. They discussed the financial aspect of rejoining professional baseball and how important the lucrative salary was to the Jensen family, grown accustomed to the good life. Although Jackie decided that night to rejoin his teammates for the 1961 season, soon afterward a reporter heard him say, "A return to baseball is highly improbable."

Apparently it took the Boston atmosphere to bring out Jackie's admission that he was returning to the sport. After baseball writers attending a meeting at Fenway Park officially learned of Ted William's retirement and the firing of General Manager Bucky Harris, Jackie announced that he wanted to play baseball again if a franchise was to be granted in the Bay area. Jackie had been authorized by friends to speak in favor of a team in the San Francisco/Oakland area. He knew all too well that his terror of flying and his uneasiness at being away from his family would be largely solved if he could play half his games close to home.

Concerning Jackie's fear of flying, an article by reporter Bud Tehaney recounted Jackie's interview with hypnotist Arthur Ellen, who had met with Jackie and Zoe after they had seen one of his stage acts at Lake Tahoe's Harrah's Club. Under hypnosis, Jackie had supposedly recalled a childhood incident when he and a friend had played crash-and-burn-the-model-airplanes. Ellen explained that when Jackie was reminded of this incident after the session, he admitted his fears were unfounded, and felt that he was cured.

Jackie became more determined than ever to play again, so he began working out at home to prepare for the next season. In November 1960 he was offered $40,000 to return to the Red Sox, which was especially encouraging since most players expected a pay cut. Jackie accepted the Red Sox offer, even though General Manager George Weiss had retired and Jackie had said that he believed the Red Sox would have difficulty becoming contenders for the pennant. Nevertheless, Jackie seemed to be looking forward to working again with Ted Williams, who had become the Red Sox batting coach. In March 1961 Jackie drove to Scottsdale, Arizona, for spring training, and his family visited him during Easter vacation.

Jackie was getting back into true form quickly, and was the leading hitter of the spring Cactus League. One sports-page photo showed him sliding head first beneath the third-baseman's glove. A fan sent Jackie the March 20 clipping with an arrow leading from his hand-written caption "He all wet," [sic] to the umpire, who he thought had erred in calling Jackie out. The next day the Boston *Tribune* printed Ed Schoenfeld's interview with Casey Stengel, who had been dismissed from the Yankees and was in the process of writing his autobiography. In "Casey Explains Jensen Trade," the old manager expressed his views about Jackie: "Jensen is a very high class and skilled man and it's a very fortunate thing that the Red Sox obtained his services to go back since Mr. Williams dropped out."

Stengel went on to praise Jackie as one of the best runners, throwers, and RBI men he had known, and he said that Jackie's one-year layoff from baseball would not affect him much. Casey explained that he had traded Jensen years before because the Yankees needed left-handed batters, and Jackie hadn't yet developed his present ability to hit right-handed pitchers. Overall, however, Casey thought it would have been in the best interest for the Yankees to have kept Jackie:

> "If I was in the American League," he said, "I would think the best thing I could ever do is give three or four men to get Jensen on the Yankee team. Because if he was with the Yankees right now, with Mantle and with Maris and with Jensen you'd have an outstanding outfield where no one could hardly have anything better."

That spring Jack was a guest speaker for the Phoenix Junior Chamber of Commerce, whose March 27 newsletter headlined "Jensen Is Guest." Part of the accompanying column said: "Besides raising a happy family Jackie is a successful restaurateur in Oakland, California, and real estate developer at Lake Tahoe." Unfortunately, the well-intentioned writer was misinformed: Harmony did not exist at home, Jackie had left the management of the restaurant to Boots, and little real estate had been developed.

As baseball season got under way, Jackie found himself at the center of controversy. Jensen was sorely needed, for without him, Manager Mike Higgins would have "a gaping hole in the batting order," and, of course, Jackie was the primary right fielder. Jackie discovered that his fear of flying had not disappeared, despite his session with the hypnotist. At the prospect of flying to Boston after a Cleveland game, Jackie left the game early and told Zoe he was ready to quit baseball again, but she managed to convince him to board the plane and return with the team. The incident did not go unnoticed, and when pressed for an explanation, Jackie said, "We're a family of champions. Zoe was one before me and she knows the trials and tribulations of competition. She could understand my feelings. I owe it all to her."

The Red Sox became uneasy, wondering if Jackie could be depended on. When on the diamond, Jackie gave 100 percent effort—he just had to get there. Higgins, the players, the fans—all wondered if Jackie would quit again, and there was cause for alarm when, after Higgins gave Jackie special permission to drive to Logan Airport rather than take the chartered bus, Jackie never appeared, although the plane was held for fifteen minutes. Printed just a few hours before the scheduled night game in Cleveland, the headline "Jensen Must Fly or Quit" led readers to believe that Jackie was on his way out, but Higgins stated simply that Jackie wouldn't play in any game for which he was late, a fair enough compromise, it seemed. Much to everyone's surprise, Jackie did make it to the Cleveland game in time, having driven 850 miles from Boston with Arthur Ellen.

As some headlines were announcing a truce in Laos, the fact that Cuba had joined the Red bloc, and that America's first man-in-space shot (with Alan B. Shepard Jr.) would be delayed two days, came the May 2, 1961, edition of the *Oakland Tribune*, which ran as its feature article Jack's words as recounted by Ed Schoenfeld: "Jensen Tells His Own Story," subtitled "Won't Accept Money When I Can't Deliver, He Says." Jack's unselfishness and honesty were readily apparent: "I am retiring from baseball because I feel I cannot play the caliber of baseball that would satisfy me in order for me to be of value to a ball club. I get satisfaction and my happiness out of baseball knowing the job I do is an asset and not a liability."

Jackie said that physically he had slowed down and that his

reflexes were poorer, although he did have the confidence he had once lacked. Another quote provided insight into his personal life:

> "My reasons for leaving the game in 1959 were listed as a desire to spend more time with my wonderful family. But I state now as an absolute fact that in no instance does my family play a part in my decision at this time. I am now firmly convinced I played baseball purely for the love of the game and not for monetary values. Otherwise I would still be in the game. I have always taken a personal pride in my playing and have admitted that once I realized I was no longer essential to a ball club, then I should find something else in which to devote my energies. I feel at this time my future lies in something other than playing baseball, and whatever it may be I shall direct my abilities as wholeheartedly as I did in the past."

Jackie had nothing but praise for the Red Sox team, its manager Mike Higgins, and owner Tom Yawkey; and he had no regrets, only thankfulness that he had been able to realize a childhood dream of playing with Joe DiMaggio and Ted Williams. As to why Jackie quit so suddenly, he made the following statement: "I was forced to take the action I did when I learned a reporter had been eavesdropping through closed doors and took it on his own that a story is worth more than a friendship." Jackie was forgiving enough not to mention the reporter's name.

Did Jack make the right decision to rejoin the team in 1961? Many years later in an interview for this book, former teammate Ike Delock made the following comments: "Everybody was *hoping* it would work because he was such a nice person and a good team player. But we all in the back of our minds didn't think it was going to work. In spring training he wasn't as fast; he'd lost that little half step, couldn't throw as well, couldn't hit nearly as well. All you have to do is lose that little edge and somebody walks right by you."

The media followed Jackie back home. In a reprint of a *Tribune* article, Ed Schoenfeld, who rode West with Jack on the train, was pictured at his typewriter alongside Jackie. Above that photograph was one of Jackie comforting "sobbing wife, Zoe Ann, upon arrival at Reno Depot." Jackie had left Boston three days before, taking the train instead of flying. He had hoped that no reporters would make a scene when he arrived, but photographers mobbed him and Zoe Ann, and in a rare display of temper he snapped, "Can't you see my wife doesn't want her picture taken?" Zoe Ann and Jackie escaped when a couple of men purposely drove their car between the couple and the reporters, allowing them to drive on to the Mapes Hotel, where their children were waiting.

In short, Jackie was disappointed in his 1961 performance. "I also made a mistake coming back in 1961," he said, "The year away didn't throw me off. I had a great spring training. It's just that the same problems resurfaced. I thought they were solved, but they weren't."

Jackie was not about to mention that he had been experiencing some problems with Zoe Ann. In the months that Zoe Ann did stay with Jackie in the Boston area, she enjoyed the socializing that naturally occurred among the players and their wives. As former Red Sox player Dick Gernert later explained, the Red Sox were a very close-knit team: The wives got together when the team was on the road, during All-Star breaks, and for special events such as a baby shower for Jimmy Piersall's wife. When the Red Sox were in Boston, however, it was not unusual for several players to get together for parties, and of course alcohol flowed freely. Zoe Ann regaled the revelers with descriptions of Lake Tahoe and would be most loquacious. Jack socialized, also, but he was content to have only a drink or two. He'd become alarmed when he saw Zoe drinking more than he, and more often than not he'd angrily force her to leave early with him, despite the protestations of other players. In a letter to the author (7-23-87) Zoe Ann said, "I didn't need much sleep and Jack always seemed to need extra. I enjoyed going and doing. He once said to me, 'You act like each time you go out it is your last.' Guess I was trying to make up for lost time."

In retrospect, nearly two decades after he quit the Red Sox, Jackie reflected in the *Boston Globe* (January 25, 1980) on his decision to leave professional baseball for good:

I was convinced the plane was going to crash. Every time I went up. A stewardess would explain everything to me, all the noises I was going to hear, all the movements the plane would make, take me all the way into the air. Then everyone else would fall asleep and I'd just stare out the window at the engine, as if [if] I took my eyes off it something was going to happen. We'd get wherever we were going and everybody else would be thinking about the pitchers we were going to face, the games we were going to play. I would be thinking about how many days it would be until we had to fly again. It was awful. Just an awful time. I had to quit, had to get away from it.

Five years after the *Globe* article was printed, Zoe Ann also reflected on Jackie's decision to quit the Red Sox: "He had another six or seven years minimum of good ball left. He had made no plans for the future, which was later proven. The flying was a deciding factor. The club would have arranged to have me fly with him the whole season, but this plan was unrealistic to me. The priorities of '3 children,' of 'home,' came first."

11

TRIBULATIONS AND TRIALS

Many people knew better when Jackie said—even after he quit twice—that he'd have nothing further to do with baseball. Within a few months he was coaching the South Tahoe Little League, where Jon Jensen was a player, and the common interest of baseball provided a good basis for Jack to get to know his elder son. But life was no longer just a game; Jack needed to find employment or make some good investments to provide his family a comfortable lifestyle. It was difficult to adjust to the changes he and Zoe faced on leaving professional ball. He still sought balance—a successful career and a secure family life. But being a businessman did not come as naturally as being an athlete. One question was, Could the Golden Boy live off his laurels? Retired professional athletes usually had a few options: Survive on invested earnings, endorse products, or enter into new business ventures. Unfortunately, Jack never had been a good money manager, and had even loaned thousands of dollars without charging interest, nor did he secure the loans with collateral. He had spent much of what he earned, but at least the house, car, and boat were paid for; and he had $800 (rumored to be $2,000) a month revenue from the Bow and Bell.

Undaunted by previous investment losses, Jack announced in April 1962 his intentions to join West Coast auto magnate Reynolds Johnson in restoring a golf course, named Ponderosa, near Truckee, Nevada. It required a hefty investment and much labor for renovation, and Jack supplied both, buying half the shares and running a bulldozer. Over the next few years Jack found himself investing more in the golf course, which eventually became a huge success, but not to his benefit. The Ponderosa was especially noted for its clubhouse, which ten years after the course had been built was the repository for 850 caps from around the world. Initially Jack and manager Alex Stewart pooled their collection of baseball and golf caps and hung them on the walls; then others added theirs, notably Arnold Palmer, Joe DiMaggio, Ben Hogan, Carol Mann, Tony Lema, and Dwight D. Eisenhower.

A few years before, Jack and Zoe had purchased a few Lake Tahoe lots, and recently had bought two one-acre waterfront lots in Hawaii, put into a trust for the children. Jack also had endorsed a few products, such as Wonder Bread and MacGregor sporting goods, in addition to his Camel cigarettes and Gillette television ads, but he hadn't kept a manager and wasn't up to soliciting additional business himself. So it was necessary for him to concentrate on finding employment.

As Jack settled into a more domestic routine, he realized the impracticality of enjoying his much-sought-after goal of spending more time with his family. Baseball still had a hold on him, and Zoe Ann was still eager to socialize, perhaps to make up for all those lonely years. In Jack's absence, Zoe Ann had endured the usual difficult time most professional athletes' wives experience; only she was not the typical housewife. Zoe Ann had matured under the gaze of the public eye, and she become world famous as an Olympic diver, accustomed to admiring glances for both her ability and her beauty. As Zoe Ann explained in a letter to the author, Jack was so jealous of her talking to other men that he even called her phychiatrist and asked him if Jay had been fathered by another man. Such incidents, combined with the increasing realization that their finances were unstable, led to tension and frequent, sometimes violent, arguments.

Suffering from back pain that had started years before, Jack began visits with a chiropractor. This aggravating disability limited Jack's capacity to do physical labor and dampened his desire to become a builder. The home that Jack and Ray Ehlers built in

Incline Village, the "House that Jack Built," did not readily sell, so they scrapped the idea of building any additional houses. Another venture that never materialized was the construction of a restaurant on a hill outside of Reno, even though Jack and friend Woody Burris went so far as to have an architect examine the building they planned to copy, Pinnacle Point, in Scottsdale, Arizona.

Realizing that his family was living beyond its means, Jack reconsidered playing ball, but he still wanted to spend as much time at home as possible. If only he could conquer his fear of flying, both problems would be less severe. Driving for many hours each week certainly took a toll on his back, and by flying instead, Jack would save much time that could be spent with the family. Therefore, Jack and Zoe Ann drove to Las Vegas and met again with Arthur Ellen in another attempt to cure his fear of flying. Ellen diagnosed Jack as neurotic and concluded that he loved life so intensely that he couldn't put his mortality into the hands of another—which is precisely what happens when you fly. In an automobile he was in control, and in a railway car there was the security of the ground. The solution would be to play for a California team that wouldn't require him to fly. Ellen wanted to keep helping Jack and said he would even travel with him, if necessary, as he had done at least once before. With such reassurance and the realization that baseball was indeed the most logical way to earn a high salary, Jack started looking ahead to the next season when he might rejoin the Red Sox or some other team—a desperate move to save the marriage.

Meanwhile, Jack's charisma and fame, bolstered by his friendship with the owner, led to a job as the public relations director for Harrah's Club in Reno and Lake Tahoe (where he was in charge of speedboat racing and such events as tennis tournaments where Danny Thomas and Frank Sinatra, among others, began their friendships with him), and among his duties was seeing that guests and especially celebrities enjoyed themselves at Mr. Harrah's resort, on his yacht, and hunting. Many people he encountered naturally questioned him about his baseball days and wondered if

Jack might again rejoin the sport, and he admitted he was considering it. Some questioned his age (thirty-six), but his reply was, "I want to play baseball on the Coast, preferably with the Giants. Physically I don't have any problem. I feel better than ever."

Jack probably knew better than to expect a team to hire him under his conditions; nevertheless, he contacted the Red Sox about his joining a West Coast team. He found that they had him on a restricted list but would accommodate him. Perhaps in anticipation of the Giants wanting him, Jack quit his job with Harrah's to become a publicity agent and salesman in an automobile business in San Francisco, which put him in close proximity to those who might be able to help get him a team position. The Giants were trading Felipe Alou, so some thought that they needed someone like Jackie for his fielding and hitting ability, and one rumor had it that Horace Stoneham was trying to sign Jackie for a salary of $65,000. A May 16, 1963, article revealed Jack had decided to stay in Lake Tahoe after all, having landed a job as sports public relations director at the Stateline casino/night club, but soon rumors surfaced that he would try to rejoin the Red Sox.

The next day Zoe Ann sued for divorce.

Jack's uncertainty about jobs wasn't enough for Zoe Ann to hang her hopes on, and he was still as jealous as ever of Zoe's male friends. She entered court claiming "extreme cruelty without provocation." When asked for an explanation of the divorce, Jack merely responded, "I wish I knew." Outwardly Jack tried to make it seem the divorce didn't affect him much—the day it was announced he played golf in a Pro-Am preliminary tournament. But although he had seen it coming, Jack took the separation hard. He couldn't bear facing Zoe Ann in court, so he had his lawyer, H. Dale Murphy, stand in for him; and he contested only one of five parts of the divorce settlement, cruelty.

The settlement went largely against Jack, who lost the debt-free house and its furnishings and the new Jeep Wagoneer that was registered with the Bow and Bell (Jack agreed to supply a new car equal in value to it annually for the next ten years). Alimony was

$675 per month until Zoe Ann's remarriage; and child support was $100 a month for each of the three children, whom Jack could see only once a week and two weeks in the summer. At least Jack was able to force an agreement that if the Crystal Bay house were ever sold, the children would be entitled to half the profits.

What was especially to present a problem (even more so with a later, second divorce) was the clause that required Jack to pay half of any medical or dental expenses for the children up to $50, then all the costs beyond that. Additionally, he was to pay for any education for the children beyond high school. Property was to be divided equally except for the one lot Jack had in his own name; this necessitated swapping lots and created problems with the Hawaiian property in trust for the children. In short, except for the investment in the Ponderosa Golf Course (and this he would have to forfeit later), Jack lost most of what he had owned and more than half his income of about $1,300 per month.

Although the divorce depressed him, Jack was not about to go into seclusion. On September 12 he returned to the Bay area to attend a luncheon for forty of the Big Six Sky-writers, who heard Cal Chancellor Edward Strong put to rest rumors that Memorial Stadium would be leveled for other university use. Jack was pleased to visit with old football buddy Jim Cullom, who was now assistant athletic director, and the *Berkeley Daily Gazette* twice pictured Jack with current Cal football players. Shortly afterward Jack was also seen at the fall Bootjack Tournament at the Diablo Country Club, where he was pictured with Jack La Lanne and Oakland Mayor John C. Houlihan. Despite these excursions to California, Jack still frequently ran into Zoe Ann in the Lake Tahoe area, so he gave up his job at Harrah's and moved in with some friends in San Francisco, a move many interpreted as another attempt to be closer to the Giants.

In early December it was reported that Jack was again wondering about playing for the Giants. When asked about Jack's chances of joining, Giants boss Horace Stoneham gave a forthright statement: "He's 36, isn't he? It's asking a lot of a fellow, even one who was Most Valuable Player in 1958, to start again after a three-year layoff. I know Jackie and he's a fine boy. But as a Giant—well, no. However, I think I'll talk to Alvin Dark about him."

Trying to get to the bottom of the speculation, Art Rosenbaum of the *San Francisco Chronicle* approached Jack, who admitted that he hadn't talked with anyone from the club, but would consider only the Giants, if any team at all; and he'd appreciate a chance for a tryout. It was not until the second week of February 1964, however, that all speculation was laid to rest. At a Baseball Writers award dinner (for Willie Mays and others) in San Francisco, Jack said: "I'm not going to play—things have developed along other lines."

Shortly after that announcement, Jack joined Ted Williams (in the Bay area on business for Sears-Roebuck as a sports adviser) and Boots at the Orinda Country Club for a round of golf, where Boots hit a hole in one, witnessed by Tony Lema in a following threesome. The next day Jack joined Boots in celebrating the tenth anniversary of the Bow and Bell, but the successful business was beginning a downhill slide. Boots suffered a personal tragedy that would change his life and the future of the restaurant: His three-year-old daughter died unexpectedly, and Boots, having the liquor readily available, developed a drinking problem that would take years to overcome.

By 1964 residuals from his national television commercials for Camel cigarettes and Gillette had run out, and Jack turned to doing regional promotions for Lucky Lager. He also obtained employment sportscasting a ten-minute weekly television segment on the *Dick Stewart Show* in San Francisco and announcing a weekly, two-hour Auto Circus (car race) weekend show for thirteen weeks. In mid-March Jack began work in public relations for a Lincoln-Mercury dealership run by Jim Wessman, a flashy high roller from whom Jack possibly got his first ideas about building his own dealership back at Lake Tahoe. Wessman reportedly was paying him $15,000 a year, which enabled Jack to "furnish a swank four-room apartment at 1800 Pacific Avenue." A reporter saw Jack with a couple of lady friends, at least one of whom was a date set up by well-meaning friends; but his mind was still on Zoe Ann.

Meanwhile, although Zoe Ann got a good divorce settlement and had income from a rental unit, she hadn't taken advantage of tax deductions and realized only a little income from giving swimming and diving lessons. It was not enough to support the lifestyle she was used to. Furthermore, her friends were of no financial help, so she offered Jack a chance for reconciliation. He had secretly hoped she had not stopped loving him, so he gave up his job in San Francisco and rejoined her at Crystal Bay. The Jensens' unannounced informal wedding (at which Jan was the mistress of honor and Woody Burris the best man) surprised nearly everyone.

With Jack's anxiety over playing ball finally put to rest and his opportunity to be around home greatly increased, the Jensens seemed to have a chance to make their marriage succeed. All that was needed was lucrative employment in the Lake Tahoe area if what Jack had said so many times about his ideal home life was true—that if he was home more, he would have a happy family. But things weren't that simple. For one thing, Zoe Ann was skeptical that the marriage would last: She refused to put back into both their names anything she had received as a result of the first divorce. Naturally Jack was upset that she didn't trust him, but he didn't trust her either. He remained jealous of Zoe's being with other men, however innocent the reason, and he would again accuse her of liaisons and of rendezvous at such places as ski lodges.

In an interview with the author (8-18-86), Jay Jensen said, "What people told me is Dad would be the one that would become jealous. Mom is a very open person with friends. She enjoys her friends—they may be male; they may be female. Mom would go skiing, sometimes, without Dad because we were trying to be family oriented when Dad was around, but I understood Dad would get upset if Mom would go skiing with some of her male friends. I always wanted them to get back together."

Jack's income was still half what he had been used to, and trying to keep the children on the right track was a problem in itself. The older children had grown up with a part-time father, and Zoe had left some of the children's supervision to a housekeeper. Thus, they lacked the respect they might otherwise have had for their parents. Jan was becoming an attractive, active teenager who sought attention by doing things her conservative father found shocking. About four years earlier, Zoe Ann and Jack had taken her to a psychologist, who Jan would later say (in a letter) recommended family counseling, which Jack refused. She sold prizes and trophies Jack had won—some he had given her; some he had not—and she got into trouble with the law more than once. Jon, although a superior athlete, had a rash temper and once was accused of breaking several school bus windows (which Zoe Ann ended up paying for). Jay, several years younger than his siblings, was finding little to do but fight boredom in rural Incline Village.

Jack's busy schedule did not prevent him from playing golf frequently and making personal appearances occasionally, but he longed for more financial security and realized he'd have his best chances in the Bay area. By 1965 Jack had come to understand that he couldn't just step into a high-paying job—he would have to work his way. So he embarked on a variety of new enterprises: He hosted his own ten-minute *Jackie Jensen Show* prior to Giant-Dodger games on Channel 2-TV in Oakland, then secured a position as color man for ABC-TV, working alongside Keith Jackson. Former Senators and Red Sox teammate Sid Hudson recalled meeting Jack during that time: "After his playing days were over, he once visited Waco to broadcast a football game between Baylor University and Syracuse. He called me early in the morning and wanted to visit with me. I picked him up at his hotel, and we rode around all morning looking over Waco. He was very friendly and seemed very happy as color man for the football games, and was extremely complimentary about Baylor University and Waco."

Jack had been working during the week in the Bay area and coming home weekends; frequently he would sleep overnight at the Bow and Bell and bring back hearty helpings of fine food for his family. However, he saw an opportunity to set up a business near Lake Tahoe that would allow him to commute from Crystal Bay. His partner in the golf course, Reynolds Johnson, was at the time the Volkswagen distributor for not only Nevada and California, but also Oregon, Washington, Montana, and Idaho. The company permitted him to own one dealership, Spartan Volkswagen in San Jose. Johnson introduced Jackie to general manager Bob Wilson, who in turn told sales manager Earl Parsons that he had a new salesman. This surprised Earl, who always had selected his own staff, but he had met Jackie before, and, having played football himself for the 49ers, hit it off with the former All-American fullback. He readily understood why Johnson was sending Jack to work for him. Jack hoped to learn the business, then start his own on property he purchased in Carson City, for Volkswagens were selling well in the West. Unfortunately, Jack was not good at closing deals, and the population of Carson City started to decline. Johnson was forced to withdraw his offer to help set up Jack, who ended up burdened with payments on the lot. At least Jack struck up a lasting friendship with Earl, who would be one of the first to console him about ten years later after Jack's worst let-down.

With his hopes dashed and income again diminished, Jack kept looking and hoping for lucrative employment to help him meet expenses. Fortunately, Jack maintained his position as sports director of KTVN-TV in Reno, an ABC sports-oriented affiliate, and as color man for ABC. Finally, he was forced to sell his interest in the Bow and Bell, and some feelings were hurt when he removed some of his photographs and trophies. In the midst of these financial difficulties his home life suffered: He appeared to resent Zoe's ongoing social life and found his own values and ideas of having a good time conflicting with hers. Furthermore, they had few friends in common, and he did not like to talk business at home. After three years of the renewed marriage, Jack separated from Zoe Ann. The kids, especially, hoped they would get back together, so the whole family decided to give it one last try during Christmas of

1967. The holiday season seemed like a perfect time for everyone to come together and start things anew, but the spirit was superficial and all knew it. Three days before the New Year, Jack filed for divorce, citing "unfortunate and irreconcilable differences."

As a result of some promotional clips for the Holiday Lodge on KTVN, the motel gave him the honeymoon suite, which overlooked the Truckee River. As part of the separation agreement, Jan moved in with Jack, and she recalls the suite as being "rather luxurious; it had a big round bed in it and a big green sun on the wall and a little kitchenette and a little dinette."

Although only seventeen, Jan wanted to marry her boyfriend of four years, and reluctantly Jack gave his consent. Zoe threatened trouble if Jack traveled for more than a few days for his job and left Jan alone. Although Jack probably hoped the marriage would be in Jan's best interest, the day after the wedding her husband, a Seabee, shipped out for Vietnam for a twenty-two-month stint; and Jan had a difficult time living by herself.

Jack needed a way to leave his troubles behind.

12

HOME ON THE RANGE

Although catering to those seeking divorce, the Donner Trail Ranch in Verdi, Nevada, brought together at least one couple. Named after the ill-fated Donner pioneers in 1846, the 3,000-acre ranch bordering on the Toiyabe National Forest at the foothills of the Sierra Nevada had been the first stop for stagecoaches and horse changes between Reno and California's gold fields. In the '60s it was run by a breeder of quarter horses and a one-time North American Rodeo champion, Harry Drackert; he and his wife, Joan, were to become close friends of Jack. The Drackerts made their living operating the Donner Trail Ranch for people to establish the six-week residency requirement to be eligible for divorce.

One such resident in 1967 was Katharine Cortesi, who had visited the ranch previously for a divorce. She had enjoyed a life of luxury in Mexico City. An attractive, articulate lady, educated in private schools in Virginia and Italy, Katharine readily found new beaux eager to make her acquaintance, but she was in a position to bide her time. Her eight-year-old daughter, Tinsley, stayed with her at the gamekeeper's cottage on the sprawling ranch alongside the Truckee River next to the two hundred-acre Sunrise Pasture. School was close enough for Tinsley to reach by pony, and nearby Squaw Valley provided skiing and ice skating.

Between hunting trips with the Drackerts in the mountains and rice fields of California, and marksmanship matches (in June she won the Nevada State Women's Skeet championship), Katharine was a commercial artist for Spencer Advertising. Her interest in rodeo led her to become secretary for the Reno Rodeo Association, where she had met director Harry Spencer, a West Coast advertising mogul who recommended she try for an opening with KTVN in Reno. Accordingly, she did apply, and began work in March as an account executive, soon working in advertising sales and the production of sports programs. Jack's life and hers were to come together. In her words:

> The manager of the station took me to lunch and said, "I think we're going to be able to get Jackie Jensen to work for us." And I didn't know who Jackie Jensen was; I said, "Oh, the golfer (I thought he was a golfer)," and the manager said, "No, Jackie Jensen the baseball player."
>
> I said, "Oh, oh, the one who was married to Zoe," for I knew of Zoe because I had been active in swimming and a couple of water ballets.
>
> The first time I remember seeing him was when he was talking to the manager of the station in the manager's office, and I walked by and here was this terribly golden-colored man, golden skin, golden hair, in a blue blazer; and I just remember thinking: sort of an unusual-looking person.

One day Katharine was introduced to Jack in a studio hallway, and by that time she had become familiar with his football and baseball achievements and learned he was a color commentator for ABC. Katharine first worked with Jack when the manager asked him to accompany her to help secure a contract with the Ponderosa Hotel, but it wasn't until their next opportunity to work together, a few weeks later, that they got to know each other. Katharine recalled:

> One day I had to go to San Francisco to get a contract signed and Jack was going to interview O. J. Simpson, and we left my car at my house on the ranch. We went over the mountains to San Francisco, did our business, had dinner. During dinner I did sort of get the message; I did sort of see Jack sitting there, for the first time, and then when we went back to my house on the farm. There was a snake on the kitchen floor, and it looked very large and very unappetizing in a kitchen. I was upset to

see it there, and I grabbed it by the tail and snapped it like a whip and chucked it out, and I think that's when Jack said, "That's the girl for me."

At the time Jack was again experiencing some difficulty with Zoe Ann, but nevertheless called her from Katharine's to let her know he'd gotten back from California all right. Katharine's first real date with Jack was on June 21, when he took her to the Nugget casino for gambling and dinner; there he told her that she was so much more fun to have dinner with than his last girlfriend, who couldn't taste anything! He had tried dating a few other girls, one a Mormon from Lake Tahoe, the other two from the Bay area. Katharine knew Jack was getting serious after they went on a weekend fishing trip to Bridgeport in the Sierras with another friend from the ranch, who told her afterward that Jack said he wanted to marry Katharine as soon as his divorce from Zoe was settled. And so the relationship escalated, as Katharine met and worked with Jack the next weekend at a rodeo, then at Reno Raceway, and had lunch with him at the Nugget the following weekend. Before long. Jack was regularly visiting Katharine at the ranch.

Once, intending to show up this professional athlete with her shooting ability, Katharine invited him to a trap shoot at the famous Harold's Gun Club near Stead Air Force Base. Much to her chagrin, but nonetheless impressed, she watched Jack take first place in a match on his first try at shooting trap! By July they would be meeting frequently for lunch or dinner at Holiday Lodge, Harrah's, or Harold's Club—all the best dining and entertainment establishments. Jack seemed to be resurrecting his youth, as he often sported a bright blue Austrian suede jacket that matched the equally bright blue Porsche he leased from car dealer Earl Parsons, and Katharine drove her new '67 Mustang, a gift from an aunt who rivaled Jack's in generosity. They often visited entertainers in their dressing rooms between casino shows. Ushered backstage one night to see Ray Charles, they were stunned when Jan, who had accompanied them, uninhibitedly threw her arms around the startled performer and told him how much she loved him. On another occasion, Trini Lopez stood on a coffee table to catch Katharine's eye as Jack looked on, and when she signaled waning attention, Lopez left the room to soon return with an autographed record album for her.

In mid-July Jack and Katharine saw their first movie together, the romantic French comedy *A Man and a Woman,* and the next day Jack invited Katharine to dine with him at the home of the Ehlerses, where Mrs. Ehlers told Katharine not to worry about being responsible for bringing about a divorce between Jack and Zoe—that it was inevitable regardless. A few weeks later Jack drove Katharine in her Mustang to the coast through the redwood forest, and they spent the night watching the fog roll in above the sea. A new life was dawning for Jack: a mixture of private moments spent hunting, fishing, searching for Indian artifacts, exploring the desert, and enjoying rodeos and such stage shows as Roger Miller's at Harrah's, and Rowan and Martin's at the Nugget.

While in Oregon in late September, Jack called Katharine and told her he missed her, and she flew up to meet him. A week later he took a train to Boston and called just before he covered a Red Sox game. Obviously they were falling in love, but would Katharine be able to accept his frequent travel? At this point Jack may have been wondering if their relationship would eventually be a repeat of what he had experienced with Zoe Ann. Traveling across the country for ABC was not much different from traveling with the Red Sox. Several years before, for the sake of his family, he had quit something he loved doing; but now, as he drifted away from Zoe and closer to Katharine, he seemed to be able to travel with less pressure—he seemed more compatible with Katharine, and so far she was supportive of his responsibilities.

The first Celebrity Golf Classic, sponsored by newspaperman Perry Phillips, was held in late September 1967, and the Hole-in-One prize was a Grand Mercedes 600 Sedan. Money that entrants paid went to support the Oakland Repertory Theater, and the event was much heralded. In the opening pages of the fifty-page brochure, printed by the *Oakland Tribune,* Jackie's image appeared with Phil Harris, Bing Crosby, Tony Martin, Lefty O'Doul, and Joe DiMaggio. A short character sketch described Jack: "Dubbed the 'Golden Boy' at the University of California after leading Cal in rushing in 1946, '47, and '48." The blurb ends: "very good golfer, long-time associate with Boots Erb in backing the Bootjack Golf Tournament. With Erb developed Jack London Square restaurant."

Other celebrities included Trini Lopez, Peter Marshall, Monty Hall, Rocky Marciano, Clint Eastwood, Jackie Cooper, and Pat Boone. Jack actually did not attend, due to ABC commitments, but he did get to the Mapes tournament in early October. Charley Mapes had grown up with the family hotel/casino alongside the Truckee River, and he became a big game hunter, accompanying such greats as Marlin Perkins. Like so many others belonging to the "in" crowd, Charley was on the rodeo committee. Jack got to know him well, since Charley kept his horse on the Verdi ranch and would hunt with Jack and Katharine, whom Charley knew from her doing the artwork for his Mapes newspaper ads and promotions.

During the Mapes Tournament, Jackie made a fine drive along the fairway and chose his next club as Katharine walked along with the spectators. To her astonishment, far ahead a souvenir hunter (or petty thief), sauntered out from among the crowd, picked up Jack's ball, and made his way into the crowd on the other side. Katharine rushed up to Jack and explained what had happened, and Jack, more amused than angry, was allowed to drop a ball without penalty. Years later, when the Jensens told Charley they were moving East, he kindly begged them to stay and offered them jobs at the casino. He went bankrupt soon after they left, however, and the hotel closed.

Shortly after the Mapes tournament Jack invited Jon and Jay to Katharine's cottage for dinner; Katharine was hoping the children would feel at home with her and was excited at the prospect of having one or both of Jack's sons living with them at some point.

They further invited the children to visit whenever they pleased and tried to maintain a close relationship with them, supporting their many sporting endeavors whenever possible. Eventually they asked Jon to stay with them at the ranch, and Jack even transformed an outbuilding near their cottage for him, but Jon never moved in.

At the end of October, Jack realized that to meet his obligations to the radio and television stations as well as ABC he would have to conquer at last his fear of flying. With Katharine's encouragement, he flew East with her to Florida, where they enjoyed the tourist attractions at St. Augustine and fishing off the coast. Katharine still had obligations at KTVN, so couldn't always fly with Jack, who otherwise preferred driving or taking the train. This malediction was, in part, to cause anguish again in a few years.

In 1968 Jack became a director on the board of the Reno Rodeo Association, for which Katharine had been secretary, and he also resumed golfing. He attended the Crosby Pro-Am Tournament at Pebble Beach, Cypress Point, and Spyglass with Orville Moody as his partner and finished second in the finals and fifth overall (having played only twice during the year prior to the tournament). Many have said Jack could easily have made his living as a pro golfer, something he later conceded himself; and his later friend, Nevada Senator Paul Laxalt thought Jack was a great golfer and said he "could hit the ball a mile."

Jack continued announcing football and baseball games and occasionally even a boxing match. Finally the long-awaited day of Jack's divorce arrived, on January 17—this time he was the one seeking the permanent separation. The settlement was financially devastating to Jack, and Katharine immediately pooled her resources with his to help out; but times would soon prove to be worse than expected. When Katharine turned thirty-three, Jack set the wedding date for a few days later, moving out of Holiday Lodge and into her cottage.

A cold, misty, rainy day was the setting for Jack and Katharine's wedding, held on February 19, 1968, during their lunch break from the television station. It was a simple, private affair, in sharp contrast to their previous nuptial ceremonies. Their Paiute Indian vows were spoken in front of a fireplace in the main ranch house before Hank Mosconi, a justice of the peace who had lost his left arm by hanging it too far out his pickup truck window when another truck passed very close. Their witnesses were Joan Drackert and a housekeeper who claimed to be Anastasia. The reception was a lunch at the Verdi Inn, their honeymoon a private night at the cottage—nothing more elaborate could be afforded, anyway.

Soon afterward, Katharine sat down with Jack to make a long-overdue financial assessment, for he had kept few records. Jack had bought—in the children's names—land in Hawaii on which he owed many thousands of dollars. He also still owned the land in Carson City he had earlier wished to develop for a car dealership, on which he owed $40,000. To complicate matters further, Jan's husband had arranged for her to visit Hawaii, where she saw the lots and recognized their value; upon her return, according to Katharine, she told Jack that Jay had given up his interest to her, which he hadn't. (Jay himself later said that he told his father to keep the land for himself.) When Katharine asked Jack if any debts were owed him, he replied that he thought someone owed him $7,000 or more, and that the note might be in a box he had stashed away. Katharine had the prodigious task of sorting through a large box: "full of check stubs and legal stuff. It was the worst mess in the world. It was crammed in without any order, and I took every bit of it, put it in chronological order, weeded out and neatened it up, and I found a *note,* and sure enough he was owed some money, and that was manna from heaven. The fellow was very difficult, didn't want to pay and had some excuses such as building a house."

Eventually, Jack did get the money owed him—a godsend, as nearly all of his income went to alimony and child support.

In addition, Katherine learned that the television station was faltering; she would spend hours with a sponsor producing a commercial, then watch at the scheduled showing time only to see something else in its place. Due to what the owner saw as declining sales, Katharine was relieved of her advertising position. She continued to produce Jack's show, one of her own, and one she and Jack worked on together. She left on the ides of March, and a week later saw her last show on KTVN. Seeking a position in the Reno area, Katharine heard employers telling her she was overqualified, so she languished on the quiet ranch waiting for Jack to return from one of his several jobs.

By the beginning of May, Katharine's unemployment checks had ceased, and with Jack's alimony payments to Zoe Ann due each month, the newlyweds found it increasingly difficult to get by. Lunches and dinners at restaurants became rare, seldom was there enough money for movies or shows, and Jack started looking for additional work to supplement his primary job at ABC. He found employment with the Reno Recreation Department, where he organized sports for teenagers. Jack gave occasional speeches at the University of Nevada at Reno and at other places, and he and Katharine even served briefly as extras for MGM.

One particularly exciting enterprise included Jack's participation in a staged mountain-lion hunt for the Central Nevada Development Corporation, produced to lure adventuresome people into the area. When the lion was flushed from a tree, and a hunter grabbed its front paw, Jack fearlessly leapt forward and grabbed its tail, which made for the action picture the company had hoped for. That photograph and others appeared inside and on the cover of the April 28 edition of the *Review-Journal's* supplement, *The Nevadan.*

In the spring Jack landed the job of head baseball coach for the University of Nevada, ran a baseball clinic in early June, and began coaching at a camp in July, a job that lasted until late August. By this time he, too, had left the local television station, but he and Katharine found excitement in hunting for the plentiful Indian artifacts in the area, such as the trade beads that had been swapped so long ago to Native Americans by traders. Katharine passed along some hunting tips she had learned from Harry Pahl, an old gold miner, and from friend Bill Fleming; these pointers soon took on practical importance, for by mid-summer the newly-weds were seriously hunting, but not for sport. Much later Katharine could still vividly recall their excursions:

> Hunting in Nevada was really thrilling; it was dangerous—to be out in the desert where it was total stillness, coyotes calling, and crows; and if you could see a puff of dust on the horizon, it meant there was someone else in the area, and you felt crowded. A 12-gauge shotgun would do for almost anything. We knew the animals' habits really well because we were both very interested in nature; we were in the eastern edge of the Pacific flyway for waterfowl coming down from Canada— Canada geese and snow geese. We were pretty darn good hunters. We'd either pothole [move from one small pond or river or spring to another] and shoot the birds as they'd come up, or creep up on a pond or holding pond or catch pond on a ranch, and the birds would get up and fly. Stalking with binoculars, we spotted game at great distances and crept within shooting range. It gets to be instinct.
>
> Jack always shot with an old pump gun (I hated that gun; couldn't even lift it), BANG, BANG. He modestly said he filled the air with lead, and hoped something would fly into it.
>
> He always got the shots, and he had terrible buck fever. He really didn't want to shoot a deer. He got so tender-hearted about animals that he didn't really want to shoot them, and he would just pull the trigger. So for most of the time we were married we would hunt for deer together, and then if there was ever a possibility of the shot, I let him take it, and he always muffed it, except for once. He'd shot a lot of deer in his day, a lot of them; but it seemed that after all he'd been through, he had become tender-hearted. I never mentioned that I knew he was missing on purpose. Hunting was such a big part of our lifestyle that I didn't want him to confront this little fact.

One of the men Katharine knew at the gun club owned a clothing business and asked her if she'd be interested in opening an outlet in Reno. On August 21 she opened what she termed a "wretched dress shop," and the income helped pay Jack's alimony and the escalating medical expense for the children—Katharine noted that Zoe Ann seemed to be ensuring her kids got the best medical and dental attention as frequently as possible. In mid-September Katharine accompanied Jack to Chicago and then New York where he reported to ABC headquarters for two days of meetings. He returned by rail alone as she flew on ahead.

The Second Annual Celebrity Golf Classic opened later in the month in Hayward, California, and this time Jack was pleased to be able to attend. The tournament brochure had expanded to seventy pages; here Jack was listed with more than thirty other celebrities, including Rick Barry, Bing Crosby, Buddy Hackett, Art Linkletter, Dick Martin, Dan Rowan, Charles Schulz, and Danny Thomas. Included was an updated biography of Jackie: "One of the finest athletes ever developed in Oakland, Jackie Jensen is one of the few men ever to play in both the Rose Bowl and a World Series. Jackie is currently putting both his baseball and football know-how to work, serving as a baseball coach at the University of Nevada and NCAA football color commentator for the [ABC] network. He is also sports director for KTVN radio in Reno."

On October 8 Jack took the train to Atlanta, and Katharine took the plane soon after. Just as the trees were turning color up North, Jack and Katharine rented a car and enjoyed a leisurely drive along the Blue Ridge Parkway, stopping at Laurel Springs, Lynchburg (Katharine's childhood home), then Charlottesville to visit Katharine's mother, and Monticello, finally reaching Columbus, Ohio, where Jack announced a game on the nineteenth. They then drove all the way to Rawlins, Wyoming, stayed overnight, and continued on to Verdi. After just a week's rest, Jack was on the road again to Wisconsin, and he finished the year by announcing three football games. At the Camellia Bowl in Sacramento, Jack, who was assisting Keith Jackson, insisted that Katharine join him in the press box, but she protested because it was crowded and because she had to scrunch down beneath the heavy camera on its turret. Jack nonetheless wanted her there and had her sketch the camera crew as they worked. (The cameraman accepted Katharine with good graces, but she had to duck every time the big camera swivelled to follow the game.)

Although Katharine convinced Jack to fly with her, she suffered a numb wrist as he clenched it so tightly during the entire flight to Florida. There he announced the North-South game, which was not particularly to their liking as it occurred on Christmas Day, and the Jensens would have preferred to spend Christmas in the snowy mountains rather than in Miami. A few days later Jack worked the Gator Bowl; then they returned for a quiet New Year's Eve.

The early part of 1969 saw little action other than occasional trips to Squaw Valley to see Tinsley ski. On January 15 Katharine had to close her dress shop—the location was inadequate—and they became so destitute that Jack had to turn down Crosby's invitational Pro-Am Tournament because he couldn't afford the $200 entry fee. Furthermore, he gave up leasing his Porsche and bought a motorcycle to save gas. By the end of February, baseball training at the University of Nevada had begun. Jack had taken over as head baseball coach and was featured in a March sports article by the *Berkeley Daily Gazette* in a column by Nick Peters. In it Jackie said: "I was supposed to be head coach last year, but I couldn't do it because of TV commitments. I said I'd stay on as assistant, so they made Jerry [Scattini] baseball coach, but his first love is football, so everything worked out. I'm not doing as much TV now, but I have one year to go on my contract with ABC doing NCAA weekly football games. I've always wanted to coach at this level, but not in the pros."

Jack liked the University of Nevada because campus life was very peaceful; his future might have been much different if only he remembered these words a few years later, when he would make the decision to coach at Berkeley. Still of interest to the public was Jack's past private life, so later in the article, Nick spoke about why Jack had left baseball: "Insiders, however, refer to his marital troubles with Zoe Ann Olsen, the former Olympic diving star, as the prime reason for his premature retirement. But now there's peace of mind for Jackie, apparently enjoying his new life with second wife Katharine amidst the mountain grandeur of Verdi."

Less than three weeks later, the IRS called Jack and said he owed back taxes on the sale of his restaurant. Jack gave the details in an interview with Glenn Dickey for *Sport* magazine:

> When I sold my 51 per cent of the restaurant in 1966, for $100,000, it was also agreed that I wouldn't open up a restaurant within 100 miles for ten years and my partner could use my name for ten years. I took my money, paid the capital gains tax on it, and I thought that was that. Then, an accountant talked to my ex-partner and told him that if he set up the deal as half of it being for the purchase of the restaurant and half being for the use of my name, he could get a tax break. But that meant half of my money was taxed as regular income. The IRS came to me and said I owed the $11,000. I told them I didn't have it, and they said they'd take my car and everything I had.
> I called up my old partner and said, "I thought we had an agreement.'"
>
> He said, "Well, that's business."
>
> "We'd known each other since fourth grade."

(Boots later said that his accountant had given him erroneous information and had been playing each partner against the other to cover his own errors.)

Later, in a lawsuit, the court found in Jack's favor, but not before great damage had been done. After the IRS called, Jack hung up the phone and told Katharine, "I feel horrible; I feel like I've got the worst indigestion of a lifetime. What am I going to do?"

Katharine replied, "Well, don't go to practice," and Jack responded, "Well, it will probably go by."

Just after he covered the twelve miles to the university on his motorcycle, he suffered an acute myocardial infarction, and few who saw him expected him to live. Members of the team rushed Jack to the emergency room of the University of Nevada Hospital.

In area newspapers the headlines once more brought Jackie's name into thousands of homes; the *Nevada State Journal* on Thursday, March 27, 1969, announced at the top of the front page: "Jackie Jensen Suffers Serious Heart Attack." It went on: "His condition was reported as critical Wednesday night at Washoe Medical Center. His wife, Kathy, said she was told 'he will be considered on the critical list for several days; and he will probably be in the hospital for six weeks.' "

More than a thousand letters, get-well cards, and telegrams inundated Jackie's hospital room. Relatives, friends, former teammates, and fans from across the country hoped the Golden Boy would recover.

13

RECOVERY

Jack was in considerable pain the first few days after his heart attack, but by April 10 he was pictured in the *Reno Evening Gazette,* sitting up in bed reading a newspaper. The accompanying caption read "Coach Recovering." The next day San Francisco *Chronicle* sportswriter Ron Fimrite wrote a column entitled "He Is Still the Golden Boy," praising Jack and making a summary statement of his life:

> I doubt if any athlete in the history of the University of California has been so revered by his contemporaries. He had a difficult childhood, a glorious young manhood and a maturity hounded by a marriage gone wrong, a psychotic fear of flying and financial defeats. He had remarried, made new investments and was back in baseball as a coach at the University of Nevada. Then he was stricken. Jackie Jensen added much excitement to my life. I owe him that. May he recover swiftly and completely.

The next day in the *Nevada State Journal,* local sportswriter Ty Cobb (not the Hall-of-Famer of the same name) wrote that Jack blamed his illness on tension due to missed practice time for his team because snow had covered the field in February, and that Jack had mentioned he'd lost ten pounds, was "down to 186, my playing weight."

A month later *Sports Illustrated* revealed a bit of wry humor about a letter Jack had gotten: "After suffering a heart attack in March, Jackie Jensen received many messages, one from former Red Sox catcher Sam White. He sent a clipping which read 'Jackie

Jensen stricken with heart attack during his team's workout.' Sam had written, 'Jeepers, Jack, they can't be that bad.'"

Another lighthearted line was in a telegram that read, "Get well quickly. You know how much you hate to fly." Many well wishes were completely unexpected, such as the one from Alabama Governor George Wallace, who recalled the hospitality Jack had once shown him in Reno; and Irving Stone, at Katharine's request, wrote Jack a note that included the famous author's appreciation for the chapter Jack wrote for *There Was Light,* a biography of Cal which Stone had edited. (See appendix C).

On April 12 Jack was home with his doctor's orders to walk a little each day to bring his muscles back to life, and he was eager to see the impending Nevada-Reno team play San Francisco State. Taking walks on the ranch every day, he soon regained his strength and felt strong enough to go fishing at Pyramid Lake Indian Reservation, where he caught a twenty-two-inch trout.

A nearby resident of the area, Abe Abrams, was Chief of the Piaute tribe and had become a good friend of the Jensens, often regaling them with old Indian tales and indicating areas of archaeological interest and good hunting. His daughter had been Katharine's maid before the marriage and the hard financial times. One day when Katharine arrived at the trading post, the chief was waiting with a cigar box full of little dried red roots, and he said, "Now you make a tea out of this, and hot as you can drink it, and feed it to Jack." She did, and as Jack's health improved, so did the chief's boast that his herbs cured Jackie Jensen.

Jack surprised many by showing up to watch the Mapes Golf Invitational in mid-May; soon afterward, the Sunday *Times Herald's* sports editor's column included details about the heart attack:

> The biggest cheers were reserved for Jackie Jensen when he
> joined a flood of other sports stars, past and present, for intro-
> duction at the Mapes Invitational stag dinner the other evening
> in Reno. The one-time University of California All-America
> gridder, who surrendered his senior year to jump into pro
> baseball, recently suffered a heart attack.

"If that guy's been sick,"said one of the golfer-diners in the
audience, "you sure can't tell it. He looks like the healthiest guy
in the house."

In that article, Jack went on to say he hadn't had a physical for
two years, that his cholesterol level was "way out of line," and that
he was smoking two to three packs of cigarettes daily. His only reference to his personal problems (the IRS) was the comment,
"Tension certainly was a factor." Jack didn't look for sympathy, nor
did he want the public to know much about his private problems;
but he did feel that people would like to know he was recuperating.

A few days later, after walking about and staying at Bing
Crosby's Rising River Ranch in northern California, Jack was
almost fully recovered. Fortunately, the university encouraged Jack
to continue as coach and suggested he complete his degree, and he
and Katharine agreed it was a good idea. He did some light sideline
coaching to help finish the spring season but didn't go on the road
again for ABC until June, when Katharine helped him drive East.
Katharine picked up copies of her aunt's book, *Flying Horses,* for
which she had designed the cover. (The book is her autobiography
of an iron ore mine operator's daughter and her rise to affluence in
France and Italy.) The same aunt, Katherine Lightner Crenshaw
Raffalovich, invited the Jensens to sojourn on the Italian Riviera at
her villa in Rapallo, near Genoa, and offered to finance the excur-
sion. After Jack stopped by his old domain, Yankee Stadium, on
Independence Day, they left New York on the luxury liner *Raffaelo.*
As they passed by Gibraltar a week later they were the only two
who stood on the deck to weather a violent storm, and they remi-
nisced about Jack's grandfather's sailing days and the Jensens'
Viking ancestry.

They arrived July 13 to find the Stars and Bars flying outside the
Rapallo mansion, for Katharine's aunt was quite proud of her Virginia
heritage. While in Italy, Katharine found time to take up her sketch
pad (years before Mrs. Raffalovich had sent Katharine to Parsons
School of Design, and she had worked for Norcross greeting cards and
become an assistant editor and illustrator for *Harper's Bazaar*), and

she and Jack reveled in the scenic hills and waterfront surrounding the grand villa. Unfortunately, Jack strained his back while lifting a rock for Katharine to sit on while she sketched an old monastery, forcing him to stay in his room while the daughter of the king of Spain (wife of Enrico Cinzano Marone, of the famous Italian vermouth company) visited Katharine's aunt. As Katharine was enjoying her cocktails with the guests, she glanced up to see Jack's wounded expression as he curiously gazed down at them from the second-floor balcony.

Back in the United States, the papers kept tabs on Jackie; the Reno *Evening Gazette,* under the headline "No Baseball for Jensen While in Italy" had the following to say:

> RAPALLO, Italy (AP)–University of Nevada baseball coach and former Boston Red Sox star outfielder Jackie Jensen is in Italy for a 45-day vacation—but no baseball. Jensen and his wife arrived in this Italian Riviera resort Sunday to stay with her aunt, Baroness Katherine Raffalovich.
>
> "The place is so beautiful," Jensen said, "that we will hardly move from here. We will be resting and swimming until we leave on Aug. 25 to return back home."

Katharine and Jack later enjoyed San Marino, Cannes, Milan, the Regina Palace Hotel on Lago di Garda, Genoa, Florence, Portofino's Castello Brown (where Richard the Lion-hearted had been imprisoned), Gothic ruins, and the best meals they'd had in months. Their honeymoon was finally being realized, and although all regretted that it came as a result of the heart attack, nevertheless it provided a tremendous psychological boost to a couple who for months had suffered from depressing conditions. In addition to being entertaining, the excursions, combined with Katharine's influence, were drawing out Jack's interest in the fine arts and would soon complement his studies in Nevada.

Jack found to his surprise that the Italian he had learned as a Cal student enabled him to converse with the locals. Jack and Katharine were having the time of their lives, but misfortune struck again. First, Jack received a telegram from ABC informing him that his contract was not renewed. Despite his improved health and the fact that he had managed—even with his phobia of flying—to cover games across the country, ABC wanted someone less risky, to its way of thinking. Jack was later to say that "It takes a knack to pick out what's important. It's no business for an amateur." This statement seemed to be true, for an inexperienced man who replaced Jack botched an assignment, prompting ABC to call and ask Jack to come back to work. However, pride kept him from returning, despite his great need for employment.

Meanwhile, the Italian Line personnel had declared a strike, and Jack and Katharine wondered how they'd get back to America. When things were finally settled, the company upgraded the Jensens from second to first class, so they especially enjoyed the return trip to the States. They arrived in New York two months after they had left it. Driving West, they had occasional car trouble, convincing Katharine they had to get rid of the classic Mustang on their return. While staying in Salt Lake City, someone broke into their car and stole valuable items and cherished keepsakes the couple had acquired in Italy.

Most of the fall was spent hunting or looking for jobs. At one point Jack applied as a night watchman for the Verdi Viking plant, which made missile nose cones, but he couldn't convince the boss he wasn't kidding when he said he needed the work. One day Jack surprised Katharine by bringing home a much-needed, two-or-three-dollar plastic kitchen colander. When she saw it, Katharine burst into tears, not because of his thoughtfulness, but because they really couldn't afford it!

They were forced to enjoy the little things in life, but found those to be just as rewarding as all the glitz and glamor had been. Free time was spent roaming the desert to explore old settlements and ghost towns, and they dubbed one place "our secret meadow," a mountain glade with an unusual variety of wildflowers and lush green grass through which ran a little creek. On their first visit they came across a grouse with her chicks, and the little birds ran to Jack and swarmed around his feet while the mother cackled with consternation. Jack and Katharine also fished as much for food as for relaxation, recalling Jack's early days in Oakland during the Depression. Occasionally they'd catch a football game where Jon was playing; and he came by the ranch a couple of times during the December holiday to visit, as did Jay. The year ended on a quiet note, with a relaxed Christmas on the ranch and a visit to Jack's mother on New Year's Eve.

Nineteen Seventy found the Jensens in dire economic straits; however, Jack did make a little money at odd jobs, including a stint as a hitting expert for a clinic held in January at the University of California at Davis. Throughout the next several months Jack was intent on completing a goal he had established when he signed on as a coach—earning a college diploma. He enrolled at the University of Nevada, and took eleven credits, attending classes when not coaching baseball. Regional papers, as well as *Sports Illustrated,* got a big kick out of his going back to school and pictured him sitting next to a coed young enough to be his daughter as he barely squeezed into a student desk. Katharine not only encouraged him but sat in on some of his classes as well, particularly ecology under Buck Wheeler, past Fish and Game Commissioner, with whom they developed a friendship.

Jack's interest in the history and environment of Nevada expanded further as he became good friends with another naturalist, Comanche Indian Raoul Dixon, who was night manager of the Frontier Hotel in Las Vegas. Once when Jack's baseball team played at Las Vegas, he and Katharine called to inquire about an exhibition of Indian archaeology as mentioned in a *Frontier* newsletter and subsequently met Dixon, a great baseball fan, who offered them free lodging. That set the stage for future visits, when the Jensens would take advantage of the fact that most guests were sleeping off a previous night's fun and frolic; they played tennis on the courts at dawn's first light, then swam in seclusion, and finally joined Raoul for a late breakfast, after which he would take them on excursions into the desert. Dixon was a largely self-educated archaeologist who was a friend of Chief Banks from Wounded Knee, and who later published *The Way of the Hunter.*

Between occasional speeches and talks, Jack again entered the Mapes Tournament and ended up with the third low net score. In May Jack completed his courses at the university, including the

Bible as literature, literature of Nevada and the Far West, introduction to audiology, and three independent studies in speech. His sons visited infrequently, and Jan rarely dropped by.

Fortunately the Red Sox hired Jack as manager of its Jamestown, New York, team in the New York–Pennsylvania League, and he and Katharine traveled East via train in mid-June. They prepared thoroughly for the trip, even bringing window cleaner and towels (Jack cajoled the porter into letting him use his portable steps so he could reach the glass), and they enjoyed favorite foods and wines as they turned their compartment into a virtual nest.

A bit of the West seemed to follow them as Katharine found an arrowhead on a golf course a few days after they got to Jamestown, and the local papers jumped at the chance to bring their readers news of Jack's arrival: The *Oneonta Star* (July 11, 1970) ran a series of four photographs with the title "Former big-leaguer does his thing in Oneonta."

Jack settled into coaching, and the Jensens moved into an apartment on the local campus. The following month Katharine flew to Virginia to visit friends, as Jack's team did well in competitions with Batavia, Oneonta, Niagara, Williamsport, Auburn, and Newark, with the last game in Chicago in late August. This happened to be the end of the rookie league, as Jack explained in an Ed Levitt column a year later: "The Red Sox would sign boys out of college and send them to Jamestown for instructions. They also sent some of their Class A league players for further training. But they finally had to eliminate the team. It cost $150,000 to operate the club just three months a year, June to August. It was too costly."

Jack said later that he "loved managing in the minors, working with young players," and he believed he had done a good job with the team. So he applied to all twenty-four major-league clubs for a job. Most didn't bother to answer, and only one had even a minor position available. He also made inquiries to fifty colleges, but nobody offered him any hope of employment. So that fall, back in Nevada, the Jensens had no promise of a better life, although they had earned enough money in New York to send Katharine's daughter, Tinsley, to Castelleja, a private school in Palo Alto, for seventh grade. Despite the cost of a private education, Jack and Katharine were determined to make sacrifices for the sake of Tinsley, who showed exceptional promise as a student.

In early December Katharine finally sold her troublesome Mustang and replaced it the next month with a new, inexpensive Volkswagen. Jack returned to his studies the beginning of February and began his fourth year of coaching. Archaeological trips continued to Washoe Lake, Carson River, Humboldt Sink, and Big Canyon Ranch at Pyramid Lake. An especially good find was in the Pine Nut Range, low hills between Carson City and the desert. There the Native Americans used to gather nuts and cremated their dead, who wore Hudson Bay trade beads. They found hundreds of these small beads, most of them white, some of them red, and a few blue, now honored possessions of Katharine's and resting alongside numerous arrowheads in a glass-covered table in her Virginia home.

Jack again took exams and was later pictured (at age forty-two) holding his diploma in Ty Cobb's column "Sweeping Away—the Cobwebbs": "This summer he reached his goal. He didn't qualify in time to go through the procession of graduates wearing cap and gown during Nevada's June graduation, but several weeks later he made it. Jack Eugene Jensen won his diploma. He had a bachelor's degree in speech, and had minors in history, and P.E. History, particularly Nevada history, is his hobby."

The same article pointed out his personal interests: "Last weekend was Homecoming at Nevada's Reno campus, but Jensen, as a newly-qualified 'Old Grad,' didn't participate. He traveled to Lovelock to watch son Jon, a competent athlete, play with Incline (Lake Tahoe) High School's undefeated football team as it won the conference championship. The next day the Jensens all went hunting near Denio, in northern Nevada; didn't bring home any deer, 'just two arrowheads.'"

Jack gave a few coaching clinics in June, and on July 1 appeared on a KOLO-TV segment, but very little money was available until a great breakthrough occurred.

14

CARSON CITY

While Jack called around asking about job possibilities, he recalled Guy Shipler having interviewed him for the *Sports Illustrated* cover. Knowing that Guy often covered government news and had long been a good friend of Governor O'Callaghan, Jack called to ask if he'd make an inquiry about state employment opportunities, for the governor was a great sports fan. Later the same day Guy ran into the governor on the street and told him of Jack's predicament. O'Callaghan's first remark was that there was an opening, and his second was that Jack might have to fly to some meetings. He seemed reluctant until Guy piped up, "Well, look, for Christ's sake, you're a jock; you ought to meet the guy anyway. You know he's a good man."

Guy set up an appointment. Katharine mended, cleaned, and pressed Jack's blue blazer and waited expectantly in the Nugget near the capitol as Jack was interviewed. O'Callaghan was immediately impressed with Jack, recognized his speaking ability, and was embarrassed that nobody in Nevada would offer him decent employment. When Jack entered the casino with the good news that some kind of job would indeed be available, Katharine was ecstatic. On July 9, Jack attended a barbecue at the Governor's Mansion, a newly refurbished, neoclassical edifice that had become the pride of the state. Jack couldn't help but be impressed with the mansion's gleaming classic columns, the foyer's Maria Theresa chandelier nearly five feet in diameter, hanging above the black-and-white Carrara marble floor, and the ornate white woodwork around the Nevada blue rooms. The place was a great contrast to the humble gamekeeper's cabin he and Katharine lived in on the ranch, and he was eager to learn what kind of job might be coming his way so they could improve their standard of living. Within a week O'Callaghan called Jack to announce he was appointed assistant director of the Office of Economic Opportunity, working under Frank Matthews. The *San Francisco Chronicle* (July 28, 1971) verified Jack's glee at obtaining the position when it quoted him: "It's definitely a turning point for me. Once I got out of baseball, my [$11,600] salary went down to an average man's and I learned to live with it. I've been just as happy these last few years as I was then. I've been poor. I know what it's like. I'll be trying to make people a little more aware that it's a problem in the whole state, not a problem you can turn your back on."

Jackie had always been photogenic, and his picture soon appeared with many officials in several papers. He gave talks to, supported, or was a member of sundry public service and public interest groups, including the Mothers Baseball Association, the Rotary Club, and the Citizens for a Better Carson. This was the era of the "Silent Majority," and Jackie proudly considered himself counted among its numbers, inasmuch as he had always been conservative. With a steady income ensured, life became grand. Jack and Katharine happened on a great buy on Division Street, a charming redwood home with colorful stone floors. It had an adjoining apartment they could rent out, and it was within easy bicycling distance from the state government office where Jack worked. Additionally, their neighbor let Jack use his backyard to raise a garden—something he had always longed to do. It was much easier that fall to afford sending Tinsley to school, and the Jensens could again dine out and enjoy the Nevada night life, although they usually preferred to stay home. However, hunting had become ingrained in them, and Jack and Katharine maintained their relationships with old friends and continued to visit old stomping grounds.

Although he had completed his degree requirements earlier in the year, it wasn't until the end of October that Jack received his diploma in the mail from the University of Nevada. Accompanying a photo of Jack wearing a graduation cap and displaying his diploma was his advice regarding college education—that college athletes stay in school to finish their degree requirements, otherwise complete their studies in the off-season. Instead of focusing on himself as an example, he referred to Bobby Brown, who had been a Yankee roommate and kept studying to become a doctor (eventually Dr. Brown would become president of the American Baseball League). Several months later, when columnist Ed Levitt asked, "Is College a Waste?" Jack took the side opposing Paul Richards, vice-president of the Atlanta Braves, who said he tried to talk high school graduates out of attending college because at that age the professional clubs could train them properly without the distractions of schoolwork and the socializing that accompanied it; but his team did give scholarships for players to attend college in winter. Jack, however, possibly recalling the debt he owed Coach Evans so many years before, said that the professional clubs were turning to colleges for players such as Reggie Jackson from Arizona State, and that college had provided Jack the opportunity to get the contract he wanted. With his degree in hand, from this point onward Jack would always stress the importance of education, and such would often be the topic of his public speeches.

Christmas with Jon and Jay was their best yet and ushered in an enjoyable and prosperous 1972, marred only by a death in Katharine's family and some problems with Jon's schooling. Jack attended Jon's graduation, then was surprised by a letter from Zoe Ann stating that Jon was enrolling in the summer session of Menlo Junior College. In another letter from her, Jack learned that Boots Erb had lent Jon $600 and that Zoe thought Jack should repay Boots, as the divorce settlement decreed that Jack had to pay for the children's schooling. This forced Jack to write Boots a note telling him he had jumped the gun in making the advance: Jack was supposed to agree to any school the children wanted to attend, and Jon had shown himself to be irresponsible with money. Furthermore, Jack couldn't afford to send Boots the money at that time. Coincidentally, now Jon became eligible to draw from a trust fund established as a result of Jack's selling the two Hawaiian lots, the last payment having been made by a Mr. Byman of Inglewood, California, who had been making payments since 1970. (Jan had already tapped that resource.) So Jon did manage to attend the school, and Boots understood and later explained that he was just trying to be helpful.

Jack and Katharine started to get out more, dining either with old friends or at the Governor's Mansion or with Senator Laxalt. Jack had become friends with Paul Laxalt when a mutual friend, sportscaster Ted Dawson, called one day asking if Jack would complete a foursome for tennis doubles—that Paul had heard Jack was a very good tennis player. Jack was honored, but somehow forgot his appointment and was immensely embarrassed. Nevertheless, he eventually did play with Paul, and Jack and Katharine became good friends with Paul and his secretary (wife-to-be), Carol, enjoying dinners at the Ormsby House and camping at Marlette Lake. Looking back almost fourteen years, Senator Laxalt, in an interview, reflected very carefully before making some remarks about the Jackie Jensen he knew at that time: "We played tennis frequently; he would come to my house in Carson City and we'd play there where I had a tennis court. We played golf occasionally, too. He was a tremendously coordinated athlete. Whatever he did was a combination of grace and power—intensely competitive. Jackie Jensen hated to do any endeavor where he'd lose; so as a result of that association we became good friends."

Paul and Jack were very much alike in their competitive spirit, conservative nature, and outlook on government. Jack not only would talk sports frequently with Paul but also would argue government policy with great concern, almost to the point of getting emotional, prompting Paul to remark about Jack: "He was not your usual jock."

Throughout the year Jack and Katharine continued their interest in Indian affairs through Jack's position and frequent contact with Native American groups; and in addition to continued trips to Pyramid Lake and Washoe Lake, they added new archaeological sites: Honey Lake, Pintail Bay, Indian Lakes, Rough Creek, Middle Lake, and Massacre Lake.

On May 2 Katharine's Aunt Raffalovich died, so a couple of weeks later Katharine went to Italy (with Joan Drackert), where she paid her respects and collected some family heirlooms. During that time Jack, as deputy director, was to receive the first monthly newsletter from the Office of Opportunity Director Frank J. Matthews, which documented accomplishments and the fact that some goals had been set. With Nevada's overall depressed conditions, small achievements took on added significance. For example, the Nevada Economic Opportunity Office had contacted Harrah's Club (where Jack had worked a few years before), securing employment for eight minority members. Jack was probably reminded of his good fortune when he read a particular statement in the report: "There has never been a concerted effort to recruit the poor for government jobs because the minimum qualifications for state hiring are too high."

An article published just after Jack had secured his job said that he admitted to having known little about the position; nonetheless he said: "I've never found it hard to adapt. I'm used to homework." However, Jack was being realistic (as well as prophetic), when he also said, "There's no security in what I'm doing."

The lack of the job's permanence did not prevent Jack from taking his work seriously—perhaps too seriously. Once, while breakfasting with the Governor, Jack looked at his watch and remarked that he had to report to work or Mr. Matthews might say something. Governor O'Callaghan assured Jack that he didn't have to worry, but when Jack again expressed his concern, the governor made up an excuse, jotted it on a paper napkin and had it forwarded to the office. The note evoked many laughs, and Jack retrieved it as a memento.

That summer Jack played in the Phillies Old-Timers game billed as a completion of the 1952 Annual All-Star Classic. It had been called because of rain in the fifth inning twenty years before, when Jack, as a Senator with the American League, had taken right field against the National League. Before Jack left for the game, a local paper quoted him as saying: "I'm in good shape, but I need to practice swinging the bat a little."

Jack would play in several other games over the years, and fellow players would always be impressed at how healthy he looked. While East, having traveled by train, the Jensens visited St. Catharine's School in Richmond, a private girls institution Katharine had attended, and there they enrolled Tinsley. The only excitement on the vacation occurred when the train engine caught fire on the route back west from Chicago.

In October Jack, along with many other prominent sports figures, attended a special program sponsored by the Greater San Francisco Chamber of Commerce: "An Evening with Pappy Waldorf," held in the Grand Ballroom of the Fairmont Hotel. Pete Rozelle, commissioner of the National Football League, was the principal speaker. Inside the program booklet was a foldout of past headlines concerning Pappy's old teams. Only three of the twelve headlines happened to mention any players' names, and Jack's was amongst two of the 1949 headlines: "Jensen Blasts for Six," and "Jensen Saves Day as Troy Treats UC Insultingly, Nearly Victoriously." Pappy, when asked to describe his biggest thrill as a coach, had the following to say:

> Jackie Jensen gave that to me in 1948. He was back to punt on fourth down and 31 to go. The rush was on. Jackie saw that his punt would be blocked, so he took off. He slammed his way through those first tacklers, dodged others, and ran on for 32 yards and a first down. That great run enabled us to beat Stanford, 7–6, finish unbeaten, and go on to the Rose Bowl. Jackie was so strong, so fast, so electric. I've always been curious about how he would have done in pro football.

A month later Jack attended a Rose Bowl reunion, and on December 1, he and Katharine enjoyed a visit to the Jack London State Historic Park north of Sonoma. Perhaps Jack Jensen recognized a few parallels with London's life, besides sharing the same given name. Both had been born in San Francisco, attended

Oakland High School, were influenced by the sea, were twice married, had three children, and became household names. One line of London's Jensen surely could relate to: "The proper function of a man is to live, not to exist." This attitude would, in fact, alter the course of Jack Jensen's life.

January 1973 began for Jack with a continuation of his government job, and much sports action and publicity came his way. In February he played in a University of California alumni game, which Jack's team lost 0–8, but he belatedly received, along with Nino Barnise and John Fiscalini, All-American certificates for the 1947 Cal season. Perhaps this game and the award prompted Jack to make a drastic change in a year, one that would hurt Katharine and eventually himself.

The family newspaper *Grit* ran an article about Jack on Valentine's Day in its news section, showing him holding a fish near Pyramid Lake, in baseball uniform during the previous week's All-Star game, and with Katharine as they held shotguns next to a tailgate full of chukka partridge. In that article Jack said he enjoyed "trying to straighten out rebellious youngsters," and he put in a plug for friend Paul Laxalt's Ormsby House across the street from his (Jack's) office: "You can't beat it for a night out. The old-time elegance is there, they have good entertainment, and the dinners are reasonably priced."

Throughout these times Jack had followed his sons' lives and had been especially pleased to see Jon excel in sports; and during one of Jon's visits, the Jensens discussed opportunities in the Army. Katharine had encouraged Jon's excellence in marksmanship and suggested he would enjoy being on an Army rifle team. As a result, Jon signed up in February, and by May was out of boot camp, celebrating with Jay at a dinner at Jack and Katharine's. He wasn't destined to stay in the service too long, however. Jack also kept in touch with Jay and Jan, and wasn't surprised that his daughter was going to remarry.

Knowing that Tinsley was about to begin her spring break in March, Jack and Katharine planned a trip to Mexico, not only for a vacation, but also to force themselves to stop smoking. The two-weeks trip was to be a reward for their self-imposed abstinence. They met Tinsley in Arizona after she flew in from Virginia, and they continued down along the west coast of Mexico to Puerto Vallarta, stopping to fish and swim occasionally in the Gulf of California. One morning they awoke in their little motel cabin to find soldiers outside with rifles drawn, and they dared not venture from their room for several hours. They left without questioning the incident but sought further adventure nevertheless.

They had heard of an isolated Indian village that could not be reached by car. From Puerto Vallarta they took a boat (reputedly a former yacht of John Wayne's) and found it had a unique accessory: a fireplace! Moving down along the coast, they came to an inlet between steep, rocky cliffs, where a river flowed from the jungle. Four or five palm-thatched huts with bamboo walls formed the little village of Yelapa, and the Jensens made camp in one hut furnished with nothing but cots and hammocks; however, they were pleased to learn that they had access to running water an hour each day. One hut served as a kitchen and dining room. A great storm the previous day had turned the water milky, and the waves came crashing onto the many huge boulders strewn along the beach. Intent on fishing, though, Jack made his way out onto one of them and got out his tackle. Having set up her easel and paints, Katharine was in the process of recording the scene when Jack suddenly returned looking rather pale, for a huge fish had snapped his line as the waves swirled all around him and threatened to engulf him. Later, while Jack slept, Tinsley and Katharine ventured into the jungle and discovered ancient pottery shards.

Having lugged much fishing gear with them, Katharine and Jack again wanted to try catching something, so Katharine negotiated with a scarlet-eyed Indian (evidently affected by a local narcotic) to take them out into the bay on his motor-driven dugout canoe. Katharine's embarrassment at reeling in a large plastic bag gave way to excitement as Jack caught a sierra, which made a delicious meal when grilled and mixed with rice and local fruits.

After three days they were back in civilization. On their return they took a side trip about fifty miles inland to an old silver mining town named Alamos, and stayed in the House of the Treasurers, an inn that had been transformed from one of the old haciendas. They returned to Nevada having accomplished their goal of quitting smoking. Loving life in Carson City, Katharine assumed she and Jack would remain there for quite some time, and Jack himself said, "I'm happy working in the Reno area. My second wife and I live a simple life." However, the allure of sports would again beckon and usher in a tumultuous period in Jack's life.

PART FOUR

1973–1977

Jack's idol and ex-team-mate Joe DiMaggio threw out the first ball for Jack's initial season as the Bears' coach. Jack recalled his first day in the Yankee outfield with Joe when he yelled at the veteran player, "Watch the wind, Joe, watch it!"

Assistant Coaches Bob Milano and Jim Darby flank Jack at the Bears' baseball stadium. Milano eventually replaced Jack and Darby maintained his interest in baseball by becoming an executive in Mizuno Sports Equipment.

Former teammate Mickey Mantle was Jack's guest at a sports banquet at the University of California at Berkeley. Mickey had a great sense of humor.

Jack donned a sandwich board and used a bullhorn to raise attendance at a Cal game as Bears' catcher Steve Bartkowski lent support. Like Jack, Bartkowski became an All-American in baseball and football, and eventually became a television host and a color analyst. Steve was the number one draft pick of the NFL in 1975 and the Atlantic Falcons' "Rookie of the Year."

Here Jack is in the center of a group at the Bohemian Club in San Francisco during Big Game night on November 11, 1970. From left to right are Dick Madigan, Jim Merrifield (in front), Tony Cortese, Noble Hamilton (in rear), Dan McGanney (wearing glasses), Mike White, Jack Swaner, Joe Ruetz, Joe Kapp (in rear), Jackie Jensen, Lynn "Pappy" Waldorf (in rear), Frankie Albert, Rod Franz (in rear), Milt Vucinich, and Chuck Taylor.

Pictured behind the Jensens is the old Bow & Bell Restaurant at Jack London Square on the Oakland, California, estuary. Opened by Jack and Boots in 1954, it was a popular hangout for athletes and sports fans. Kids menus were shaped like baseball mitts, and if children ate all their dinner, they received gifts such as small Jackie Jensen bats made by Louisville Slugger.

Jack at his home in California, with his son Jay, who played baseball at Incline High School, and later for the University of Nevada at Reno under Coach Gary Powers, who had been one of Jack's players. Jan (right, in 1968 picture), frequently wrote Jack and Ralph Kerchum and described Jay as "quite the man with the ladies at school."

15

CAL AGAIN

In April 1973, just before Nixon aides Haldeman, Ehrlichman, Dean, and Kleindienst resigned because of the Watergate cover-up, Jack learned that the president was eliminating funds for the Office of Economic Opportunity, and since for the last few months "we did nothing but take coffee breaks and read books," Jack feared the governor would have to let him go. Besides, Jack felt that because of excessive bureaucracy the office could not be effective, although he had personally created a lot of goodwill and started many Native Americans and rural Nevadans in educational programs.

Not since the end of June 1971 had Jack seen sports columnist, caricaturist, and friend Dave Beronio. Dave, who often wrote flattering portraits of Jack, had learned that George Wolfman, head coach of the University of California baseball team at Berkeley, was retiring. He met Jack for dinner and asked if he'd be interested in coaching again, and when Jack said yes, he told him of the opportunity at Cal. Beronio called Dave Maggard, the athletic director, who in turn offered Jack the job. Jack was ecstatic and threw all caution to the wind. Katharine was greatly against the idea of Jack's switching jobs, though, and sensed that something wasn't right. For a couple who were so compatible, one might not have expected the scene that developed that day. According to Katharine:

> Well, we had arguments, but that was the argument to end all arguments; that was really a bad one. I remember I had on a quilted, red paisley zip-up bathrobe, short like a dress. It was thick; it was a sort of Chinese thing, and he took it by the back of the neck and *bounced* me on the floor because I was so beg-

ging him not to go. I said, "Please don't follow this up; please
don't go. I just can't see it; let's not leave Nevada. Please,
please, please. You left California—things weren't right in
California; let's not go back."

He was so strong; I was like a dishmop, just being bounced
on the floor—I remember he was strong enough to hold me up
and down, but I managed to say, "Look! If nothing else, please
call the governor before you go, before you say 'yes,' before
you say anything."

Although Jack consented, the governor was out when he
phoned. So he didn't wait to call again but immediately drove to
Berkeley to talk with Maggard, and agreed to take the coaching
position. When Governor O'Callaghan got back in touch, he told
Jack he always would have had a position for him, even if the OEO
were abolished, but Jack wouldn't think of rescinding his decision.
Word of Jack's return to Cal hit the papers on May 25. The previous year the team had finished 21–31; Jack had some work cut out
for him. When asked about the appointment, Jack replied, "I
couldn't be happier. If you want to be a coach, there's nothing quite
like returning to your alma mater."

With the profit from selling their Carson City house combined
with an advance from Katharine's mother, the Jensens sought a
good buy on a new home not far from the college. At the end of
June they moved into a condominium on what had been the old
Moraga Ranch in the Coast Range. The residence fit their needs,
since it was only twenty minutes from work, included a swimming
pool, and had not yet succumbed to urbanization; in fact, the
rolling hills around the homes were still dotted with cattle and
wildlife. As much as he loved Nevada, Jack was thrilled to be back
in California, for the cool wind rolling in the fog at night brought
back youthful memories. To celebrate their move, Jack and
Katharine held a party on the Fourth of July. What Jack would
learn, however, was that Cal was not the same place he had left
nearly twenty-five years earlier. Attendance at games had dwin-
dled to a quarter of what it had been when he played there, and

budget cuts limited the number of players and what the team could do. To learn more about the team and Cal's program, Jack and Katharine dined with the Wolfmans. The retired coach shared ideas with Jack, and happily handed over the reins of power.

Much of Jack's summer was spent recruiting, which he did not relish, although he recognized it as necessary. "The quest for talent has created a monster," he said, "and it starts right out in the Little Leagues. There is pressure to compete, pressure to win and often the fun element is forgotten."

Despite his lamentations about the business end of coaching, however, Jack's private thoughts about his new position were positive, as he wrote in a letter to Katharine's parents (7-22-73): "My return to the University has been busy and happy. Most of all of the old teammates and acquaintances have reappeared to say hello and wish me luck. Naturally the school has changed a great deal but then I have also. The players are still enthusiastic and look younger than ever. It's hard to believe I looked that young at one time myself."

At the end of September Jack spoke at the Sigma Alpha Epsilon football dinner, where he admitted that Cal had been going through some rough times with student demonstrations and NCAA probations, and with no chance of going to the Rose Bowl. Jack himself attended a Rose Bowl reunion about a month later, and his holidays were largely spent visiting family and friends. As 1974 began, Jack was faced with a dilemma few coaches ever experience: Would he play with fellow alumni in the upcoming game against the varsity, or instead be the young men's coach? Scorewise, he made the right decision, as the varsity won 16–0!

At Jack's invitation, old friend and teammate Joe DiMaggio spoke at the alumni banquet, then threw out the season game ball the next day and signed autographs for many of the 2,000 spectators. Just before then Jack had been pictured with football and baseball standout Steve Bartkowski on the front of the *Cal Athletic News* (2-5-74), and the two quickly established an enduring relationship. The previous season, with twelve home runs, Steve just beat Jack's record which had stood for more than twenty years.

Like Jack, Steve left college early, but to play a different sport in the pros. Bartkowski signed a contract of over $600,000 to play football for the Atlantic Falcons! Jack's team did have other stand-out players—all-Pacific Conference players Al Derian and Randy Hooper—and hopes for the season ran high, though Cal hadn't won a conference championship since Jack had been a player.

When Jack returned to Evans Field, he found things hadn't changed much: The bullpens were still on the playing surface, there was only one batting tunnel, and the same old wooden bleachers awaited the next season's fans. Although the cement wall forming the back of the track stadium was still extant, a portable fence (which had to be periodically removed for football practice) demarcated home runs that previously had to be hit into the street or over the wall 535 feet from home plate (over which Jack had supposedly short-hopped with a fly ball—a legend he denied). On arrival in his office, Jack found a stack of papers more than a foot high congratulating him on his new position. His assistant, Bob Milano, who was hired largely as an assistant athletic director, was impressed that Jack answered every one.

One thing Jack would find much different, however, was the attitude of the players: They seemed more sensitive than those Jack had coached at the University of Nevada. They didn't like criticism and wanted reasons for a coach's decisions. Jack's philosophy was that the game should be played primarily because it was fun; but without necessarily saying so, he expected all players to put out 100 percent—the way he used to. Unfortunately this was unrealistic for that era. Overall, the players were glad to have someone of Jack's caliber coaching them (even though he made them get haircuts), as a couple of newspaper interviews attested. Player Gene Little said, "He has been around baseball a long time and sees the little things most coaches don't see"; and his teammate John Hughes said, "What's great about playing for him is that he runs things like a professional team. Some coaches treat twenty-one and twenty-two-year-olds as if they were still fifteen. He doesn't. We don't have curfews. He doesn't try to control our outside lives."

Jack himself said, "Where other coaches are strict disciplinarians, my discipline is training my players hard in fundamentals, so that when the game comes, they can do things on reflex."

Of course Jack still golfed, and occasionally visited Bing Crosby's Ranch with Katharine. A letter from Crosby dated February 18, 1974, illustrates their close friendship:

> I was delighted when I heard the news that you were to be Baseball Coach at California. I hope you are inheriting some good talent, and I believe this to be true—from what I've heard.
>
> If you find anybody who looks real good, let me know and we'll have Pittsburgh take a look at him. I'm still one of the owners there. I remember the call to you at your fraternity in 1949—when I was trying to get you interested in signing with the Pittsburgh Pirates. Never have forgiven Del Webb or the Yankees for getting in ahead of me on that! Well, you had a good career while you were up, so I guess it was all for the best.
>
> I do hope the season is successful there for you.
>
> All best wishes,
>
> Bing

Exactly a month later, a letter from another friend, Governor O'Callaghan, showed that there were no hard feelings that Jack had precipitously left his employ. He wrote in part: "There is no doubt the Golden Bears have one of the finest coaches in the nation and should improve as the season progresses. Best of luck during the present season. Stop by and visit the next time you are in town."

In an interview for the *Providence Journal,* Jack was asked how he looked on coaching again. His response: "Today's program gives a true perspective of what college sports should be like. We'd like to have an outstanding team, but we don't want to sacrifice any fun doing it." He recalled that back in 1949, "college athletics were everything. Because there were no big-league teams in the area, the community revolved around the college teams."

With his team compiling a winning record by the end of April—

a considerable improvement over the previous year's performance—Jack bought a new Toyota, and Katharine planned for a Mexican vacation. In an early May article *(Los Angeles Times,* 5-4-74) titled "Fame, Failure, and Finally Reality," Jack reminisced about his playing days and said he missed Nevada somewhat, but that he enjoyed his job because the players were easy to work with. Just three days later the UCLA *Daily Bruin* ran three photos of Jack coaching, and ran the following caption: "Mr. Cool—Jackie Jensen has proven to be a popular coach at California, where many players express delight with the skills of the former major league star."

Shortly after the baseball season ended (25–24 overall, 8–10 conference), Jack, Katharine, and Tinsley headed again for Mexico. Before crossing the border they stopped at a tavern that was obviously the hangout for many prominent citizens. Recognizing the former baseball player, the mayor rushed up and asked, "Aren't you Jackie Jensen?"

After confirming the fact, Jack remarked that he and Katharine were worried about where they would leave their car, and the mayor offered the police parking lot.

The couple traveled by train to various points and were enthralled by the lifestyles of the Indians, who used the trains as a means of time travel from the old desert valley way of life to the relatively modern cities. The three weeks spent in Mexico were so entertaining that they didn't want to leave. On the last day of vacation, Katharine, who was always a meticulous record keeper, argued furiously with Jack and Tinsley that they had one day left before they had to catch the train North. Finally, to prove her point, she bought a paper, which she had done daily during their stay, and showed them the date. Not convinced, Jack questioned the vendor, who said, "Oh, all papers are a day late!" They missed the train for which they had tickets, but making her way through the station crowded with colorfully dressed Indians from Copper Canyon, Katharine spoke Spanish to the stationmaster and evoked his sympathy enough to get tickets for the next train.

Jack's sons visited frequently throughout the summer, and the

Jensens often traded dinner invitations with his brothers' families. Jack, Katharine, and Tinsley drove the scenic route through Colorado and Utah to Atlanta for a Braves Old-Timers game in August. Jack was one of four college coaches who played, joining Bob Cerv from John F. Kennedy College in Nebraska, Enos Slaughter from Duke, and Bobby Richardson from South Carolina. Not long after the game, Furman Bishop's column in *The Sporting News,* Sept. 14, 1974, described Jack as: "47, his features boldly Grecian, the yellow hair having given way to a gentle hue of brown, and the body athletically admirable. The ravages of distress and marital chaos left no traces."

In September, an unexpected public appearance for Katharine greatly embarrassed her, but she and Jack would look back on the incident and laugh. Katharine relates the story:

> At the condominium there was no washer or dryer; so I was at Laundromats with washing, and I really wanted a washer and dryer. A friend of Jack's from Los Angeles called and said, "Jack, I'd like you to be on this show I've got called *The Girl in My Life.*"
>
> And he said, "*The Girl in My Life*; What is that?"
>
> And he [Jack's friend] said, "Well, it's about ten o'clock in the morning, and you come on there and you say that you've had problems in your life; and some woman really helped you out."
>
> When Jack said, "Oh, God forbid; no way would I go on your show," the guy said, "Well, Jack, listen, you know, it's not that bad; nobody watches, number one, and number two we give really wonderful prizes, but this has to be a secret from your wife."
>
> And Jack said, "Like what?"
>
> And he said, "Oh, trips, Maytag washer and dryer."
>
> Jack said, "You said the magic words, 'Maytag washer and dryer'; What do I have to do?"
>
> So we went down to Los Angeles. Jack said he had to be interviewed on some sports show—which was a very usual event. We went out to the television studios, and people from

the network took Jack and sent somebody with me and said
Jack had to go backstage for makeup, and said, "You join the
audience here for this show, and that way you'll be there for
the next one. We do these shows two at a time, and you'll be
in the audience for the next show, the sports show."

And I said, "All right, fine."

And so I went, and my head was bothering me a little bit,
for we'd been out late with friends Peg and Sid Gilmore of the
Los Angeles Angels. And I was sitting there and I thought, 'oh
God, this is the worst show I've ever seen in my life,' and I
thought, 'Oh, my stars; let me out of here—this drivel!' And so
I started to get up and leave and the usher came up and said,
"Oh, you can't leave."

And I said, "Oh, mercy; I don't want to sit through this."

He said, "Well, I'm sorry; we don't let anyone out."

And I thought, 'Oh, dear; I have to watch the rest of the
show.' As my head was throbbing, I looked up and said to
myself, 'now what?' And they had a silhouette of this man
behind the curtain, and then this terrible thing had happened
and my wonderful wife, and I thought, 'Oh, my God; that's
Jack's voice!'

And then the lights go on, and the lights all shine on me,
and I hear "his wonderful wife" and there I'm sitting with this
dreadful hangover, feeling trapped in this ghastly show, and I
thought, 'This is a living nightmare; I can't believe this,' and
I'm sort of hefted onto the stage, and "Oh, wonderful wife,
here's your trophy."

Afterwards, the people who produced the show said, "We
thought we'd never keep you in that seat long enough."

We got the washer and dryer, and Jack said, "Promise
you'll never tell anyone we were on that show."

I said, "Are you kidding; never will I admit that."

But by the time the show aired, Jack's team had gotten wind of it.
They were in hysterics as they watched it in the locker room. Jack did
indeed give much credit to his wife; he was quoted as saying, "I'm

lucky to have Katharine. She's very strong, and intelligent. Without her I would have had a real bad time. She's shown me so much."

Having learned that Jack and Katharine were participating in that show, their friend Sid Gilmore visited them in their hotel and introduced them to Filmore Crank, husband of Beverly Garland (wife on the TV show *My Three Sons* and the mother in *Scarecrow and Mrs. King*) and owner of two Howard Johnson's hotels. They invited Jack and Katharine to stay in a suite when the Cal team later visited Los Angeles for a game. Months later the couple took advantage of the invitation and the opportunity to host a Westwood Hotel party that began after Jack and Bob Milano bedded down the Cal team in another hotel. Besides Bob, guests included sports announcer Ted Dawson (who used to broadcast with the Jensens in Reno), Peter Paxton (builder of Laguna Niguel Tennis Club), the manager of the Los Angeles Coliseum, the Gilmores, and a couple whose family used to own the Donner Trail Ranch. They ordered pizza, fruit, beer, and wine for a party, and Jack had the time of his life. About eleven at night the phone rang: A Cal player had broken curfew, rented a car, and had an accident. Jack was tipsy and asked Milano to pick up the boy, which he did. The story was hushed up, since Jack always felt uneasy that he had to ask Bob for help.

In December the Jensens purchased a new Audi and traveled East through the southern states to New York, visited relatives in Virginia, picked up Tinsley from St. Catherine's, and did some sightseeing at Colonial Williamsburg. This was the first of a few trips the Jensens would take over the next couple of years, but it was not just for pleasure. At the University of Virginia, Jack spoke to the athletic director, whom he had met earlier in California and had discussed the possibility of Jack's coaching at Virginia—but that chance would never come to fruition due to what Jack and Katharine believed were suspicious circumstances.

By the end of the first week of January 1975, Jack was back at Cal, but he and Katharine were disappointed when Maggard told him a lack of funds would prevent Jack from attending meetings in

Washington, D.C., as had been expected. In fact, the team (including junior varsity) had to be cut from fifty-six to thirty-six players, and the budget crunch would create some serious problems. On February 8 Jack was pictured in the *Oakland Tribune,* standing alongside Mickey Mantle and Cal player Gene Little as Mantle appeared as Jackie's guest at a Big C luncheon for ex-baseball greats held in the Faculty Club on the Cal campus. Jack related how he had played both with Mickey and against him, but particularly recalled standing in right field and watching his 565-foot hit over the center-field scoreboard in Griffith Stadium. Mantle amused the group with the story of how Casey Stengel once told team members at a meeting that there were two cases of gonorrhea on the club, to which Yogi Berra responded, "Hey, that's great. I'm tired of drinking Gatorade anyway."

Jack responded to a question about how often he was recognized when traveling by saying people between thirty-five and forty-five would often know who he was, but not the younger crowd. This paralleled his own words in a previous article: "The players see my picture on the walls and they know someone named Jackie Jensen was supposedly a star here, but I think they're firmly convinced that the guy and me just happen to have the same name. Occasionally, I run into someone downtown my age who recognizes me."

In March, the team came off a 5-year NCAA suspension for recruiting infractions, and with a shortage of funds, a reduced squad, and the loss of twelve senior players, Jack had his work cut out for him. The challenge, though, didn't bother Jack as much as the apparent apathy of the Cal students toward baseball. Out of frustration he resorted to doing something that took much courage and that truly embarrassed him at first, but it brought an unexpected bonus as several newspapers caught wind of it and gave his efforts publicity—more than what he had hoped for. Jack donned a sandwich board that read BASEBALL GAME TODAY/2:30 EVANS FIELD, and he carried a megaphone to get the attention of passersby. On being interviewed, Jack referred to Foghorn

Murphy, who allegedly had been dubbed such by Jack London and who had ridden a white horse around the Bay area announcing the Seals or Oaks were playing ball that day. Jack said that his pitch started to be fun, especially when he ran into people he knew; newspapers across the country carried an AP photo of him talking to Steve Bartkowski, and all who knew him recognized his under-lying sincerity.

Perhaps the publicity spurred one person in particular to show up unexpectedly at a game. One of his players came up to Jack and said that there was an old man in the stands who wanted to say hello. It was Stengel, who told him to "tell my players to get around the bases like I used to do."

Also in March, Steve Bartkowski was pictured on the cover of *California Monthly,* but this time not for baseball. The 6'4", 215-pound quarterback had led the nation in passing the previous fall—2,580 yards with only seven interceptions in 325 passes. However, on folding open the publication, the feature article con-cerned not Bartkowski, but another football player, one nearly his size but older and more distinguished: Jack's old high school and college buddy John Najarian. After Cal, he had studied at the University of California School of Medicine and later "pioneered the kidney transplant service at UC." At the University of Minnesota, he replaced retiring chairman Dr. Owen Wagensteen, who had trained Dr. Christian Barnard of South Africa. Furthermore, he had developed an antirejection serum and organ-storing machine, and had performed more than 700 kidney trans-plants. For these accomplishments he was awarded the title of California's Alumnus of the Year.

During the spring season Jack's team won about half its games. The players might have done better were they to have freely accepted Jack's method of coaching. Jack became good friends with the head football coach, Mike White. They both had problems working for Maggard, whose primary concern was making the athletic program profitable. Some players grumbled at Jack's way of helping them: He would answer questions with questions, forcing them to look to themselves to solve problems. They favored speaking to Milano; he made things easy for them. If a student needed help with a subject, Bob would get on the phone and try to get him a tutor, whereas Jack would tell the student that this was his own responsibility.

Unfortunately, some players either expected too much of Jack or used him as a scapegoat for their lackluster performances. When Jack spent a week of his vacation during Cal's spring break as a guest training coach at Scottsdale for the Angels (where he also sought to learn some new coaching strategies), they said they felt he had abandoned them. Jack naively assumed that those students remaining on campus would study. Eligibility had been a problem before for the baseball team; but when Coach Milano offered to hold practice, they believed Jack to be shunning his responsibilities, when in essence he was not only doing as he pleased during his own free time, but was also talking to managers and scouts about Cal players who were likely professional prospects. Returning to Berkeley and hearing Maggard complain about his absence during practice, Jack explained that he gladly would have stayed there during the break had he known what the players wanted. The incident was the first sign of trouble brewing.

As Jack realized later, when comparing notes with football coach Mike White, communication was often a problem in the Cal athletic system. Only once in four years of coaching did Jack have a substantial meeting with Maggard, and that was over a lunch to which Jack had invited him. Although Jack was frequently asked to speak at various functions outside of Cal, Maggard gradually ceased to ask him to represent the university, and later Jack would also learn that Mike White, whom he considered a better speaker than himself, had also been passed over for such engagements.

In May Jack was pictured with Rod Franz (former teammate and three-time All-American football player) at the Sacramento Rotary Club luncheon, where Jack was a guest speaker. The team finished the regular season 22–24 overall and 7–9 in the conference despite having had some students benched for eligibility reasons, but the players looked forward to a tournament in July, which would be followed by the Robert Goulet show. Jack didn't attend the July Yankees Old-Timers Day, but a picture of him and Mantle did appear in *Pinstripes,* the monthly newsletter; and that same month he was presented a Certificate of Appreciation from the Kiwanis Club of San Jose.

The July tournament in Las Vegas was played in a sandstorm, and afterward the players traded their uniforms for garb many were less accustomed to: coats and ties. Jack had arranged with his friend Robert Goulet for his team to go to his dinner show at the Frontier Hotel, and finally the moment arrived for which Jack had been anxiously awaiting—Robert Goulet's appearance. Goulet had the habit of coming down off the stage and walking amongst the audience; but unexpectedly, when he made his way to Jack's table, instead of singing, he called for the spotlight to shine on his good friend, and he went on to mention the presence of the Cal team and Jack's accomplishments. In an apparently festive mood, one of Jack's players made a flippant remark to the entertainer, saying in a sense that he was carrying the praise too far. Much to Jack's surprise, Robert, a robust individual who lifted weights, put his microphone behind his back, leaned over to the young man, looked him straight in the eye in the most serious manner and said, "Do you want a fight?" Fortunately for all concerned, the lad had enough sense to avoid an altercation, and the show continued with the audience unaware of what had just transpired. Returning to Berkeley, Jack immediately wrote Goulet to apologize for the player. Goulet answered:

Jackie,

Thanks for the sweet note and we'll get together at my place in July. My best to you both and to your team Captain.

Robert Goulet

In August Jack made a speech at a veterans home in Yountville in the wine country just north of Napa and attended a Padres Old-Timers game on the Leather team with Bobby Richardson, Enos Slaughter, and Al Gionfriddo, among others. His team opposed the Lumber, who had the really big names: Stan Musial, Mickey

Mantle, Roger Maris, and Yogi Berra. Jack also continued his interest in baseball by working with a Little League. Throughout the fall he played golf, did some Indian research, saw Goulet again in Vegas, and traveled through Arizona to watch the Dodgers, Athletics, Padres, and Angels play winter-league ball, followed by a visit to an Apache reservation, where he and Katharine felt uncomfortably white and unwelcome.

Near the end of the month, Jack announced a game at Palo Alto. He spent his Thanksgiving with Katharine in Carmel, at Aunt Lil's. During the Christmas season he and Katharine entertained Governor O'Callaghan and other friends and had Jay and Jan over for dinner. They anticipated that the Bicentennial year would be another pleasant one, but 1976 turned out to be a year of extremes for Jackie. On the one hand he would be honored by appearing in a national magazine article; on the other, he would suffer indignities not just from his players, but also from a columnist who had been a longtime acquaintance.

Optimism was the tenor of the January 1976 *Cal Athletic News,* which quoted Jack as saying he had a very good baseball team—with "experience, speed, power, and pitching." However, what Jack didn't mention was positive attitude, and this was the one thing that would hurt the players and Jack himself. Perhaps the major leagues' spring lockout contaminated all of baseball, for in referring to it in a late-February interview before a game with Fresno State, Jack said, "I'm fed up with baseball; not just with this thing that's going on now, but with what's been going on for years." He went on to criticize the plethora of lawyers in the sport, the players who demanded too much, and the high price of tickets that kept fans from going to the games, which is why he furthermore stated that the Bay area couldn't support two teams (Giants and Athletics). Jack went on to lament, "Baseball is no longer the national pastime. It's lost its luster."

His words were unfortunately all too prophetic: Soon after, the Golden Boy himself would be described as having lost his luster.

16

LOST LUSTER

Soon after Jack had publicly criticized contemporary baseball, a complimentary article in the February 1976 *Baseball Bulletin* referred to Jack in its front-page headline as "Yesterday's Hero." In that article Jack said he had no regrets about anything he'd done or anything that had happened to him. He did admit he didn't see many of his old playing buddies except during Old-Timers games, but he was still getting about twenty letters a week from fans seeking autographs. An article in a March *Los Angeles Times* seemed to echo the *Bulletin*'s tone, but perhaps with a touch of melancholy as columnist John Hall sought to describe the current status of baseball: "College baseball is Jackie Jensen, American League MVP in 1958 for the Boston Red Sox, coming home to coach the alma, the Cal Bears, and walking around campus with a sign on his back to attract attention to his game," he wrote." Didn't the Golden Boy bat and pitch the Golden Bears to the Golden title in 1947? Doesn't anybody remember?"

The April 12, 1976, special baseball issue of *Sports Illustrated* devoted fourteen columns to the life of Jack Jensen. Entitled "A Fear of Flying," Ron Fimrite's article was the most personal story yet published of Jack's life. Although it highlighted Jack's early accomplishments, it essentially took up where Al Hirshberg's biography left off, while interweaving accounts about Jack's phobia. Jack had known months ahead that the article was forthcoming, but had no idea the amount of attention it would get. Jack was deluged with letters reflecting how much Fimrite's article touched responsive chords from fans and friends. Above all else, Jack's ability not only to survive but also to surmount his difficulties impressed everyone, jogged some memories, and inspired a few hopes. A look at some excerpts from letters illustrates the impact the article had.

From a student at Cal from '46 to '49:

> I was one of the thousands who sat in the stands—marveling at your footbal playing prowess. When anyone says "football" to me I think of Jackie Jensen. Let me say that your experience is very inspiring to me, and your life is far more meaningful to me and, I'm sure, many others than had it been all bliss and roses. Life's pathway is not always one of ease, and through experiences of people as yourself who are willing to share them with others, we can take courage and continue to do our best.

From a University of Kentucky coach and former Cleveland Indians player:

> Certainly many people can identify with the ups and downs that you've faced. I have long considered you right up there with Jim Thorpe and Jackie Robinson as the greatest all around athletes this country has ever produced. I'm so glad that you're coaching and passing on your knowledge to young people.

From the President of the University of the Pacific:

> I am pleased to enclose my check for $20 in support of the baseball program. You are certainly to be commended on the way you have handled adversity in earlier years and I am delighted things are going so well for you at this time.

From a former University of Nevada player:

> Many memories quickly passed in front of me. It made me realize how much I missed your presence on a baseball diamond and how I treasure the season while playing baseball at the University in the spring of 1971. I really enjoyed your article and it makes me proud that I was fortunate enough to play baseball for a man of your caliber.

And this letter from Saudi Arabia:

> I can remember listening to the Cal games when I was in high

school in Eureka, California. Jack, when you thought you were "at the top"—you weren't—you're there now.

As usual, Jack took the time to answer every letter. He did feel as though he were on top of the world, but had no idea how quickly he would plummet. In reality, Jack had found the coaching life less than ideal. A few years before, when coaching the Jamestown rookie farm team, Jack admitted he was frustrated at players who came to him lacking the fundamentals, but at least some made up for that with their enthusiasm. A trend had been gradually forming over the years that can be easily recognized in retrospect. Unlike Jack's early baseball days, when he coached in Nevada (according to later the University of Nevada head coach Gary Powers, who played for Jack and coached his son Jay) some players would question a coach's methods but usually would not confront him. However, by the '70s many players not only did not hesitate to question a coach but would go so far as to demand that he coach the way they felt best. Unfortunately, Jack was inflexible in his approach. As Bob Milano (later head coach at Berkeley) and Jim Darby (another assistant to Jack and later an executive for Mizuno Sports) pointed out, Jack expected players to put forth the same amount of effort *he* did during practice. He would demonstrate, not just instruct, and would not coddle anyone: A player was expected to try his best and not let personal problems get in the way. Jack enjoyed hard work and the rewards it brought, and he mistakenly thought the players felt the same way.

The team seemed to overlook the fact or just didn't know that Jack was working on a limited budget, but he did arrange for them to play in the prestigious Riverside College Baseball Tournament, where they performed well. However, a few seniors who were disappointed in not having had a spring-break trip influenced other members of the team to lodge complaints. Seven players, after talking to Coach Milano, who neither encouraged nor discouraged them, took a petition of complaints to Athletic Director Maggard. Just a week after the *Sports Illustrated* article rekindled Jack's fame, and a day after his team beat Stanislaus State, came headlines that shocked the sports world: "Players Petition for Jensen's Ouster" and "Cal baseballers gripe about Jensen's coaching."

Actually the petition, reportedly signed by twenty-two of twenty-five players, had been delivered to Maggard on April 9. He read it and destroyed it, but the grievances were made public by outfielder Marshall Johnson, who listed three complaints: player-coach relations, skill instruction, and road trips. Johnson said Jack was aloof from the players and related better to some than others, that he didn't teach fundamentals, and that he kept them from attending a tournament at the University of Hawaii. Jack responded briefly to each accusation, saying that he did spend a lot time with each player, performed the job as only he knew how to, and didn't go to Hawaii because of budget limitations (airfare was $300 per player). Jack was called in for a conference with Maggard just an hour after the players appeared with their list of com-plaints. Maggard told the players (in response to a question) that such grievances were common and "some of our most successful coaches have had personality conflicts."

Although Jack said, "I have my way of coaching and I don't know any other way. I can't be someone else," he met with the players and placated them to some extent. Furthermore, five of them went to him on their own and said his instruction had been adequate if not excellent. Jack felt pressured to state publicly, "There is no way my aversion to flying will prevent the team from taking part in any tournament," and Milano later attested that Jack did indeed fly with him to Los Angeles, helped by Dramamine and John Brody, who happened to be on the same plane and talked to Jack the entire way to keep his mind off the flight.

To Jack's defense came his catcher Len Patterson with a com-promising appraisal of why some players might not have been taught skills in depth: "I think he tried to make us realize that we're 21 or 22 years old and we should be able to pick these things up. Maybe it's because he was good enough to do it by himself."

This statement paralleled one made at another time by George Maldonado (in a *Gazette-Journal* article by Dan McGrath), who had played for Jack at the University of Nevada at Reno and explained why some UNR players had thought Jack impatient: "I thought he took a very professional approach. If you went to him for help, he'd work with you all you wanted, but he didn't seek you out. He pushed us to improve. He stressed fundamentals and little things like moving runners over because they help you win. And I noticed when I got into the pros they harped on the same thing."

But perhaps most important was Patterson's statement that the issue should have been kept within the team and not made public, for it hurt everyone. Friends and fans rallied to support Jack, as illustrated in an April 28 letter from a San Diego lawyer, who wrote:

> I simply want you to know that I and thousands of others totally support you, your dedication to athletics and athletes and hope you hang in there. I would consider it a great privilege for any son or daughter of mine to be coached by you for I think you would be an extremely fine influence upon them. A copy of this letter is being sent to Dave Maggard simply to let him know my sentiments which I think are undoubtedly echoed by many, many others. Good luck and I sincerely hope this issue is resolved and that you have many happy, successful years at the helm of Cal's baseball team.

A fresh perspective of Jack's plight was offered by Wells Trombly, of the San Francisco *Examiner and Chronicle,* describing Jack as a man caught between time zones. Trombly told how Jack had entered baseball during an era when athletes were heroes and well respected, but stopped playing when "The new athlete slouched, swore, chased women, smoked dope, took pills to get up and pills to get down." Trombly stated, accurately, that Jack coached the way that he had been coached, and that the complaints were based on petty resentments.

Jack could have seen the criticism coming had he focused on the last lines of a previous article entitled "Overcoming adversity top Jensen feat." Nick Peters, who for years had lauded Jackie, used most of his column to summarize Jack's life up to the time he started coaching at Cal, then said that it was he who had called

Jack and asked him if he'd be interested in applying for the vacancy when it occurred. He carefully led into an animadversion:

> Because of his [Dave Maggard's] need and his [Jack's] name, he was hired. Today's seers have mixed emotions about their new skipper. His recruiting intensity is questioned and so is some scheduling which carefully avoids any flying. But when you're a Jackie Jensen, any negative aspects of your behavior are easily swept under the rug. When you have meant so much to a school that hungers for athletic glory, you can always come home again.

This thinly veiled criticism would be far surpassed by later diatribes of Peters. A letter from Katharine to her parents dated April 28 demonstrates her viewpoint of the whole affair:

> The baseball team is 28 wins & 14 losses & 1 tie. He had a blow when most of his team went to the Athletic Director with complaints about him (instead of going to him) & it went on & on; on T.V. & in the papers. Berkeley seems to be breeding these blasted self-important kids who are students of anarchy. They ended up looking silly & everyone from all over have called & written support for Jack—The gov. of Nevada called & said "I could have told you they'd be like that down there!"

The incident soured the Jensens some on the University of California, for in the same letter Katharine described how Jack had told Tinsley she should attend Cal. Katharine pointed out the good reasons for her daughter to attend Berkeley: "Cal is a beautiful school lavishly maintained on our tax money and the cost for attendance is low. So that means no pinch instead of pulling in our belts to send her elsewhere. It will be fun for both Jack & Tin; his office can be her headquarters & she can go to school with him each day 'till such time as she might join a sorority & can fill the time she doesn't have to study with the many activities and sports."

Jack's team finished the season 9–14–1 in the California Intercollegiate Baseball Association and 24–6 in nonleague play. Meeting with Maggard to discuss his future, Jack was essentially told he needed to win more games to keep his position. With the decision of whether he'd be rehired up in the air, Jack took a much-needed vacation to the East Coast, leaving with Katharine in early June. Their California problems behind, they attended Tinsley's graduation, then went on to Stockbridge, Massachusetts, where they tried unsuccessfully to locate the Norman Rockwell painting the artist had done of Jack for the *Saturday Evening Post* cover during his Red Sox days. They continued on to Newport, Rhode Island; Martha's Vineyard; and Ogunquit, Maine—where they stayed at the Island House near the yacht basin at Perkins Cove. They enjoyed a Red Sox game at which Jack was interviewed by an Oakland A's television announcer. (Upon calling his brother Bob, Jack learned that many people back home had seen him). At the end of the month they finally headed back West to see what else could be in store.

On his arrival, Jack learned that Maggard had decided to rehire him for the next year (starting July l), but that news was surely dampened when Nick Peters struck again in a *Berkeley Gazette* article (6-26-76). His vitriolic tone left little doubt how he felt about the same man who had graciously agreed to be interviewed for the previous personal article. Jack was no longer "Jackie," but "Jensen," as Peters opened wounds with such statements as these: "Maggard is giving Jensen just enough rope to hang himself. A poll of players clearly indicates that Milano is the respected leader of the Golden Bears and not Jensen. It strongly suggested a lack of respect for the onetime 'Golden Boy' of Cal."

The article also begrudged Jack's taking an earned vacation, saying that Milano had confirmed Jack was on vacation, and that a player thought Jack should have been out recruiting instead. At least Bob wouldn't comment any further. Although he admittedly would have liked to take Jack's place, he was friends with him, respected him, and recognized that his positive coaching qualities outweighed any negative aspects.

The other coach, Jim Darby, later provided some insights into the issue of Jack's recruiting. Jim had finished playing baseball at Cal the year before Jack arrived (1973), then as a graduate assistant coached with the junior varsity squad, followed by a year as varsity assistant in charge of pitching at St. Mary's. He was invited back to Cal by Jack, and the men developed a warm friendship. As Jim said later, "This is the guy who when I was a little kid I used to hero worship; and for my birthday my parents used to take me to his and Boots's restaurant."

Jim explained that indeed Jack didn't like recruiting but realized it was something Maggard required because it was good business. Whereas Jack tended more to act as a father to the young men, Bob "jived" with them. Invariably they associated with him more than Jack because Bob always rode with them on the bus or plane to games; Jack occasionally drove by himself. Bob had to fulfill his duties as assistant athletic director so couldn't recruit much, but he did handle a lot of everyday activity as directed by Jack, who was always tactful about suggesting what Bob's responsibilities were. Jack and Bob were different, but together they presented a good coaching situation. Jim, not much older than the players, kept a low profile.

Despite the students' complaints, the team finished with a 33–20 overall and 9–14 conference record; the .623 win statistic was the team's best in ten years, even though several games had been forfeited due to the ineligibility of a player who had falsely claimed more credit than he had earned. With such a performance, Jack was offered (and signed on June 30) a 12-month contract for $19,000 to coach the '76–'77 year, which included stipulations that he could not make any public appearances resulting in unfavorable reflections on Cal, needed the athletic director's permission before engaging in any "commercial activity," and could not accept any gratuities. Furthermore, his thirty-day vacation time had to be coordinated with Maggard. With employment ensured, Jack returned to mundane office work and commenced the summer with speaking engagements and attention to his family.

Although Tinsley had been doing quite well as a Cal student, her stepsister was leading a difficult life. Jan had married for the third time and was raising three children. Jan and Jack had drifted farther apart since Jack's marriage to Katharine, who had tried her best to accept her. By her own admission, Jan was a tomboy. She was the antithesis of Tinsley the lady; and Jan saw Katharine as taking time away from her and Jack. She had not only suffered through divorces but had also gotten involved in drugs and experienced financial difficulties. Her liberal life-style contrasted greatly with Jack's. As Jan later recalled, "I was not the petite little young woman that needed a white hankie to wave bye-bye with. I had my own baseball uniform, and I could outfish my dad, and I could gut my own fish and cut lizards and newts and frogs and wasn't afraid of worms."

Jan said it wasn't until she had her second child that she really got along well with her mother, Zoe Ann, a disciplinarian who she felt resented Jan's closeness to Jack. Jan had grown up living a lie as a model child of an all-American family, and for the rest of her life she sought acceptance from her father. Despite Jack's largely ignoring her, Jan kept trying to communicate with him, writing him at his school address as she was unnecessarily paranoid about Katharine seeing the letters; and she chided him for once forgetting her birthday, for not visiting her when he was in the area seeing Jon or Jay, and especially for not expressing much joy at seeing yet another grandchild when she took it to a Cal game one day.

Again Jack was caught in the middle; he had a marvelous marriage but was tied to his past by his children. His relationships with Jon and especially Jay were comfortable, although both sons would develop their own marriage problems. Jan was destined to be married four times and never to have a true reconciliation with her father. The sorry state of affairs was made evident later in the year when she sent Jack photos of herself and her children with a sad note on a Christmas card: "Dear Dad, Here's a few reminders of a part of the family I guess you'd rather forget."

In July Jack began to repay an invaluable debt to Jan's godfather, Ralph Kerchum. Ralph had left the Oakland Public School System after thirty-five years to become a full-time ranger for the United States Park Service and had regularly kept in touch with both Jan and Jack over the years. He was a railroad buff—had traveled on and studied railway systems across the country and in Europe and Asia and was a charter member of the National Association of Railway Passengers. When he heard of a vacancy for the post of consumer representative to the Amtrak Board of Directors, he wrote Jack for a recommendation, having already obtained one from his good friend and former classmate Edwin Meese III. Jack moved ahead full throttle and wrote to the right people, many of whom he knew personally: Nevada Congressman James Santini, Senator Paul Laxalt, and Governor Mike O'Callaghan. Ralph received the appointment, which he continued to hold for many years.

Eager to repay Governor O'Callaghan, that fall Jack forwarded to Maggard a purchase request for eight tickets to a UCLA game for the governor, his aides, their wives, and himself and Katharine. He volunteered to turn in four complimentary tickets of his own, so only four more would have to be bought. However, Maggard looked on the request as an attempt to get free tickets and, much to Jack's chagrin, provided very poor seats for the governor, for which Jack had to apologize. This seemed to point to another year of friction ahead.

On August 6 Jack spoke to a crowd of 350 people at the launching of the Pacific Southwest Regional Babe Ruth Baseball Tournament in Elko, where teams from California, Nevada, Arizona, Hawaii, and elsewhere competed for the right to progress toward the Babe Ruth League World Series. The tournament director, John C. Miller, had scheduled Sandy Koufax as the guest speaker, but he canceled at the last minute, forcing John frantically to scour the West for a replacement. Miller contacted Nevada Congressman Jim Santini, who in turn called Jack. In his speech at the banquet Jackie praised, among others, Johnny Mize, whom Jackie had known when he was playing with the Yankees. A series of baseball cards had been printed extolling Mize's achievements and lamenting the fact that he had not yet been elected to the Hall of Fame (something Guy Shipler said Jack's friends in Nevada used to kid Jack himself about). Ernie Lombardi, Allie Reynolds, Gene

Woodling, Hal Trosky, Phil Landrum, Enos Slaughter, James "Cool Papa" Bell, Ted Williams, and Ken Keltner gave their reasons, on respective cards, why Johnny Mize was noteworthy. Jack's promotion, titled "Mize Belongs with Baseball's Best!," read as follows:

> Unlike many who have played with and against Johnny Mize, I feel it is a great injustice that "Big Jawn" has failed to be elected to professional baseball's Hall of Fame. Mickey Mantle, Joe DiMaggio, Ted Williams, Yogi Berra, Whitey Ford and other members of the Hall of Fame—were my teammates, and I can honestly say that John Mize could proudly take his place among such men and feel sincerely deserving. Once in 1951, when many said that John was all through, he somehow reached back for that extra strength that champions possess and hit three consecutive home runs. I will never forget that day, coming so late in John's career. I sincerely hope that the powers in charge will see their way clear to reconsider Johnny Mize for HOF status. He truly deserves the honor.

(Johnny Mize was inducted into the National Baseball Hall of Fame in 1981.)

A day after the Babe Ruth Tournament, Jack hit a double during an Old-Timers game at Hughes Stadium, and a newspaper article a few days later revealed that he had a six golf handicap and had played in the Bing Crosby National Pro-Am at Pebble Beach on fourteen occasions. A few days later an article gave Jackie's version of why Ted Williams never tipped his hat and mentioned that Joe DiMaggio had just given him a Mr. Coffee machine. Furthermore, an article at the end of the month, picturing his life and entitled "The Golden Boy Has Mellowed," revealed he was still smarting from the players' criticism of a few months before. Jack made a prophetic statement regarding earning a living: "That's why I admire a rancher or a farmer. They work so hard...I think I could have been happy doing that."

A year later he'd find himself in that very position.

17

REMOVAL

At the end of the summer of 1976 Jack had said, "Somewhere there is a point where you start to appreciate your life more. You see that somewhere down the line it will end."

Whereas in August Jack had written letters of recommendation for Ralph Kerchum, his mentor since junior high school, in early December he did the same for someone he himself had supported financially. Bert Padell was seeking admittance to the California bar, so Jack wrote a glowing recommendation to William Morris, director of the National Conference of Bar Examiners. Bert would later represent Jack in a legal matter and go on to be famous in his own right as an agent of celebrities, profiled in an article in The *New Yorker* and in other magazines.

As a member of the board of directors of the Northern California Chapter of the National Football Foundation and Hall of Fame, Jack attended the Scholar-Athlete Awards Dinner. One of the winners was Craig Landis, a back from Vintage High School in Napa County, who had decided to attend UCLA instead of Cal because chances of developing a talent in football were better there, he felt. Like Jack, he had been a good baseball prospect, and a couple of months after seeing Jack at a banquet, Craig wrote him a letter that included a look at Coach Jensen's recruiting efforts: "I want to thank you for all the time you spent talking to me and recruiting me for Cal. I have heard my dad talk about you for many years and it was a pleasure talking to you. Thank you again for all your time and effort. I really appreciate it." Jack responded to the note, and for the next several years privately hoped he himself would be inducted into the College Football Hall of Fame.

By the middle of January, baseball scrimmages had begun, and Jack continued in his free time to play golf and attend banquets. The season was looking pretty good for Jack, according to the *Oakland Tribune* article (2-10-77) entitled "Cal Baseball's Biggest Fan," for beneath a photograph of Jack smiling was the caption, "Jackie Jensen Happy Again." The article quoted Jack: "When I get up in the morning and know we'll be playing that day, I'm the happiest guy in the world. I'm a fan. I can't help but like seeing my team play."

On reflection, Jack said that the previous season's problems with the players' petition had been due to Cal's high-powered program, and that he had delegated too much authority to his assistants; consequently, he hadn't become as involved with the players as he had in Nevada, where he had coached alone. He went on say that he had modified his way of coaching somewhat and that five of the students who started the petition had lost their eligibility as seniors. Jack said, "It's easy to forgive. You just don't forget."

Jack explained the difference between baseball in his day and in 1977: The player wasn't different, just the recognition he received, for players in the '40s were noted by the papers much more, but in the '70s it took true dedication to remain on a team because virtually nobody except scouts would watch the players. Playing was not so much for fun, but rather for business. In an August 19, 1986, interview, Jim Darby, who was in charge of junior varsity baseball, had the following perspective of Jack's coaching at Cal: "Jack wanted a fun program for the kids, wanted a feeling of joy in their experience at Cal; I think it meant an awful lot to Jack Jensen that the kids who came into the program graduate." Although Jim went on to say that Jack was "very much against those guys who just came hoping to go on to a pro career," Jack said that four or five of his juniors were talented enough to be drafted by the majors and that 95 percent of Cal players were recruited. His optimism was apparent when he remarked, "This will be the best team of the bunch."

A week after that article appeared, Jackie's team played the Bears' alumni, coached by George Wolfman. By mid-season the

Bears were winning about half their games—about the same as Incline High School in Nevada, where second baseman Jay Jensen was finding his picture in the paper, too, as he tagged the bag and prepared to throw to first.

George Sullivan was an associate professor of journalism at Boston University when he wrote a lengthy article about Jack in the *Boston Sunday Globe* (3-20-77). He later would author two books that included excerpts about Jack—illustrated histories of the Yankees and of the Red Sox. His *Globe* article recounted Jack's ups and downs and his current situation, which included a total record of ninety wins and eighty losses at Cal. However, that winning record wouldn't be enough to satisfy the athletic director, whom Jim Darby said looked upon baseball "as a business."

In April the ever-vigilant sports columnists and reporters gave mixed reviews of Jack's team. By mid-month the team stood with twice as many wins as losses in non-league games, but 0–6 in Pac-8 play. However, as Larry Stone of the *Daily Californian* pointed out, the team gave "glowing praise" to Jackie, and said Jack's honesty might have been helping to condemn him, since he had mentioned that his salary would never make him wealthy, that he didn't enjoy the hustle and bustle of the Bay area, and that he didn't like the pressure to win. Perhaps Athletic Director Maggard read that article or ones like it, but regardless, the season's final statistics rang the death knell for Jack: 29–27 overall, but only 5–13 in conference play.

Just after they returned home, on May 25, 1977, came the public announcement by Maggard that Jack's contract was not been renewed. He had given Jackie the chance to resign gracefully, but Jack refused. Maggard told reporters "What made it [the decision to fire Jack] especially tough is that Jack and I are such good friends—and I'm sure it will remain that way." However, Mike White told the author that Maggard "crushed Jack as a person," and that the athletic director should have helped Jack rally the alumni and bring back the glory to baseball.

When Darby found Jack in the locker room "just pale as a

ghost," the day of the announcement, he thought Jack would have a heart attack. Completely devastated by the turn of events, Jack purposely could not be reached for comment. Larry Stone, at the *Daily Californian,* noted that some speculated Milano did not want to return to Cal if he did not get Jack's job, and he was a logical candidate for the position. One of the players, using language Jack wouldn't approve of, said he would love to see Milano as coach: "The man is a winner, he works his ass off." Unfortunately, Jack was the loser. His 109–95 overall record was overshadowed by the 29–45 conference figures. But those numbers meant little to him compared to the great loss of having to leave the college to which he had dedicated himself and had brought so much fame. Jack was so depressed that Katharine worried he would have another heart attack, and fortunately friends and relatives again came to his aid. The day after the announcement, Jack's brother Bob visited, and soon afterward sportswriter Ron Fimrite came to dinner.

On June 1 Stephanie Salter, a columnist for the *San Francisco Examiner,* wrote what a poet would term an apology for Jack, more an explanation of what had transpired than a justification. She first of all returned fire on another columnist who had gloated at Jack's misfortune, who had called him "seemingly paranoid, fraught with insecurities." and who had delivered the ultimate insult: "his lengthy list of employment failures offers ample proof of his instability." After sardonically referring to her arch rival columnist as an astute amateur psychologist who had fired shots usually reserved for the likes of Idi Amin, Salter put Jack's coaching record into perspective, noting how in 30 years the team had won only two conference championships (one of those being in the year Jack starred), that Cal's competition was outstanding, that three of its pitchers were lost to injuries, that Cal turned away talented players who lacked high academic standards, and that two of the team's best players preferred to play basketball. Salter was one of the few people to whom Jack would speak the day after he was fired. Jack himself then put baseball at Cal into perspective: "Coaching at Cal is a little different from coaching at some other schools. There are a lot of boys here for other reasons. Baseball is not necessarily their top priority. Other places, a fellow is generally there because of baseball."

Over the next couple of weeks, the newspapers served as a forum for both writers and readers to express their views, views that reflected in some way a love for the "old" Cal of traditional values—epitomized by Jack—and the "new" Cal that stressed individual freedom and student rights. Some time before, Jack and Katharine had discussed what they would eventually like to do with their lives. They had decided they might return to Katharine's native Virginia and buy a small farm or build a house: They had even gone so far as to obtain a few collections of floor plans. In fact, Jack had even mentioned their intentions to others at Cal, and that he had thought about coaching baseball at the University of Virginia. They wondered in hindsight if such admissions could have been added to Jack's having been fired, for some Californian administrators sincerely believed that nobody could ever find a better place than Berkeley to work. That an alumnus might prefer working elsewhere was sacrilege. So Katharine, in correspondence with her mother, now living in Charlottesville, learned that she wouldn't mind having Jack and Katharine stay with her for a while as they looked for a new place to live. On the advice of a real estate agent, they put their condominium up for sale at a price twice what they had paid for it a few years before, and immediately a wealthy Arab purchased it for $95,000, which gave them a great head start for what lay ahead.

On August 1 the movers arrived. They loaded up the next day, setting out ahead of Jack to put their goods directly into storage at the Woolen Mills warehouse near Charlottesville. Along the way, Katharine was reminded of Lennie in Steinbeck's *Of Mice and Men,* for Jack would entreat her to tell him about how there really would be a farm and a vegetable garden and serenity. Jack and Katharine made their first stop at Reno to say good-bye to friends, then attended a party given by their lawyer, John Miller, in Elko, Nevada, where the bank president presented them a fistful of silver dollars by which to remember Nevada, and then they had dinner at the old Stockmans Hotel.

By the ninth they arrived at the home of Katharine's mother, Comilla Payne, where they stayed a month while searching for a new home. The Charlottesville area seemed ideal for Katharine, who had friends there; for Jack, really any place would do, as long as he was distracted from his unpleasant memories. What Jack and Katharine sought was a relatively inexpensive farm that provided solitude and an opportunity to generate revenue, as neither of them was assured of employment. Finding a suitable place to live was placed in the hands of a real estate agent who would become a close friend and fellow coach, Jim Herndon. Jim happened to be an assistant baseball coach at the University of Virginia and had been in real estate about three years. In the car the first day when showing the Jensens around, he mentioned his interest in baseball; and Tinsley, who had come along for the ride, said, "Oh, Jack was the baseball coach at Cal," and it was only then that Jim realized exactly who was riding with him. He said, "I've got cold chills. You're really *the* Jackie Jensen?"

Of course Jim knew the athletic director at the University of Virginia, Gene Corrigan, who in a meeting with Jack gave him the impression that he could very well use Jack in coaching baseball, with Jack's highest hope being the head position. Soon afterward Corrigan attended a meeting of athletic directors in the Midwest, and Katharine and Jack wondered if Dave Maggard attended, too, for upon Corrigan's return, Jack was told he would not be considered for any coaching position (although Jim West continued as head coach for a few more years anyway).

Jim later recalled that the Jensens did not want him to show them the usual prestigious properties: rather they were looking for a place with a view, trees, wildlife, and a few good neighbors. Jim maintained his friendship with Jack and frequently golfed with him, always amazed at Jack's even disposition and athletic talents. On a few rare occasions Jack sat down and talked with Jim about the past, revealing that what he missed the most was that he had never established a good relationship with his children and regretted not having remained in baseball for just a few years more to prove his ability and to qualify for a better pension on retirement (something that would have also helped Katharine cope much better in the future). What few people knew was that Jack was corresponding with Gene Autrey about teaching a baseball clinic with the Angels.

Despite Jack's desire to find a quiet place to settle down, his heart attack at Reno, and his dismissal from Cal, he still felt compelled to participate somehow in baseball. In just a couple of years he would realize that dream in an ideal situation that was the best of several worlds.

The Jensens finally settled on a Federal-style farmhouse named Twelve Oaks (originally Oakland), cut from an old 900-acre tobacco plantation. Perhaps something in the name's association with Jack's hometown prompted them to consider it a little more than they did other properties. Katharine had owned a historic home in Connecticut and was eager to put her artistic talents to work with the finishing touches on the restoration, which was completed by the former owner, Virginia Moore, author of biographies of William Butler Yeats, Emily Bronte, and a book called *Scottsville on the James* (Scottsville was the James River town so often referred to in the television show *The Waltons;* it lies five miles from Twelve Oaks and twenty miles from Charlottesville). The house was made from heart pine and its bricks had been fashioned on the plantation. It featured high ceilings and seven-feet-tall windows. The interesting history of the home included a visit by Sheridan's army, which had raided its stores of food and destroyed what it couldn't use (but missed the hams which the lady of the house had hidden beneath her large skirts).

Besides the tenant cottage, on the seventy-five acres surrounding the white house overshadowed by magnificent oaks were three streams, many fruit trees, berry bushes, numerous varieties of flowers, another cottage, five outbuildings, and the remains of cabins that once helped house the ninety slaves who worked on the early plantation. Jack had always wanted a large garden—in fact that was mostly what he talked about during the trip East, so he called for a soil test. Unfortunately, the ground had been largely played out by tobacco, but it was well suited to the growing of pines; so Jack and Katharine, looking for ways of investing some of the money they retained from the sale of the condominium, the income from Jack's baseball pension, and land they had sold in Carson City, discussed the prospect of raising Christmas trees. This was the first well-thought-out investment (with potential for good tax breaks) Jack had ever made.

In the spring the Jensens—by reading articles, attending seminars, and joining forestry associations—learned much about the soil and what kinds of pines would stand a good chance of proliferation. They soon began the arduous task of clearing the fields and planting hundreds of white pine and Scotch pine seedlings, and even pressed the reluctant Tinsley into service. They hoped to produce salable Christmas trees within six to eight years, but they also realized the risks involved: disease, insect damage, drought, fire, and even spraying of adjacent fields with herbicide. Renting out the tenant house, in need of some renovation, suggested a way to supplement whatever earnings Jack could make coaching (if such a job would ever present itself), and he utilized his carpentry skills learned long before in Nevada to help renovate that building.

Katharine was already known by many in central Virginia, for she had attended high school in Charlottesville, and many of her old friends and classmates were now in business and government there. One would have thought that the Jensens, having been accustomed to dinner shows and the limelight, would have some trouble adjusting to farm life, but such was not the case. The old days of living together at the gamekeeper's cottage in Nevada, and before that Jack's humble life in Oakland, prepared them for hard work and humility. Whereas Jack drove an ancient Ford truck and did most of the farm chores himself to save money, the couple nevertheless enjoyed the country social life. They continued their friendship with people such as Senator Laxalt, and made friends with George Allen, future governor of Virginia.

By moving East, Jack had escaped what would have been a

painful experience, for on October 1 the tax collectors auctioned off items in the Bow and Bell to settle a debt of nearly $48,000 in unsecured property taxes. The pier supports, which had been sunk into the bottom of the estuary only a few years after Jack was born, had outlived their usefulness, threatening to doom the restaurant supported above. Everything inside was to go on sale, but fortunately Boots and Jack had removed the dozens of trophies, photographs, and other memorabilia that had adorned the eatery since as early as 1954. Actually, Boots had a fifty-year lease with the city of Oakland, but when they condemned the pilings, the lease was automatically broken. The restaurant had been closed since November 2 of the previous year. Boots and others had hoped the city would approve a plan for constructing concrete pillars to replace the rotting ones, but the city of Oakland wouldn't agree. When Boots finally did win an option to start anew with financial help from his friend Ren Hofmann, an environmental agency dragged its feet so long that a favorable decision was not able to be made. Boots ended up working at the Big "C" Athletic Club, where he continued to be employed for many years.

Perhaps part of the readership of California and Nevada papers had gone too long without seeing Jack in the news and were still eager to recall the golden days when he and Zoe had been together, for a few months after Jack's departure, the San Jose *Mercury News Magazine, California Today,* featured on its cover Zoe Ann, her dark hair in contrast to the golden-haired image on the cover of *Collier's* reproduced in the lower right-hand corner. The synopsis in the table of contents gave a tight picture of her marriage to Jack:

> The legendary marriage between All-American halfback Jackie Jensen and national diving champion Zoe Ann Olsen was the saga of the post-war era, a time when everything had a happy ending. Caught up in the enthusiasm and euphoria of victory, the world had time to write the storybook romance. But even as people were forced back to the tasks of daily living, the story of the real marriage had gone sour. What went wrong, and why it did, makes an absorbing story.

Written by Sunny Merik, the extended article incorporated eight photographs and quotes from other publications, such as *Sports World,* but some of the things Zoe Ann said seemed to be making their debut in the article. She wasn't afraid to let her feelings be known about not only Jack, but also her parents: "The main thing I remember about my childhood," she said, "is being tired, always tired. Mother was a slave driver. She had me doing tap, ballet, adagio, piano, drama, radio skits, swimming, diving."

Zoe Ann said Jack pushed her to get married and that if she had gone to Stanford (she had been granted a four-year scholarship), he never would have dated her again. The turning point, however, had been a violent argument with her parents, immediately after which she called Jack and asked him to pick her up so they could discuss wedding plans. She said that she had rebelled, that the only means of escape was marriage. Little details that added up to the whole picture were revealed:

> Six months after the wedding he lost the ring, [Jack had taken off the ring and put it into a suitcase before playing a game and, on returning to the hotel room, found it gone.] and I was very hurt. It was no big deal to him. He just came home and said he'd lost the ring and that was that. But it really hurt me. The wedding was just so big and overwhelming. I didn't want TV taking pictures. Neither did Jack or Daddy. But they came. They had big lights and rattling cameras. It was just horrible. During our first year we were together for three months. Baseball just split us up. We were both very lonely for each other. All Jack had ever wanted was a family and here we were separated. Two months after the wedding I got pregnant. We hadn't wanted a baby that soon. But neither of us knew anything about sex. We had our first big fight about the baby. I wanted to stay with Jack in New York for the birth. But he wanted me to come back home to Oakland because my folks were here and he didn't know where the Yankees would be when I went into labor. I wanted him, that's all.
>
> He didn't ever want to talk about the games at home. It was one of his rules—no baseball at home. [Jack later regretted

this, telling Katharine that for years he was simply following the advice of an old friend not to bring work or troubles home.] I felt shut out completely. We should have talked about it, it could have been an avenue of communication. Jack dominated the marriage. He decided for both of us what we would and wouldn't do. He didn't want me to work so I didn't.

The article went on to state that Zoe had ulcers by age twenty-one, that she underwent an abortion so she could train for the '52 Olympics, and that she faced a jealous husband who always doubted her fidelity since she had appeared not to be a virgin on the night of their marriage. She and Jack experienced difficulty in coordinating times and places and often ignored the children. She also revealed the seriousness of Jack's fear of flying: "His whole body and system would go into trauma. He'd get bad chest pains. His blood pressure would soar. He couldn't eat. He'd shake and break out in a sweat." Although later Zoe Ann said in a letter to the author that she was misquoted on some things, some of the article's lines were damaging to Jack's reputation:

When Jack at his young age quit [baseball], well, I lost respect for him as a man. Not as an athlete, but as a man. One night Jack and I were up really late. Everyone else had gone to bed, and we were in the living room and he started hitting me. I can't remember what the argument was over, but Jack pinned me down and kept hitting me over and over.

Evidently the interviewer had called or written Jack and asked him about the fight, for he was quoted as responding: "I didn't feel that a married woman should be doing things that could cause doubt in the minds of others. You know how you slap someone to bring them out of that? Hell, that's all it was. I was trying to shake her out of it. I had no anger by any means."

Zoe Ann's outlook on the entire relationship explained how Jack, as well as others, might have looked on their marriage: "Jack and I were living with the moral code of our parents. That generation expected the impossible in many cases. And often it put too much blame on the woman if things didn't work out."

(Ten years later some ideas relating to baseball wives would shed some light on the relationship of women to their husbands, who, of necessity, had to be away from home so much. The July 6, 1987, issue of *Sports Illustrated* (page 38) quoted a statistic from Maryanne Simmons, married for seventeen years to Atlanta Braves catcher Ted Simmons. She wrote a quarterly called *The Waiting Room* for baseball wives. In it she reported that 72 percent of all ballplayers' wives live somewhere other than the city in which their husbands play. She wrote, "Women in this game tend to be judged by their husband's importance.")

A few months later, Ed Levitt, who had written frequently about Jack, featured him again in the *Oakland Tribune* in a two-page interview with Zoe Ann, titled on the first page "It was a storybook marriage" and on the second, "An All-American marriage that failed." After so much romanticism about Jack and Zoe over the years, here again was realism as Zoe spoke frankly about her relationship with Jack. Some of the things she said were similar to the *Mercury News* article, but also she caught the readership up to date with her life and revealed some things about her and Jack in various statements:

> This is the same house Jack and I lived, loved and battled in. When the marriage failed, and the three kids could handle themselves, I walked over to the Cal-Neva Lodge nearby and asked for a job. They taught me how to deal 21 and I worked there for three-and-a-half years. It began getting difficult to communicate. We had little to talk about. He shut me out of his career and my career was finished. He wouldn't even allow me to continue my diving. And he didn't want me to work. He just wanted me to be the wife, the cook, the mamma. I handled the home, the bills, the kids, the discipline. He didn't want any of the family responsibility. I became bitter after the divorce. I never hated like that in my life. I hated Jack. I hated all men. Reading about him in the papers made me furious. Last time we spoke together was nine years ago. We screamed at each other across the divorce table.

Since that divorce, Zoe married Don Branham, an underground construction executive, and seemed to be pleased with her current life. She denied the accusation that Jack left her because she had turned into an alcoholic but did admit to smoking three packs of cigarettes a day during their marriage. Zoe said that Jan had just remarried and had three children, Jon was a dealer in the Nugget in Sparks, Nevada, and Jay was in college. When all was said and done, three short sentences summed up her marriage to Jack: "We just weren't meant to be married. We should have stayed on a buddy-buddy relationship. That way we could have been dear friends all our lives."

Jack's first visitor from the West Coast was ex-teammate Jim Cullom, who enjoyed a dinner at Twelve Oaks in mid-January 1978. A couple of weeks later in Waynesboro at the Touchdown Club Jack said he felt fortunate to have played at the end of a golden era of the game. Looking back, Jack put contemporary baseball into perspective for the audience:

> Times have changed and baseball, as I remember it, sometimes seems like a relic of the distant past now. The bigger parks take some of the feeling out of the game. Riding the trains instead of flying made the players much closer together back in the days I played ball. I think TV has destroyed the lower minor leagues from a standpoint of spectator interest, and major league baseball is at a definite crossroads right now. The lure of soccer offers a big threat to the game and may be robbing baseball of the wealth of talent for the sport in this country. Baseball must start to sell itself by means of public relations. The fantastic salaries and pensions are starting to cut into the integrity of the game. We have to start bringing back memories to initiate tradition. The next couple of years could be crucial.

The memories and tradition to which Jack referred soon became an important part of a new enterprise.

Part Five

1978–2000

Twelve Oaks, near Scottsville, Virginia, had been a tobacco planta-
tion which General Sherman's troops had looted on their way to
Richmond. Jack and Katharine purchased the farm soon after arriv-
ing in Virginia from California. McLean Faulconer, Inc. photograph.

The Jensens
cleared fields and
planted thousands
of Christmas trees,
selling timber to
finance the opera-
tion. This picture
was taken shortly
before Jack's
death.

Jack found his niche at Fork Union Military Academy in Central Virginia where athletics was valued alongside cadets' education and spiritual development. Here he works with varsity team members.

When not coaching, Jack worked as assistant director of admissions in Hatcher Hall. Next to Jack are Major Lowell S. Pitzer, Lt. Col. Evan H. Lacy, Capt. William C. Clark, and Mrs. Jessie D. Snead. Fork Union Miltary Academy photographs.

Jack with Katharine's daughter, Tinsley, by the fireplace at Twelve Oaks. While a student at Berkeley, she was a faithful fan at baseball games when Jack coached. When the Jensens moved East, Tinsley transferred to Sweetbrier College in nearby Amherst.

Posing with ex-teammates Ted Williams and Bobby Doerr during the first Red Sox Old Timer's game.

During an Old Timer's game, Jack appeared to be in excellent health, having recently undergone a physical at the Greenbriar Clinic. He was looking forward to attending the first All-Star Old Timer's game in Washington, D.C., and to being honored at the Bay Area Sports Hall of Fame when he died suddenly at age 55.

Jack's gravestone in Amherst, Virginia, its simplicity belying his fame. Katharine devised the wording on the stone to sum up Jack E. Jensen's life with the words, VIR FORTIS ET CLEMENS ERAT *(he was a strong and gentle man). Author's photograph.*

Katharine Jensen by the plaque honoring Jack in the Bay Area Sports Hall of Fame. Broadcaster Curt Gowdy, who had been a personal friend of Jack's and had announced many of Jack's games, delivered the induction address. George T. Kruse photograph.

Left to right: Dick Erickson, Frank Brunk, Jim (Truck) Collum, and Paul Andrew, were all teammates of Jack's when he was All-American at Cal Berkeley. They honored Jack at the dedication of the press box in his name at Clint Evans Field.

18

GETTING ACQUAINTED

Within a year of having moved East, Jack was getting used to the easy pace of Fluvanna County, where taxes were low and the talking was slow. He would occasionally drop in for a beer at the Skyview, a local establishment whose one room served as a combination bar/sandwich shop/motel office. The place was owned by a neighboring farmer and former Red Sox fan from Boston, Claude Marsilia, and there Jack met an independent thinker who raised and trained hawks when not employed as a junior high teacher and fencing coach at the school (ten miles from Jack's home) around which, arguably, the town of Fork Union found subsistence: Fork Union Military Academy (FUMA). George Anderson mentioned the academy's prominence in athletics: numerous alumni had obtained full-ride athletic scholarships to universities and entered the pro ranks. FUMA boasted as a graduate the runner Kip Keino, winner of gold and silver medals in the 1968 and 1972 Olympics in 1,500 meters and 5,000 meters. Also, Vinny Testaverdi and Eddie George were each to win a Heisman Trophy.

George felt the baseball team would truly appreciate Jack's help. Still smarting from his last school coaching experience, Jack was a bit reluctant to consider this new enterprise, yet he felt the old pull of baseball, and here was an opportunity to share his expertise and become involved in the sport again. Jack did not mind, then, when George mentioned the possibility of Jack's coaching to Conrad Aasen, commandant of the junior school, who called Jack and invited him to lunch at the academy. Shown around campus, Jack was immediately impressed by the orderliness of the students and the appearance of the grounds. What struck him the most, however, was that the cadets showed him respect. Here was the antithesis of Cal: students saying "Yes, sir," and wearing short hair and clean, neat clothing. Furthermore, Jack saw that a volunteer coaching staff didn't have the pressures normally associated with men who were expected to earn their salaries by compiling winning records. A competitive atmosphere surely existed, but winning was not as important as good sportsmanship and athletic fitness.

The next meeting was with Athletic Director Bill Blair, a man very unlike Dave Maggard. Here was a modest man with whom Jack had much in common: age, childhood experiences, and most important, philosophy about sports. Both had come to believe in sports as a means to the end of overall positive development of a young man's character—not an end unto itself—and this philosophy would become evident later when the two men founded a baseball camp. Blair instantly hit it off with Jack, but he had one reservation: the academy had maintained a policy that only current staff and faculty could coach (and they did so without additional compensation, although their hiring often depended on their coaching capability). Colonel Whitescarver, the academy president, had to be consulted. In late March Jack met him in his office, and the colonel recognized that Jack would be a valuable addition to the staff. Arrangements were made to employ Jack as an assistant director of admissions, and it was agreed that he would help with all levels of baseball, although he would work primarily with the postgraduate team with Blair (postgraduates being students who wanted another academic year before college to raise SAT scores and get more athletic experience and exposure). Just a week later Jack began the baseball season. He found himself rapidly becoming assimilated into Fork Union Military Academy, for very little adjustment was necessary.

A couple of weeks after the team's May road trip to the Naval Academy, Jack received a phone call from Bob Rosen, who was prepared to do a television movie about him. Jack agreed; but where the film concerned her, Zoe Ann refused to cooperate, so it was never produced. A week after that call Jack attended a Richmond Braves (minor league) game and visited with the general manager, John Richardson. Over the next few seasons Jack would attend several Lynchburg and Richmond minor-league games, becoming good friends of the owners and managers and occasionally seeing one of his former players from the New York–Pennsylvania League he had coached in Jamestown, New York, or a player who had made it up from one of Jack's teams in Reno or Berkeley.

At the end of May, Ralph Kerchum found his way to Twelve Oaks, only a few hours' drive from his Washington Amtrak Board of Directors' office, for a visit. After the military academy's graduation exercises, Jack spent his summer working in the garden and in the fields, made a few side trips for pleasure, attended a Christmas-tree growers meeting, played a few rounds of golf, and hosted a couple of parties at the house with Katharine.

The first big trip of the year for the Jensens together was to Massachusetts in mid-August for a three-day Christmas-tree growers convention at the University of Massachusetts at Amherst. This was followed by visits to Vermont in another, futile search for the Rockwell painting of Jack for the *Saturday Evening Post* cover of twenty years before, and Fort Ticonderoga (where Katharine, as a guest of the Pells, had helped them many years before in restoration work when she was a teenager). Soon after their return, the Jensens and Twelve Oaks were featured in the "Homes" section of the *Charlottesville Daily Progress,* where a large article gave the history of the plantation and information on how they had come to own it. By fall Jack had invested $1,600 in a mower, and the plantation was shaping up so well that he ordered four varieties of more than 1,500 trees in anticipation of the next spring's planting. With field preparation largely completed, Jack turned to carpentry, an avocation that would last until the cold weather set in.

The last vestige of troubles from the West came in late October, when Jack received a summons concerning tax debts he reputedly still owed in California. Jack had turned over the problem to old football teammate-turned-lawyer Jack Swaner in 1977, and the exchange between Jack's former lawyer for Bootjack (the restaurant business) and Swaner became strained. Robert H. Moran, who had represented Jack and Boots, threatened in a letter to take action against Swaner and Jensen for "recklessly attempting to involve [him] in litigation to protect Jensen." Jack wrote to Bert Padell, then a lawyer in New York, who filed suit against Moran for failure to perform legal services. Such lack of action arose out of Jack's having sold his shares of the restaurant business, which had been done with a contract that had included a "hold harmless" provision against liability. The summons Jack faced amounted to nearly $15,000 in taxes, interest, and penalties. More than a year and a dozen letters later back and forth across the continent, Jack and Katharine settled out of court with the tax bureau to avoid further complications.

During the fall, Lloyd Canton and two other friends visited from California, and a few days later Jack and Katharine drove to Atlanta to see a 49ers game, where Jack saw Falcons Coach Mike White (ex-Cal coach who had also been fired by Maggard) and his former star baseball player (a quarterback for the 49ers) Steve Bartkowski.

When Jay came East to stay through the Christmas holidays, Jack felt the closest he had ever been to his son as they cut wood side by side and toured the Blue Ridge Parkway, visited Wintergreen Ski Resort, and dined and shopped in Charlottesville. Jack topped off his first full year in Virginia with a New Year's Eve party at a neighbor's farm with family and friends. The next day Tinsley and Jay attended a New Year's Day party together and visited Jefferson's home, Monticello. A few days later Jack dropped off Jay at the airport and visited with the Laxalts in Washington.

Jack and Katharine largely spent the first month of 1979 trying to keep warm as the temperature dropped to zero. At the end of the month Jack was bothered by word that Zoe Ann was trying to put her home at Lake Tahoe into her new husband's name. Letters (1-31-79) to his children reveal why such an impending move bothered him:

Dear Jan, Jon and Jay,

    I'm addressing identical letters to each of you as this is an issue that concerns you equally. When your mother and I were divorced in 1963 and again in 1968 it was stipulated in our divorce agreements that one half of the value of your home at Crystal Bay would be held in trust by her for you three children as outlined in the enclosed copies of those agreements.

    This is my legacy to you and now I fear that it is in jeopardy. Also enclosed is a copy of a Nevada attorney's advice which can guide you to help you secure your interest in the property. This unfortunate situation requires that you seek legal advice right away. I hope in working together you can conclude this to your satisfaction....

With that trouble momentarily out of the way, Jack faced a frightening February: A fuel line froze in the truck, pipes froze and burst in the house, and Katharine's stepfather, William Payne, suffered a serious fall. Jack took Willie to the hospital, where he later suffered a massive heart attack. Jack spent most of his time on the farm tending to the house and in Charlottesville visiting Willie; nevertheless, he was able to get out to speak on two occasions: at George Mason University and at a sports club in Charlottesville.

Willie died In the middle of March, and the day of the funeral Jack started work at the academy again. Within three weeks of Willie's death Jack decided to have his own heart checked, and he got a clean bill of health following a stress test in Charlottesville. In April Jack saw his name appear in a *New York Times* baseball quiz, and he was a special guest at the Sports Breakfast during the Shenandoah Apple Blossom Festival in Winchester.

That spring Jack attended a sports breakfast in Charlottesville with Jim Herndon and enjoyed watching the Lynchburg Mets play, and occasionally he and Katharine would visit the Laxalts in Washington. Parking was often a problem there. Once, afraid they would be late for lunch in the Senate Dining Room, Jack just parked in a handy place and hoped he would not get a ticket. What he got instead was a note from Massachusetts Senator Ted

Kennedy expressing the hope that in the future his parking spot would not be used.

The last day of May was graduation for the junior school of the military academy, and Jack was honored to be the commencement speaker. Also the academy newspaper, *The Sabre,* had given a favorable accounting of the varsity baseball team Jack helped coach to a 7–5 record, and he was pictured giving batting pointers to player Reggie Steppe (who went on to become a basketball star for Virginia Tech).

After much work around the farm in the early part of the summer, with a little golf for relaxation, Jack had a physical July 13, when he again was told he was fit. The next week he drove to Dulles Airport and flew with Katharine to Los Angeles to attend a Dodgers luncheon and Old-Timers Game—his first trip back West and first flight in years. The flight was naturally a cause of worry for Jack, but he took a Valium before boarding and concentrated on the pleasure of meeting family and friends several hours later. Holding Katharine's hand tightly, Jack smiled at the stewardess and told her he and his wife were celebrating, so they wanted drinks. She returned, only to spill an entire tray of drinks onto Jack's suit, but fortunately he was spared much embarrassment; few people were on the plane and he had a complete change of clothes in his carry-on luggage.

The Dodgers put the Jensens up at the Biltmore, where they had a romantic candlelight dinner. The next day they enjoyed lunch at Dodger Stadium with the Gilmores, and Jon and Jay joined them for dinner that night after Jack played in Chavez Ravine for the first time. They drove to see Bob and Diane Garsen at Hermosa Beach, and Jack played golf with Bob Hope at Lakeside Country Club as wives Katharine and Peg Gilmore went swimming. They completed their sojourn with a train ride up the coast to see Aunt Lil at Pebble Beach, and Jack enjoyed a game of golf at Spyglass.

The next month Jack's image appeared in the newspapers again as he planned to attend the Mets Old-Timers game in

Lynchburg, and in an interview he said that he enjoyed coaching but did not miss playing. Another paper pictured him with Al Worthington (former major-league pitcher and coach with the Minnesota Twins) and Dave Campbell (of the Lynchburg, Virginia, team). Here he disclosed that he'd "like to get back into pro baseball in some capacity." During the game, Jack hit a line drive to the wall for a double.

With Katharine's encouragement and support, Jack flew to Boston August 15 to see a Red Sox game as a guest of *Sports Illustrated,* which had invited athletes pictured on past covers of the magazine. *Sports Illustrated* hosted a party at Faneuil Hall for the visiting sports celebrities for its twenty-fifth anniversary; among the guests were skater Tenley Albright, basketball greats Bob Cousey and John Havlicek, Redskins coach Otto Graham, and runner Bill Rodgers. Jack and Katharine were honored when the publisher, Kelso F. Sutton, requested to sit between them at dinner; and later that night back at the hotel they were amused to see themselves on the late news.

An article appearing the last day of August in the *Richmond Times-Dispatch* entitled "Jensen's Roots in Virginia Now" suggested Jack was at home in Virginia with his new lifestyle. However, Jack's visit to Boston, followed by one to Lynchburg shortly afterward for a ball game, might have stirred latent desires, for a couple of days before that article appeared, Jack was in Lynchburg visiting former teammate Dick Gernert, farm director of the Lynchburg Mets, again hoping he could do some minor-league coaching (especially as a hitting instructor). Nothing materialized, however. A week later Jack returned to Massachusetts to attend the Pro-Am banquet at the American Optical Classic Golf Tournament at Pleasant Valley Country Club, joining Joe DiMaggio and about six hundred others, including Governor Edward King, Mayor Thomas Early, and the president of the American Optical Corporation, Glenn A. Hastings. The *Worcester Telegram* (September 6, 1979) pictured Jack, television commentator Jack Whitaker, the Bruins' Jean Ratelle, and Football

Hall of Famer Otto Graham wielding golf clubs during that day's play. The opening paragraph asked the question: "And whatever happened to you, Jackie Jensen?" It went on to state:

Neither DiMaggio nor Jensen, both well-tanned and seemingly quite well rested, looked too worse for wear considering it's been a long time since their last swings in the big leagues. Jensen still looked as if he could hit a ball or two over the wall at Fenway now and hardly the 52-year-old Christmas tree farmer that he is.

Both DiMaggio and Jensen, who spent a good part of the day signing autographs, were almost as good on the golf course as they were on the diamond or at least they inspired their partners to be. Jensen and his teammates pro Bill Kratzert, Holy Cross basketball coach George Blaney, radio sportscaster Bob Lobel and Ted Carangelo combined for a 14-under-par 57 and a tie for fifth place. Jackie Jensen, too, hadn't played golf in a long time. "I've only played about six or seven times this year."

Jensen still has an aversion to flying, but does take an airplane when he positively has to. After a baseball college coaching stint, Jensen has settled down in Virginia where he and his wife are raising Christmas trees.

"You have to be very patient in that business."

It was suggested that Jensen might have felt more at home playing on Lou Graham's team that included none other than Kriss Kringle, who's an AO executive when he's not working Dec. 25th.

In another article, a week later in the Boston *Herald American,* Jack was again asked about his golfing and explained that he didn't play much because the farm kept him too busy, mentioning that he and Katharine were raising about 3,000 trees. He admitted that although he had driven up to Massachusetts, he had flown a couple of times that year. However, golf seemed to have become Jack's favorite pastime, and he said that if he were starting out in sports again, he might try to make it as a pro.

At the end of September the Jensens drove to Washington for a one-day orientation at the Smithsonian Institution, which was sponsoring a Folklife Program to which Jack and other celebrities would lend their names and support. A week later he was back sitting under a tent near the Washington Monument with Mickey Vernon and a couple of other former Washington players to reminisce with and sign autographs for die-hard Senators fans. All about them was much pageantry, including colorful island dancers, Native Americans, and an Italian sculptor who explained how he had created gargoyles for area buildings and demonstrated his skills on a block of marble imported for the occasion. This was the same time that Pope John Paul II was in the Capital, and Jack pulled Katharine through the crowd to get a glimpse of the man he so greatly admired. That same month former football teammate Paul Andrew and his wife Ginger visited from California, and later the Tuckers from Atlanta. Jack and Katharine hosted a party for thirty-five people and attended one themselves for Parents' Weekend at Sweet Briar. Among all the excitement Jack was troubled by an injured shoulder, which immobilized his arm. He visited Coach Blair at the academy and began heat treatments, but a couple of days later had to have a cortisone shot, which solved the problem.

In early October Jack turned to Bert Padell to help him with both a public and a personal matter. He wrote a letter enclosing a baseball card that he had "not given permission to anyone to use," and he asked Bert to find who was distributing the card and to "take whatever actions [were] necessary to protect [his] rights." Bert in turn wrote to James E. Holland, vice-president/general counsel for the Office of the Commissioner of Baseball, who informed him that the Major League Baseball license agreements regarding baseball cards extended only to active players, and that he could find nothing about the origin of the card other than noting the name Renata Galasso, Inc. on the back of the card and the company name, TCMA Ltd. Evidently finding that information inadequate, Bert replied with what Holland called "crude demeanor on the telephone"; nevertheless, Padell prompted some action on Holland's part, for the counsel wrote the associate counsel of the Major League Baseball Players Association, who in turn referred to a September letter that concerned the same complaint from another player. A lawyer for TCMA Ltd. forwarded the following reply: "It is hard to believe that former players might actually think that they have any sort of exclusive rights to the public information about their playing careers."

He went on to quote three legal cases in which such procedures were protected by the First Amendment. However, Bert was not discouraged from pursuing the matter further. He contacted a fellow New York lawyer who informed him that while it was legal to state biographical data about a baseball player on the back of a card, it was in violation of the New York Civil Rights Law to use Jackie's name and likeness on the front of the card without "a license to do so." Finally, the young woman who had produced the cards as a way to work her way through college agreed to stop printing the Jensen cards, and Jackie didn't seek any reparations.

19

SETTLED IN

January 1980 found Jack again traveling to Boston, this time by train, to attend a banquet of three hundred people who saw him surprised to be awarded a statuette as an outstanding former Red Sox player. Jack noted how several landmarks had disappeared since he had left the team two decades earlier. The *Boston Globe* reported that Jack had responded to an interesting question by Leigh Montville: "If he hadn't quit the University of California football team before his senior season, wouldn't he be in line right now to be installed in the National Football Hall of Fame?"

Jack's response was, "I get a form every year from the college Football Hall of Fame. There's a huge list of all the people who are eligible and if you're on it, the Hall of Fame just wants to know if you're at a new address or whatever, just in case. Every year there's a little flutter while I fill out the form that maybe, just maybe, but I know how it is. If I'd played as a senior I would have a much better shot."

Jack couldn't know that before too long he would indeed be inducted. When Montville asked if the Red Sox had been a country club compared to the Yankees, Jack had to agree, and realized that had he played on a more demanding team, he might have performed even better. He admitted that before Katharine had pointed out Boston's museums, he had never given a thought to visiting them, nor any in Washington, for that matter. Then Jack revealed the story behind his having posed for the cover of the *Saturday Evening Post* during his Red Sox years: "Rockwell's agent came and asked Sullivan, White and myself to go up to Stockbridge to pose. We said: 'Stockbridge? Painting? What's in it for us?' We finally went, but none of us was happy. We grumped all the way. Stockbridge. All we thought was how far that was. God, Norman Rockwell and we didn't want to go."

During the spring Jack was an honorary guest at the Winchester Apple Blossom Festival, and shortly thereafter consented to Tinsley's request that her father (David Place, Katharine's first husband) be invited to visit Twelve Oaks, for he had always been an avid Red Sox fan and wanted to meet Jack. David and his wife arrived at the Jensens' home and began talking everything but baseball with Jack as Katharine prepared dinner. A storm came, and a lightning bolt knocked out the electric stove, forcing Katharine to finish preparing the meal on a woodstove. During that spring, Katharine's second husband (international industrialist Adalberto Cortesi) also visited Twelve Oaks.

A couple of months later, Jack would be in South Boston, not in Massachusetts, but in southern Virginia. That city was the hometown of Gus Lacy, admissions director at Fork Union Military Academy, where Jack served as an assistant director. Jack and Gus drove to Lynchburg, where Jack was to give a speech, and he announced his intentions to play in an Old-Timers game at Yankee Stadium on June 21. Jack's admissions duties included promotional trips for the academy, where his presence was often made public in newspaper articles; but back at the school he made a point of never telling any visitors of his fame, which made them all the more impressed when they discovered just who had shown them around campus.

Between those respective Boston trips Jack attended a February sports club banquet in Lynchburg and listened as Paul Laxalt gave a speech at Sweet Briar. The Jensens had selected Sweet Briar for several reasons. Tinsley had transferred largely because she wanted Twelve Oaks to be her home, and she and the Jensens were impressed with the well-groomed lawns and gardens surrounding the classical brick buildings, constructed in the old Virginian tradition. The buildings had a bit of family history in them, for some of the supporting timbers were marked with a "T" for Tinsley, the name of the lumber company run by Katharine's ancestors. She had spent some of her childhood in that small community, where, she would later point out, the family of Senator John Warner, a Tinsley relative, bought a stained-glass window for the Episcopal church Katharine's daughter attended. Lynchburg was nearby, and just before Tinsley graduated, Jack drove there to throw out the first ball for its Little League program.

Corresponding with Bert Padell, in March 1980 Dr. Robert T. Obojski, author of *The Rise of Japanese Baseball Power,* asked if Jack would be interested in having a book written about him. Jack told Katharine, "My story's not over yet," and in a letter to Bert stated, "Re. a book about J. Jensen, I have been giving it a great deal of thought and have decided that I would like to do a book on hitting." He and Coach Blair did work on such a book and wrote a few dozen pages, but were in no hurry to have the work published.

On the way to the June Yankees Old-Timers Game, Jack and Katharine lunched at the Pentagon with a distinguished FUMA alumnus whom Jack had met earlier at the academy. General Jack Chain (later commander in chief of the Strategic Air Command) and his wife were joined by Senator and Carol Laxalt and Warren Nelson (owner of the Cal-Neva Clubs at Lake Tahoe and Reno) and his wife. The very conservative yet outgoing group were in a festive mood until columnist Jack Anderson approached the table, leaned over to Laxalt and said, "Why don't you introduce me to all your friends?" Paul reluctantly did, but when Warren Nelson was introduced, the steadfast friend of the Senator said to Anderson, "Jack, you don't treat our friend Paul here too well, do you?"—referring to occasions when Anderson had publicly criticized Paul. Everyone hoped the event was a bad dream, as Anderson just excused himself and returned to his seat a few tables away. He effectively put a damper on the gaiety until Tinsley brightened the scene with comic relief, having just come from a dentist and an encounter with laughing gas.

In the Yankees Old-Timers game, Jack enjoyed playing along-

side Billy Martin and Mickey Mantle again but arose before dawn
the next day to drive back to Virginia, eager to get home to the
farm. Two weeks later Tinsley set out on a trip to Mexico to stay
with Katharine's ex-husband, and a couple of months later jour-
neyed to Scotland, where she would cement relationships with her
future husband. While she was gone, Jack kept very busy between
admissions work for FUMA, both on campus and away (traveling
with Gus Lacy to meet the parents of prospective players), and
work on the farm: mowing, fertilizing, spraying, building an arbor,
chopping and stacking wood, spreading gravel, and tending a garden. The garden itself presented problems in the form of varmints:
groundhogs, opossums, and raccoons. Jack's date book told a tale
of ongoing confrontations during the summer:

> 8/4/80 Groundhog is eating corn. War has been declared on him
>
> 8/5/80 Traps set for coons and groundhog. Killed another pos-
> sum at grapes.
>
> 8/7/80 Still fighting coons, etc. over garden.
>
> 8/9/80 A gd. hog was caught in trap. Died of H. attack.

In the evenings Jack became an avid reader of Virginia history
and embraced his new home state with all his heart, as he came
to idolize Jefferson and Lee. He and Katharine were drawn to
country auctions, where they chatted with neighbors and looked
over farm equipment while eating ham biscuits the church ladies
provided. After tedious days of outdoor chores, Jack and Katharine
never ran out of talk, continually making plans for developing the
farm business. Nights would often end with dancing to radio music
in the kitchen, clad as they were in boots and blue jeans.

Jack's date books also indicated "no church" on the several
Sundays he couldn't go because of so much work on the farm, indicating, probably, that he felt a little guilty about not attending.
During the week, however, he occasionally got Blair out to pitch a
few balls to him. He pulled his groin; he, however, true to form,
discounted it as a minor injury. Much of the summer was hot and
humid, although it didn't rain much, and farm work was very tax-
ing as Jack continued spending most of his time in the fields

through September, when the cadets returned to the academy. In October he traveled to Pittsburgh for a wedding. The next month Jack was tempted with an invitation to visit California.

Cal's 1950 class was holding its thirtieth reunion at the Claremont Country Club the day before the game with Stanford. Jack surely would like to see Pappy Waldorf and his old buddies again, but Nancy Soule, an organizer for the event, told Robin Orr of the *Tribune* that Jackie might not attend because he didn't like to fly. Although he had largely conquered that fear, he used it mainly as an excuse not to attend (even though the article suggested he could take a train), for he was quite settled into a routine in the East and wasn't yet ready to succumb to the draw the Bay area still had for him. Instead that weekend he spent stacking wood, attending church, looking for a turkey, and going to the dentist. It seemed that Jack was being converted into a genuine farmer. He didn't necessarily want to shake off the glamor of his former days in the limelight, but he recognized that for some people those days would never be forgotten, and that some good for himself and others could occasionally come out of his former associations. Most of that fall Jack divided his time between the academy and the farm, preparing for winter and staying in shape much the same way the candidate he supported for the upcoming Presidency did—splitting wood. Thanksgiving, however, was a time to splurge, and Jack and Katharine lunched at the Homestead, a luxury hotel in the Virginian mountains that substituted for the Greenbrier since it was so much closer. In late fall, Jack and Katharine were particularly eager to hunt for the deer that had been destroying some of the white pine, but the hunting was fruitless, for Jack could not bring himself to kill the marauding animals.

A week before Christmas, Jack met with Colonel Whitescarver and Bill Blair about starting a summer baseball camp, an idea the two baseball coaches had bandied about for several months. Not since the football camp of Sonny Randall (a FUMA alumnus) had ceased over a decade before had anyone considered such an enterprise. The academy did have a nonmilitary summer-school session and early football practice, but the camp would be designed to conflict with neither of those. It was important to Blair and Jackie that the camp be topnotch, as Bill recounted to the author: "He wanted to have the finest baseball camp for youngsters in the country; so we set that as a goal when we started. We didn't want it to be exclusive. Since he and I both came from very poor family backgrounds, we wanted to fix it so we could have boys who could not afford to be there. As well, we had to break even or make a dollar. We started with the idea of just central Virginia, from Lynchburg to Norfolk, that included the Richmond area. We wanted it for youngsters primarily below fourteen years old."

Nineteen eighty-one began with farm work limited by cold temperatures and some snow, with further frustration realized as a result of finding nearly two hundred trees damaged by deer. About the time of Reagan's inauguration and the release of the American hostages in Iran, Colonel Whitescarver approved the summer camp, and gears were set in motion to work out the details. Jack met Jim Herndon for lunch and asked him about helping out for the upcoming baseball camp at the military academy—something to which Herndon agreed. Katharine's birthday on the sixteenth was celebrated with a trip to Washington, where the Jensens left off some firewood for the Laxalts. A week later Jack and Katharine attended an old-timers game in Atlanta, arriving back home the day before Mike White showed up for a visit. Jim Darby also visited sometime in 1981 and recalled that Jack asked him, "Would you like to come out and help me split some wood?" Jim replied, "Sure, I'd like to do that," but within five minutes he was totally exhausted, "and Jack just pounded away for next fifteen, twenty minutes; the guy was in great shape physically."

As the weather became warm enough that Jack could transplant some trees when not working at the academy, he received an invitation to what would be the most impressive luncheon of his life, hosted by a man who for five years was a Chicago Cubs broadcaster. All but one of Jack's thirty-three fellow guests (pitcher Don

Newcomb) and he were Hall-of-Famers, and Jackie was quite honored to have been included in perhaps the largest group of Famers
ever gathered for one occasion. The host, who had been not only
a broadcaster but also an actor who played Grover Cleveland
Alexander, a Philadelphia pitcher, in a movie biography was none
other than President Reagan, who thoroughly enjoyed himself, and
among others was surprised to hear the normally reticent
DiMaggio talk it up with everyone. Also present was the childhood
friend of Ralph Kerchum, Ed Meese, and Vice-President George
Bush, who recalled his 1947 NCAA championship game against
Jack (a columnist later suggested that it was he who had added
Jack's name to the guest list). Jack's date book simply referred to
the occasion as "Great fun." Just three days later the president was
shot by John Hinckley, Jr.

In late March baseball practice began, and with it more planning and attention to the upcoming baseball camp. One incident
relating to Jack's coaching bears mention. A cadet in the junior
high school who had established a reputation for lying wrote home
to his father that Jackie Jensen was coaching a baseball team at
Fork Union. The father wrote the headmaster, Connie Aasen,
demanding that the boy be punished for yet another lie; instead,
the Headmaster asked Jack to pose with the boy for a photograph.
He did, and also signed the photo, which was sent home to prove
the boy had, at least this once, told the truth.

Jack suffered one mishap during coaching that Katharine didn't
hear about until several years later. As Blair was working with
players outside, Jack entered a gym where batting cages were
strung up, and contrary to Blair's insistence that a ball never be hit
when someone approached the cage, a player gave a ball a good
wallop as Jack walked toward him. The ball struck the netting with
such impact that it drove the cord into Jack's cheek, knocking him
down and out. Players ran out frantically onto the field, fearing
that Jack had been killed, but when Blair returned to the gym, Jack
had awakened, the imprint of the netting firmly embedded in his
face. Evidently Jack downplayed the injury; he knew Katharine

was likely to overreact.

The rest of the spring work on the tree farm was intensive, as Jack and another man one day planted 1500 trees in two and a half hours during a cool spell, which resulted in his catching a cold. As if he didn't have enough to do, Jack also had become chairman of the Fluvanna County Cleanup Committee and was pictured in the local paper with several students who had won poster awards. The baseball team wrapped up June 3, just three days before graduation, and then Jack took up a new baseball role—that of umpire, for a charity game in nearby Cumberland County. This was followed by participation in the Lynchburg Old-Timers game, where he saw Lou Gorman of the Mets.

Most of June was fully occupied with either admissions or farm work, perhaps draining Jack's energy, for he noted in his date book (7-2-81): "Tired. Took nap." The same day he threw out a ball in Charlottesville for the start of a Little League; and the next day he noted: "Still not feeling up to snuff." A few days later he visited a doctor, who told him to take it easy and go on vacation, to which Jack replied "Ha!" in his date book: He had to prepare for the baseball camp. In July Tinsley returned from Scotland, where she had earned a master's degree from the University of Edinburgh. With her came two friends, and the arrangement was that in the mornings they would all do farm work, and their afternoons would be free so they could swim in the nearby James River, where they became fast friends with Ned Hocker, last of the old-time ferry boatmen.

While baseball fans across the country were bemoaning a strike, months of planning and preparation for just one week were paying off as the Jackie Jensen Baseball Camp started without a hitch on July 19 with sixty-five boarders and thirty-one day campers. Working for Jack and Bill were a dedicated group of men (including Jim Herndon); and all displayed great concern for the primary goal of the camp—promoting character development. To that end, rules and schedules were explicitly laid out. To encourage players to read, bookcases were installed in the dormitories and filled with sport magazines and worthwhile books (Blair had been an English and Latin instructor). The academy mess hall provided sufficient food at a reasonable rate, and provisions for entertainment were made for the players during their free time, as not only the academy but also the community were fairly isolated from the cities to which most of the players were accustomed.

Having looked at other camps and talked to many people who ran them, Jack and Bill knew what would make the difference between a mediocre and a first-class camp: the little things most people take for granted. Each boy was measured and fitted with a complete camp uniform and name tag, so pride in the uniform and a feeling of camaraderie were easily established. Jack concentrated on batting instruction, although he covered all areas of baseball before the session was over. As a result of planning instructional strategies and devising a booklet for the camp, Jack and Bill started to amass information that was leading naturally to a book they wished eventually to coauthor. Both men enthusiastically believed that such a book would become one of the best baseball books available for youngsters, for it would address not only skills, but also behavior: what kind of person it took to become an accomplished baseball player. Blair was bringing his many years of coaching, teaching, and management experience together with Jack's professional expertise.

As a result of this activity and his coaching of the academy's team, Jack found he was rapidly understanding the total picture of baseball, from the ground up. He worked well with and enjoyed dealing with young players, whose elementary physical abilities were changing before his eyes into fundamental baseball skills. Here also was a chance to mold the character of each boy—something that had been so difficult to do with his own two sons.

At the same time Jay was developing on his own into a skilled ballplayer and respectable young man. Back in Reno, Jay stood out as a baseball player in high school, coached by none other than a coach who had himself played under Jack at the university, Gary Powers. Powers had followed Jack's problems at Cal and wondered how he could have been treated so badly, and perhaps he took a special interest in Jay because he wanted to see the Jensen name carry on in a positive fashion. Both Jay and Gary would show their dedication to Jack in special ways a year later.

Jack had run the camp at fever pitch, even staying in a dormitory with the boys to help ensure its success, and his efforts and those of Bill and the coaches and counselors paid off—word of the camp spread rapidly and calls came in for next year's camp from all across Virginia and also from adjacent states. However, Jack was not eager to expand too rapidly, not only because of the transportation concern, but also because he didn't relish the idea of additional pressure. He had very much enjoyed the camp and was pleased with its success, but his journal notation gave an honest appraisal: "Whew! It's over."

The remainder of summer was a mixture of work and play. The week following camp was spent alternating between mowing on the farm and doing admissions work, after which Jack and Katharine celebrated with a Sunday party at the house as a send-off for the erstwhile foreign farm workers. Drudgery was pleasantly interrupted by trips to Baltimore, Alexandria, and Lynchburg. News came that Pappy Waldorf had died. Pete Rozelle, commissioner of the National Football League, called Waldorf a major force in creating harmony between college and professional teams, and Jack also was asked to comment about his former coach for the *Oakland Tribune*. He recalled Pappy's great ability to organize his football team, and said, "Also he had good judgment to have assistant coaches of exceptional ability around him."

A month after Waldorf's death, Jack received a letter from old friend and teammate Paul Andrew, who noted that Pappy had enjoyed a dinner at Trader Vic's recently with Cal teammates Cullom and Erickson. Accompanying the letter was an article that quoted George Bush when he threw out the first ball at the All-Star Game: "I remember one year in the national finals at Kalamazoo, Michigan. [Yale Coach] Ethan Allen walked the eighth hitter to get to the Cal pitcher. That pitcher turned out to be Jackie Jensen. He hit a ball that's still rolling somewhere out in Western Michigan."

The end of shearing and mowing on the farm called for a proper celebration. In September Jack and Katharine splurged with a four-night sojourn at the Greenbrier, where Jack golfed and enjoyed a "good party with champagne and dance." Soon afterward the admissions work at the academy began again, but that ended by mid-September, when the Jensens attended a Republican Party get-together at John Warner's Atoca Farm in Middleburg, after which they swung by Washington via the Winchester Country Club and met Senator Eugene McCarthy. Two weeks later Jack was back in northern Virginia giving a speech and lunching with Paul Laxalt. During that trip he dropped by the WTOP radio station and became a guest on Phil Wood's "Sports Talk" show.

In November Jack and Katharine drove to Beckley, West Virginia, for a weekend visit with family and friends, stopping by the Greenbrier on the way home. Having noted much deer damage to the trees on his return, Jack set about building a deer stand, resolved to catch the culprits in the act and to do something about it. When he lined up deer in his sights, however, he found he *still* had no will to kill them; so finally he sprayed the section farthest from the house with a repellent. Thanksgiving Day was spent at Tinsley's in Alexandria, followed the next day by dinner with Jack and Judy Chain (at that time her landlords). Somewhat worried about his health, Jack went to the Greenbrier Clinic just before Christmas. The doctors there pronounced him fit.

20

FINAL INNING

Jack traveled to Whippany, New Jersey, to be the special guest celebrity for a baseball card show, stopping on the way with Katharine to have lunch with Tinsley and the Chains in Washington, D.C. A local paper (*The Daily Record*, 3-28-82) caught people's attention with the caption "In Jensen's Day Ball Was No Bull"; it revealed that Jack was getting three or four requests daily for autographs at home. He was asked to comment on current baseball salaries: "The salaries get to a point where they are a little embarrassing," he said. "Putting a player's value over a captain of industry or a scientist makes no sense. But my biggest complaint in conjunction with high salaries is that the players might lose sight of what's important to them."

He went on to say that he enjoyed the Old-Timers games, at which, "you forget the 0-for-4s." He probably had in mind the upcoming Red Sox game of May 1—Boston's first. Indeed Jack—having finally conquered his fear of flying—took a flight to Boston for the game. He was delighted to meet his old trainer Jack Fadden, now eighty-three years old. When interviewed by the *Boston Herald-American,* Fadden still rated Jackie the toughest player he had ever seen play while hurt. He recalled a day when Jackie's shoulder was so sore he could not throw, but Fadden encouraged him to stay in the game; Jack went three for four, and fortunately he didn't have to attempt to throw anyone out. In the *Boston Sunday Globe* Jack said, "You forget that this is just an Old-Timers Game, and you almost swear it's for real. It's just the little boy coming out of us, and things don't work out the way they used to."

Indeed, many of the 32,763 fans, and thousands more listening to announcer Curt Gowdy over the airways, were sympathetic to the former players' physical conditions, for the star of the show, Ted Williams, sixty-three years old, did not get a hit, nor did many other players, for that matter. Jack did get a hit, though, and fielded almost effortlessly. What was important was nostalgia and recaptured camaraderie and entertaining the fans, many of whom had probably been the "boo-birds" of a quarter century ago. Several comments Jack made in front of a video camera would be used in a Fenway Park documentary a year later and also in a tribute to Jack himself. Following the game, Jack and Katharine attended a party with the other players hosted by the Red Sox owner, Mrs. Yawkey. The celebrated Yastrzemski arrived in unusual dinner attire: a cream-colored sateen jumpsuit. Bobby Doerr, Piersall, and Williams joined Jack and Katharine for drinks in the clubhouse before the dinner party—a baseball fan's dream of anecdotes and fellowship ensued. Ted invited the Jensens to join him in the fall for fishing in Florida.

Only two weeks after the Old-Timers game, the *Sports Collectors Digest* listed "The Ten Most Aggravating Lifetime Statistics"; among the players was Jack, with 199 home runs. Comments made in the article certainly seemed to say something about the personality of the players listed: "You can't be a team player and worry about your personal stats too, the baseball theory goes. That's what makes Pierce [1999 SOs], Jensen, and Jay [99 wins] unusual; virtually everyone nearing a personal milestone is going to drag himself through one more season to go for it." About that time the Jensens' peacock Maximilian and his consort Chloe produced a clutch of eggs that yielded several tiny chicks, which Chloe proudly paraded from her nest in the hayfield. Jack came running in, hugged Katharine, and exclaimed, "We're grandparents!" He dragged her out to see the tiny peachicks, one of whom became the handsome Beauregard (a name Tinsley would later choose for her son).

In April Jack was a guest at the annual Welcome Home Dukes

banquet sponsored by the Alexandria, Virginia, Club of Grandstand Managers. At the end of the month Jack accepted two more invitations. The first was to appear as a special guest at Richmond's 3rd Sports and Paper Collectibles Show on July 25 to chat with fans and sign autographs. The other was to play in the 36th Annual Old-Timers Day game scheduled for August 7, when Jack was asked to represent Boston. The rest of May was busy for Jack as he went to the Greenbrier again, starred at the Atlantic City baseball card convention, and bush-hogged, planted, and sprayed at the farm. He was interviewed by local columnists Abe Goldblatt (May 30) and Ed Richards (June 5) just after the Michelob-Kingsmill Celebrity Golf Classic, which was attended by more than fifty sports celebrities. Jack seemed to be in the best of health, and he and Katharine had enjoyed the opening party with Bob Prino, "voice of the Pittsburgh Pirates" and Kyle Rote Jr. (professional soccer player, coach, and author). They felt right at home the end of the second day as they attended Las Vegas Night, and during the awards festivities of the last evening Jack and his team walked off with a first-place trophy.

On June 10 Jack received a letter from Dick Cecil, managing director of the Cracker Jack Old-Timers Baseball Classic, thanking him for agreeing to play in that first game July 19 at RFK Stadium in Washington, D.C. The summer schedule seemed to be filling up Jack's calendar: He was also asked to attend the Dixie Pre-Majors Baseball World Series, where the Lynchburg Mets were scheduled to play the Alexandria Dukes. Jack was invited to the banquet and opening ceremonies scheduled for the night before, but as the letter said, "no speech." A month later Jack received a letter from the White House signed by C. Carson Conrad, Executive Director, and ex-Redskins coach George Allen, chairman of the President's Council on Physical Fitness and Sports. Jack was flattered by the letter, which read in part: "In planning for an expanded physical fitness and sports program we have reviewed the performance and potential of a number of individuals who have outstanding expertise and have been supportive of physical fitness and sports. As a result we would like to invite you to serve as a Consultant to the President's Council on Physical Fitness and Sports (PCPFS)."

Jack responded immediately, enclosing his vitae and saying he was "grateful for this honor and hope to make any significant contribution that I can."

The second Jackie Jensen Baseball Camp began Sunday, July 11, with a day of orientation that included a speech to more than a hundred boys and their parents about the expected behavior of the campers and the importance of sportsmanship and respect for each other. Jack spent the night in the dormitory with the boys and a few other coaches and counselors, as he had every night the previous season. The next day Bill Blair began a session with the whole camp on throwing and catching fundamentals, and the following day Jack ran the hitting session while Bill interviewed someone who sought a position with the academy. The temperature reached 100 degrees and the humidity was high; nevertheless, Jack ran both a morning and an afternoon session, demonstrating techniques as usual, and at the end of the afternoon he made his way to Bill's cool office to rest. When Bill came back from the interview, he found Jack sprawled out on a chair facing the air conditioner, looking ashen. Bill asked, "Jack, are you okay?"

He replied, "Yes, I'm having a little trouble getting my breath."

Blair repeated, "Well, are you feeling okay?"

"I'm fine," Jack responded; "it's probably all that hitting I was doing this afternoon."

Just then the postmistress called to say that Jack had a special delivery package, and looking at Bill, Jack said, "Come on, go with me; I think it's those posters." (Having been invited to the upcoming Crackerjack Old-Timers Game in Washington, Jack had sent for some posters of the game, for the baseball office had been very good about supplying such things as films of World Series games. Furthermore, he planned to get some autographed balls and give them to the campers who displayed the best attitude during the session.)

They climbed into Jack's truck and had gone only a few hundred feet when Jack slowed down, grabbed his chest, and said, "Man, it's really hurting." When Bill suggested he do something about it, Jack waved him off and said it was just soreness from hitting so much. They continued to the post office, where the posters were indeed waiting, then went to supper at the academy mess hall. After eating, they went back to Bill's office. Bill said, "Jack, this is the strangest thing; we've never had time to sit down and talk during camp because we're always so busy." But the boys were finishing dinner and heading back to the dormitory where the counselors could settle them in, so Jack and Bill just shot the breeze for about an hour, speaking mainly about the way their friendship had developed and what their association meant to each other. They also talked about how well the camp seemed to meeting their goals; but Jack went beyond that, lamenting his earlier problems with Zoe Ann, having left the Red Sox, the restaurant, and the petition of the players at Cal. Finally they met with all the campers and explained the setup for that night: They had made special arrangements for viewing an All-Star Game that night on televisions across the campus. The meeting over, Jack said, "Well, everything seems to be going so well, I think I'll go home tonight. I'll see you tomorrow."

When he arrived home, Jack went into his and Katharine's bedroom upstairs and lay on the four-poster bed. Katharine noted how fatigued he looked and asked if he'd rather lie on one of the twin beds in Tinsley's room, the "pink room," for it had better cross ventilation and was much cooler, but he said no. They brought up a television, and he started watching the All-Star Game as Katharine half-watched and read a book. After a while he commented, "I've got terrible indigestion," and when Katharine asked him what he had eaten that day, he replied that he'd had seven soft drinks, which was unusual because he usually didn't drink any. Subconsciously Katharine was concerned because she had heard Jack say something similar a dozen years earlier just before his heart attack. They turned out the light and went to sleep, but about 2 A.M. he woke up and said, "This pain is really bothering me."

By then Katharine was so worried she was tingling. She told Jack to lie down on Tinsley's bed while she got him a nitroglycerine pill, for she had always made a point of knowing where the bottle of pills was (but didn't know they had become outdated). Jack looked worse, so Katharine called the Scottsville rescue squad, which was about five miles away, and two men and the rescue van arrived immediately. They asked him if his arm hurt, if he felt numbness, and other questions associated with a possible coronary problem, but all his replies were negative. Not knowing whether they should take him to the hospital, they looked at Katharine, who told them to hold on while she called their family doctor, who was well aware of Jack's medical history. On receiving Katharine's call he urged, "Go immediately to the hospital."

Eyeing Jack's frame, the men asked if they had to carry him downstairs, and Jack replied that he could walk. He made his way in his bathrobe down the stairs after the volunteers, with Katharine behind, and continued to the ambulance with its expectant doors open. She could see that the inside was very narrow, and much as she wanted to ride with Jack, he said she should follow in the car. Back in the house, as the ambulance sped down their long driveway, Katharine gathered some clothes and Jack's wallet and called the hospital. She felt as though everything was going in slow motion, as if it took an hour to do a couple of simple tasks, but a couple of minutes later she was out the door into the pitch-black night. Just as she was getting into the car, she was startled by a bobcat's bloodcurdling scream, and she thought how fitting the cry was.

On the way to the University of Virginia Hospital some twenty miles away, she kept thinking that Jack had not looked right, and when she arrived, the ambulance was sitting outside the emergency room's entrance with its doors open and all the lights on. She thought they must have been there for quite some time and wondered why everything was taking so long. Walking into the reception area, she told the woman behind the desk that she wanted to see her husband. She was told to wait in a small adjacent area.

Katharine answered firmly, "I would like to see him right now, please." The reply came, "Well, the doctor wants to speak with you."

So Katharine crawled the walls for eternity until a woman doctor came and said that Jack was dead—he had expired at 4 A.M., just about two minutes after he'd left the house in the ambulance and at the same time that the bobcat had screamed. Katharine's response was, "Just let me see him; just let me see him right now." But she was told to wait a few minutes more, so she called Tinsley in Washington (where she had been training for a State Department job), and her daughter responded that she was on her way.

Katharine finally got to see Jack:

> He looked not like a person anymore to me; he looked so gone, and I thought, 'Oh, dear, this is the last bit of peace I'll have for so, so long,' and I kept saying, "You can't leave me; you just can't leave me," and I hugged him, and he was so gone, and I put his hand around my arm, and I thought I could feel a gentle pressure. I didn't mention it to the doctor, who was standing with me, or the orderly. I don't know why I didn't, and I should have; and it always bothered me, but I was so sure they'd tell me that it was just a muscular reaction, and I didn't want to hear that.

Katharine stayed with him as long as she could; then they told her she really had to leave. She drove to her mother's not far away in Charlottesville, and Tinsley arrived soon after. Later that day they went to the funeral home to execute preparations they had made long ago. The mortician was an old family friend and knew the Jensens would not want anything fancy. He finally led them to an attic, and there in a corner rested a plain old-fashioned coffin that Katharine realized was what she wanted.

The day after Jack's death Katharine called his children, and naturally all of them were shocked. One, however, was especially affected, since he was determined, in his own small way, to pay tribute the best way he knew how. Jay Jensen, resembling his father but smaller in stature, had hoped to follow in his footsteps. Unfortunately, Jay could not make the team that Powers had inherited at the University of Nevada at Reno. Still, Jay loved the sport and attended a Cincinnati Reds tryout camp in June, but again he was cut. Steve Sneddon, from the *Reno Gazette-Journal,* located Jay shortly after Jack's death, asking for the twenty-three-year-old's comments, and his admiration for his father was evident in his response as he recounted how he had visited Jack in Virginia (Jon and Jan never had), had seen him play in a Los Angeles Old-Timers game three years before, and considered him the "greatest person that ever lived."

Undaunted by his failures to make a college or professional team, Jay had continued to play for the Reno AA slow-pitch softball team, and he was scheduled to play in a game the day after Jack's death. Having grown up admiring Jack largely from afar (he was four years old when Jack and Zoe first divorced), Jay nevertheless knew of the hardships his father had overcome; and he himself was determined to persevere. His teammates were startled when Jay Jensen arrived on schedule, so soon after the loss of his dad. But he had something to prove—that a Jensen could go on despite any hardship—and he committed himself wholly to the task ahead: helping his team. Before he walked to the plate, he spoke five simple words: "This one's for you, Dad." And he hit a home run.

Back East Katharine was completing funeral arrangements; she sought just the right inscription for Jack's tombstone, something elegant, yet simple. She recalled that Bill Blair had taught Latin several years before becoming the athletic director at Fork Union Military Academy, so she enlisted his help. He turned to Professor Graves H. Thompson and John Brinkley, eminent Latin scholars at Hampden-Sydney College, Blair's alma mater. What they were looking for was a translation for "a gentle Dane," but appropriate Latin words for the Danish or Viking didn't seem to exist; even the Danish embassy was unable to help. Finally, all involved agreed upon the epitaph VIR FORTIS ET CLEMENS ERAT [he was a strong and gentle man], which was inscribed below Jack Eugene Jensen's name, and US NAVY, MAR 9 1927, JUL 14 1982. The obverse of the white marble read: BORN IN SAN FRANCISCO DIED IN SCOTTSVILLE VIRGINIA—the simple stone and few lines belying the full life Jack had experienced.

Interment was in Katharine's family plot in Amherst, not far from Sweet Briar, where Tinsley had graduated from college. Coincidences concerning its location in relation to Jackie's life made it a fitting resting place: The verdant cemetery on the edge of the Piedmont Plateau, swathed in mist so reminiscent of the Bay area, looked out onto the Blue Ridge Mountains in the west, and his grave lay between a huge oak tree on one side and a tall pine on the other. (Katharine also noted that Jackie had died 26 years to the day after his cousin Peter Jensen had been knighted by the King of Denmark for development of amplified sound, on the fourteenth of July.) Only a few joined Katharine and Tinsley for the private ceremony: Tinsley's godmother, Ellen Broaddus, and several of Katharine's other close childhood friends from Virginia; Mike White from Illinois; Aunt Lillian Meglan; and the Gilmores from California. As the wooden coffin was lowered into the grave, the creaking ropes gave Katharine and Tinsley pause. They looked at each other with the same thought in mind—that the sound resembled the creaking of rigging on an old ship: a Viking's funeral.

Although Tinsley had thought of Jack as her own father and had been so close to him—even sharing the same birthday—she nevertheless remained collected through the ordeal and wrote Jack's obituary, asking that contributions be made to a scholarship fund she immediately set up with the academy. After the funeral she and Katharine returned to Twelve Oaks to start answering the six hundred letters of sympathy that were pouring in from around the country, many of them completely unexpected, like the ones from Senator Ted Kennedy and Governor George Wallace. The grieving women were further surprised with a call from George Bush. A few days later, Katharine obtained a copy of the death certificate, which listed the cause of death as acute coronary insufficiency due to coronary atherosclerosis, which in turn was due to generalized atherosclerosis. On reflection, Katharine regretted that

Jack had been taken off an anti-cholesterol drug by his doctor a couple of years before.

Jack was certainly not to be forgotten by Zoe Ann, Jay, Jon, and Jan, who gathered at Zoe's home in Crystal Bay for a private ceremony honoring and remembering him. Joining them were Ralph Kerchum and Ray Ehlers, and all reflected on what had been and what might have been. Jan read a eulogy she had composed. It would have been impractical and perhaps unwise for those present in the old Jensen house to travel East. Jack belonged to Katharine and the land of Virginia.

His former family had sent their sympathies to Katharine, and she would meet the children again several months later in a formal tribute to their father. Zoe Ann had been interviewed over the phone a couple of days before. Her hurt over the recent loss was added to the hurt she had suffered over the years, for she admitted that they never should have married. She said some things that some didn't want to hear and that she was reluctant to recall, mentioning Jack's jealousy and her own drinking problem. However, at the end of an interview with Dave Newhouse (*Oakland Tribune,* 7-15-82), she said: "There were lots of happy times. There really were. Give Jack a nice story."

21

Afterlife

Soon after news of Jack's death traveled across the country, a sensitive column was written by a sportswriter who had defended Jack five years before, when he was ousted from Cal. Entitled "Paying Tribute to a Friend," Stephanie Salter's column in the *San Francisco Examiner* contained gems of description that flowed from the heart. She described her first meeting with Jack after having been bored with so many articles about his prowess in sports:

> My first reaction to the nearly-50-year-old Jensen was, quite frankly, "What a hunk!" About three pounds over his major league playing weight, he was a man who exuded vitality. His roots may have been Scandinavian, but his looks were American male, and his eyes really did what many people say they do—they twinkled. That I was almost simultaneously swept off my feet by Jack's second wife, Katharine, quickly made my admiration for Jack's physical attributes of the same type [*Sports Illustrated* feature writer Ron] Fimrite had for him.
>
> We were two strangers in their home, digging into their personal lives, but before we left Katharine had showed us the family photograph album and Jack had shyly, but proudly, showed some of his collection of Indian arrowheads. Katharine had gotten him interested in them and "a whole new world," as he put it, when they lived in Nevada. As husband and wife they were affectionate and good-humored with one another. Jack was clearly in awe of Katharine's intellect and gentle, cultured ways.
>
> [After looking through some items Jack had sent her from

Virginia] I found a five year-old card from a florist that had
accompanied a bouquet Jack sent me. It arrived the day after
I railed in print about him being fired. All it said was, "Thanks,
I needed that."

Now he doesn't need me or anyone else to go to bat for him
in print, and he certainly doesn't need this tribute. But I do.

The following week *Oakland Tribune* columnist Perry Phillips
revealed a little-known anecdote concerning Jack's early restaurant days. Phillips noted that Jack had impressed him with his
"taste for quality music and entertainment, his keen wit, the pre-
mium he placed on loyalty and his long, and sharp memory." He
recalled a trip the month before when he (Phillips) stayed at the
Hilton in Reno where the Craig Evans's Trio was playing. Just
before Jack's death, Perry called him to have him guess to whom
he had just spoken. Amazingly he replied, "Cork Proctor"—a
mutual friend, since Cork, Katharine, and Jack had just finished
talking about Perry, when they met at an Atlantic City baseball
card show and shared dinner. Cork was a Reno native whose
lounge act of music and comedy was known throughout Nevada.
That telephone conversation was the last time Perry would hear
Jack's voice, but Perry went on to a more important and revealing
anecdote in his column:

> Sam Vassiliou's first restaurant job here was at the Bow and Bell.
>
> "I had been in this country only eight months and this was
> my first dining room job as a bus boy," Vassiliou, who now
> owns the Savoy in Pleasant Hill, told me.
>
> "They gave me a black jacket, black pants and a white shirt
> to wear. One night, some man asked me, 'how come you're
> wearing brown shoes?'"
>
> "I answered that 'I don't have any black shoes.' A fellow
> waiter later informed me 'that was Jackie Jensen.'"
>
> "I hadn't the slightest idea just who Jackie Jensen was, nor
> did I know anything about him. When Jensen left the restau-
> rant he gave the bartender an envelope. The bartender gave it
> to me when it was time to go home. I opened the envelope and

found 40 dollars along with a note which read, 'go out and buy yourself a pair of black shoes.'"

"I have since learned everything there is to know about Jackie."

Throughout the fall Katharine dedicated herself to making the Christmas-tree farm a viable operation, and fought constantly to convince herself that her life could go on without Jack. After Jack had become involved with the academy, Katharine had taken on most of the business of tree farming herself. Now, though, she also had to do the tasks Jack would usually do in his spare time, such as operating the tractor and other equipment. In spite of various adversities, including a hurricane, Twelve Oaks developed into a successful plantation, and Katharine immersed herself in community and forestry interests, receiving a gubernatorial appointment to the Virginia Board of Forestry.

One thing that affected her life in a very positive fashion was her introduction to the martial art of Tae Kwon Do. She and Jack had been Bruce Lee fans while in California, but had never seriously considered learning any martial arts themselves until they heard of a class being offered in Scottsville, a branch studio of a Korean master instructor, Seung Gyoo Dong, who lived and taught in Charlottesville. Katharine had suggested Jack take the class to increase his flexibility—that was the one physical trait he lacked—but he didn't want to make the twice-weekly commitment to classes, for he was too content to stay at home nights. After Jack's death, Katharine enrolled, realizing that the class could keep her fit in the winter months. She found the class offered unlooked-for benefits, as well. The mental attitude associated with the Tae Kwon Do helped Katharine take her mind off her loss, which would continue to haunt her. Furthermore, her association with one member who taught English at the academy and became her friend and Tae Kwon Do instructor eventually led to the writing of Jack's biography and her achievement of black belt status.

Jack had been scheduled to play in the First Annual Cracker Jack Old-Timers Baseball Classic at RFK Stadium July 19, and that night a moment of silence was observed in his remembrance, the first of several public tributes. Fork Union Military Academy held in its chapel a memorial service attended by the local community, and in October Ron Fimrite wrote an article about Jack in *California Monthly.*

On August 12 Jackie was honored in a memorial service at Clint Evans Diamond. It was a gorgeous day, with just enough wind to make the flags stand out from their poles. As Garff Wilson later related, behind the participants in the service, who sat in chairs on the grass, were floral tributes and pennants from Cal, the Yankees, and the Red Sox. In the bleachers were Jack's aunt Lillian and her husband Frank, his brothers and their families, and other friends solemnly awaiting the ceremony. After a men's choral group sang a medley, Ralph Kerchum, Dick Larner, Frank Brunk, and Ron Fimrite paid tribute to Jack with eulogies. Professor Wilson, who thirty-five years earlier had heard Jack reciting for him in speech class, read A.E. Housman's poem "To An Athlete Dying Young," which had been a favorite of Jack's; and the service ended with the playing of Cal's school song, "Hail to California."

On the twenty-eighth of that month, a pregame tribute to Jack aired on Boston television, where he himself was quoted, as were players who reminisced about Jack:

Phil Rizzuto:

> I had heard of Jensen's football fame. I remember the first time I saw him he had blond, curly hair; he wore a sweater with an open sports shirt. He and Billy Martin were exact opposites: He was sort of the Golden Boy and Billy Martin was like a kid from the wrong side of the tracks—a little scrapper, where Jensen had all the athletic ability. Then he went to Washington; then I became close to Jackie when I was broadcasting the Red Sox and he came up here.

Gene Mauch (Californian manager):

> Jackie Jensen was my roommate with the Red Sox at the end of the 1956 season and all through the 1957 season. When I think of Jackie Jensen I think of a most talented and highly sensitive

man. Most athletes have a toughness about them—especially a
guy that played both football and baseball like Jackie did. Jackie
was the most sensitive, gentle man I ever played with.

Carl Yastrzemski:

It's [Jack's death] just a shock to me because at the Old-Timers
game, when I saw him he was in fantastic shape. Mentally he
was so glad the game was taking place. He was a quiet guy
when I played, and at the Old-Timers' here afterward, he was
very outgoing and talking to people. Baseball will miss him;
Boston will miss him.

Ralph Houk:

I think I remember mostly how he tried so hard. I got to know
him quite well; I roomed with Gene Woodling then and Jackie
and Gene and I were more or less new to the ball club, so we
ran around a lot together and had dinner a lot together and
played tricks on one another. He was just an outstanding guy.

Curt Gowdy (the play-by-play announcer for the Red Sox when
Jack played):

Here's a man that would run right through a wall, physically
unafraid. About two weeks before he died I had a phone call
one day at my home, and it was Jackie on the phone; and he
said, "Curt, I have just been inducted in the Bay Area Hall of
Fame. Is there any chance that you'd go out and give the
speech that would put me into the Bay Area Hall of Fame?"

I said, "Jackie, I'd be honored to."

Although Katharine was unable to attend the events in California
and in Boston that August, she was able to enjoy one in Washington
the next month. Jack's former friend Warren Nelson had under-
written a $3,000 subscription to Ford's Theater in Jack's name, and
Katharine was invited to attend the Ford's Theater Benefit, hosted
by E.G. Marshall, which featured comic juggler Michael Davis,
magician David Copperfield, and singers Liza Minnelli, Lou Rawls,
Larry Gatlin, Loretta Lynn, and Wayne Newton, among others. She
stayed as a guest at the Madison Hotel with a car and driver at her
disposal. Katharine saw the Laxalts and Edwin Meese, who talked

much with her about Jackie before the festivities; and she also met Caspar Weinberger, Tip O'Neill, and President Reagan (with whom she had her picture taken). After the show she enjoyed a splendid reception at the Organization of American States Building before retiring for the evening. The next day, back at the farm, she thought of the glamor she had just experienced, as she landed in the dirt from a fall while greasing her tractor.

Katharine tried to leave her grief behind with a Christmas vacation in Bermuda, and in February 1983 convinced herself she should attend the 4th Annual Bay Area Sports Hall of Fame banquet in San Francisco. The festivities, relayed to the public by Joe Angel of Channel 44, followed a dinner and a film explaining the nature and purpose of the Hall of Fame, which not only honored athletes from the Bay area, but also sought to raise money for athletic equipment for local youths ($40,000 had already been raised for that purpose by that time). Jack had received notice of his selection shortly before he died, the same day that Lou Spadia, president of the Hall of Fame, had received from Jack a letter needed for his enshrinement. During the plane ride to California, Katharine composed the acceptance speech she would make in her husband's place, and the words seemed to flow onto her small notepad, perhaps because of the earlier struggle she had deciding what would be inscribed on Jack's tombstone.

Ollie Matson, football player; Frank Robinson, Baseball Hall of Famer and coach; Ann Curtis Cuneo, Olympic swimming champion; and James Corbett, heavyweight boxing champion—these were the names of others selected for the Bay Area Sports Hall of Fame along with Jackie. The master of ceremonies was John Madden, a native Californian who had played football and baseball in college, was drafted by the Philadelphia Eagles, and became the American Football League's youngest head coach in 1969 at age thirty-three. As a player, coach, and football commentator (also well known for his Miller Beer commercials), he was well suited to lead the inductions. He introduced the man who would present Jack's award: "Presenting the award for Jackie Jensen is a man who has covered more sports events throughout the world than any other broadcaster. If they played it, this guy covered it. The President of the Basketball Hall of Fame and who last year was inducted into the Sports Broadcasting and Writers' Hall of Fame, Curt Gowdy."

Gowdy took his position behind the podium and began by making fun of Madden's weight, saying the toughest thing for the team he had coached to a Super Bowl victory was lifting him to their shoulders after the game. However, he became very serious from that point onward:

> It wasn't all golden for the Golden Boy, though. The man at this table knows what I'm talking about. [Madden had a similar phobia.] He had a fear of flying. A lot of people thought it was funny—even hired a hypnotist to travel with us. And I remember one day in Boston, on a Saturday, he got into a car at our parking lot at Fenway Park. I said, "Where are you going? We're catching a plane."
>
> He said, "I'm driving."
>
> And he drove eleven hundred miles to Detroit and got four hits in a doubleheader the next day without one hour of sleep, but he really had this phobia about flying. And John Madden knows what it's about, and he quit. [Some laughter.] Now that's not funny. This was a very serious thing and is what forced him out of baseball in 1960. And then he came back and the announcer said "He had pride."
>
> He didn't want to play and be a .250 or .260 hitter. And he quit four or five years before his time, just like another man in this audience quit before his time with a spot in his eye, one of the most underrated players in the history of major-league baseball, from your city, Dominic DiMaggio.
>
> But I sincerely believe that if Jackie Jensen chose any sport, he could have been a great athlete in whatever he did. He had a fantastic body, he had power, he had speed, and he had great coordination. And he had a furious pride to him, but on the other hand, he was the most sensitive athlete that I have ever

known. He had a charisma to him and a quiet, shy pride that I really adored. Yes; there was really a shining quality about the Golden Boy, a shining quality as an athlete and as a man. And it's a terrible thing here that just a few days later [after receiving notification of his award] he died, July 14, and could not be here in person tonight at still a very young age of fifty-five, to be inducted into your Bay Area Sports Hall of Fame. And so it's my great honor to present for induction to the Bay Area Sports Hall of Fame, Jackie Jensen, and here to accept his award is Mrs. Katharine Jensen.

Katharine, her brown hair cut short and brushed back, wearing a black dress accented with pearls, made her way from the end of the head table. She had altered and rehearsed her speech several times. Laying her notes on the podium, addressed the audience:

Curt, thank you so much, and I thank Jack's family and friends and well-wishers who are here tonight. Two weeks ago at a forestry conference in Virginia I mentioned my apprehension about tonight and complimented one of the speakers on his ability, and he said to me, "Katharine, no guts—no glory."

And I thought to myself, 'Well, if Jack had the guts to do what he had to do to win this award, then the least I can do is have the guts to accept it for him.' And I wish to God Jack were here tonight. He was looking forward to this so much, and it represented to him having come full circle. Last year when someone approached him about doing a biography, he said, "No, my story isn't over yet."

"Well, now unfortunately his story is over—though what a good story it was. In 1967 I met a wonderful man with whom I was privileged to spend the rest of his life. If those who elected Jack for this honor could have seen him last summer just before he died so suddenly, you would have been doubly sure in the correctness of giving it to him. Through difficult times he came back, a strong, and handsome, kind, and very intelligent man who always tried to help others and who strongly believed that sports at every level was a vehicle to higher achievement. And Jack's favorite song was "A Country Boy Can Survive" by Hank Williams Jr. And that was the theme for his new life and skills, but he always missed the foggy nights of San Francisco, and he was looking forward to flying back here and being with you all tonight. And he had conquered his fear of flying. Jackie Jensen wasn't one in a million—he was one of a kind. And for Jack, thank you all so much.

As Katharine, barely able to hold back the tears, returned to her seat amid the applause, the cameras cut to Joe Angel as he spoke at the San Francisco Airport beside the large plaque displayed with Jack's image in bas-relief: "Jackie Jensen, the Golden Boy, just putting a little more shine into the Bay Area Sports Hall of Fame." Beneath Jack's bust were the words that honored him:

JACK EUGENE JENSEN

"JACKIE"

UNIVERSITY OF CALIFORNIA 1946–48

OAKLAND OAKS 1949

NEW YORK YANKEES 1950–52

WASHINGTON SENATORS 1952–53

BOSTON RED SOX 1954–61

Those bronzed words were followed by a brief account of Jackie's accomplishments, written by Dave Beronio. After the banquet, Katharine and Tinsley met with Jan, Jon, and Jay. Katharine then presented each of Zoe Ann's children with commemorative jewelry that had belonged to Jack.

Katharine rode out the winter until spring demanded planting and tending the trees, which was interrupted by an invitation to join Mark Moseley, Gary Hogeboom, Dexter Manley, and Fulton Walker (professional football players) at the annual sports breakfast at the Shenandoah Apple Blossom Festival, where Jack had been honored and remembered as a special guest himself in 1979. On May 1, 1983, Jack was posthumously received into the Alumni Association of Fork Union Military Academy following a nomination by Bill Blair. In a letter dated January 25, 1983, board of trustees member Charles Snead explained his reasons for nominating Jack Jensen:

> In the few short years that Jackie worked with the academy in our admissions office and with the baseball program, he endeared himself to all of us as a person who strongly believed in the principles and policies of Fork Union Military Academy. He so stated this on many occasions. He was a firm believer in the patriotism, discipline, spiritual life, and academic emphasis which Fork Union stands for. He took a personal interest in the life and progress of each cadet with whom he worked, and he would always have friendly words of encouragement with each boy as he checked on their activities at the academy. No boy was too big or too small for Jack to be concerned with. He made himself interested and available to the smallest Junior School cadet to the biggest postgraduate athlete, and he always had a marked positive influence on these boys. He was a friend to each of us on the faculty and staff. Of course, Jack was one of the finest athletes in the history of college and professional athletics in this century, being recognized on a national level in both baseball and football.

As well, an annual baseball scholarship was established in Jack's name, and later a memorial baseball camp. On July 1, 1983, Boston station WSBX aired the television documentary *Fenway Park — Home of the Red Sox,* which chronicled the history behind "one of America's oldest and smallest ballparks." It featured "never before seen footage" of Jack's final interview. In that interview, Jackie, wearing a dark blue blazer and gold-and-red striped tie, had described his love for the park and its uniqueness [see appendix G].

A week before the news was released to the press on February 10, 1984, Katharine had received a letter saying that Jack had been elected posthumously into the National Football Foundation's College Hall of Fame along with Johnny Bright (Drake halfback, 1949–51), George V. Kerr (Boston College guard 1938–40), and Emil Sitko (Notre Dame fullback, 1946–49). It was not until December 4 that Jack was honored at the Annual Awards dinner at the Waldorf-Astoria, and Katharine received a plaque during halftime of a Cal football game before a packed Memorial Stadium. A month later (on January 24, 1985), Jack was again honored for his football achievements—this time by the National Football Foundation and Hall of Fame at its twenty-fifth anniversary scholar-athlete awards dinner at the San Francisco Hilton. In February Jack's name appeared in the *Los Angeles Times* as a one of the "baseball players who just missed career milestones" with his 199 home runs.

Katharine donated to the University of California at Berkeley's Men's Athletic Hall of Fame a sweater and scrapbook of Jack's, which came to rest alongside the 1947 NCAA Championship baseball trophy Jack had helped Cal earn. On October 17, 1986, Jack and others elected as charter members to the Hall of Fame were honored at a banquet for 450 people held in Berkeley. Eleven months later Nick Peters of the *Oakland Tribune* wrote a three-page synopsis of Jack's life for the *Touchdown Illustrated* brochure printed for the UCLA vs. Fresno State game. The man who had so hurt Jack's feelings ten years before glossed over the former Cal coach's difficulties and the attacks he had made on Jackie, saying simply: "Dissension among his players led to his dismissal. The Golden Boy was gone from Cal for good, but the image of his prowess as an athlete never will be tarnished."

In 1987 a newly constructed press box overlooking Clint Evans Field at the University of California was dedicated to Jackie's memory, and his name and fragments of his story still appear from time to time in magazines, on the Internet, and in reruns of such shows as "Home Run Derby." At Katharine's request, Curt Gowdy, busy preparing new television shows, graciously wrote the foreword for the book that would take a more than a decade to complete, to honor and help perpetuate the memory of Jackie Jensen.

Finally, at the time *The Golden Boy* went to press, the Red Sox announced that Jackie Jensen was voted into the Red Sox Hall of Fame.

APPENDIX A

Actual transcript of Ralph Kerchum's record of Jack stating goals:

R: Ralph Kerchum
J: Jack Jensen

R: March 20, 1942. What's your name?
J: Jack Jensen.

R: How old are you, Jack?
J: Fifteen

R: When were you born?
J: March 9, 1942.

R: 1942! Come on boy, wise up.
J: 1927.

R: What City?
J: San Francisco.

R: Jack, we'll conduct this on more or less a question-and-answer basis tonight. What's your favorite sport?
J: Baseball.

R: What's next favorite?
J: Football.

R: Let's take baseball first. How's it feel to make the varsity in the tenth grade?
J: Feels great.

R: What position do you like best?
J: Aw, pitching and right field.

R: Good combination; stick to it. How 'bout football; what would you like to do in football?
J: Oh, I'd like to play left half.

R: Have you ever given any thought to basketball at all?
J: I have, but, well I just can't play it half as good (as) a lot of other guys.

R: What do you think you'll do in it?
J: Well, I might take it in my senior year.

R: What position are you going to go for?
J: Guard.

R: Atta boy! How did it feel to get into the Key Club, being the only low ten that got in in many, many years?
J: Oh, I don't know; it feels swell.

R: Do you really enjoy it?

J: Sure.

R: What does the nickname "Varsity Double A" stand for?

J: Varsity, ah, ah, ah.

R: Come on, ah, ah; what is it? Come on, Double A.

J: Oh, um, A in citizenship; A in scholarship.

R: Don't go giving me that stuff; you know it stands for "All-American." You're just trying to be modest. How many blocks before you graduate from senior high, Jack?

J: Seven.

R: Atta boy; make it an all-time record. You know that, too.

J: Yeah, yeah.

R: Just "yeah?"

J: Yeah.

R: Yes, indeed.

J: All right, yes indeed.

R: Okay, boy. (Something said, trailing off.)

J: (Said as an afterthought, it seems.) Will that be a record?

APPENDIX B

Content of Ralph Kerchum's record according to the movie *The Jackie Jensen Story*

R: Ralph Kerchum

J: Jack Jensen

R: You're on.

J: What am I supposed to say?

R. Suppose I make it easy for you; I'll just ask you questions, and all you have to do is answer them, and the only prize you're going to get is that record. What did you tell me you were most interested in? [The rest of the record represented what Jack and Ralph had said just before Ralph set up the recording device. Ralph asked Jack if there was anything he wanted to retract. In the movie Ralph had called Jack to his home to inform him that the former was joining the Navy and that Jack needed to start making his own decisions.]

J: I guess my interests are mostly about sports, but I guess I ought to do something else, too?

R: Like what?

J: You'll think I'm crazy.

R: No, I won't; come on, come on, like what?

J. Well, I expect to make seven letters in sports before finishing here at Oakland High.

R: After that?

J: After that I'm going to the University of California.

R: Well, that's what I had hoped. What are you going to major in?

J: I'm not sure—maybe physical education or boys work, kind of like you. I'm going to play varsity football, and I'm pretty sure I'm going to make All-American.

R: So am I. After that?

J: After that I'm going to play professional baseball, in the major leagues.

R: But you'll finish college first.

J: Oh, yeah, coach. I've got to do that because, well, if I ever get the chance I want to do for other kids, well, what you've done for me; and I've got to be prepared. [At the end of the film Jackie himself appeared with a child named "Timmy," from Boston, who was going to live with the Jensens for a while—probably a reference to Bert Padell when he was a bat boy for the Yankees.]

Copyright 1956, Four Stars Films, Inc. Ralph Kerchum: Ross Eliot; Jackie age 13: B. Norman; Jackie age 16: Gary Gray; Mrs. Jensen: Vivi Janiss, The View from Right Field.

APPENDIX C

The Home Run Derby

In an on-line article in the Internet site SABR (February 2000) entitled Home Run Derby: Looking Back at a Television Sports Legend, David Gough explained how the "short-lived but long-remembered television program Home Run Derby" began in 1960 as an idea of veteran sportscaster Mark Scott. The idea was that the winner of each week's "Home Run Derby" would return the following week to meet another challenger in Wrigley Field, which had been dormant for two seasons.

Nineteen sluggers from fifteen of the sixteen major league clubs agreed to participate (all but the American League champion Chicago White Sox, which had hit fewer home runs than any other team in baseball in 1959: just 97).

The player with the most home runs after nine innings was the winner, and received $2,000. The loser received $1,000. A player who hit three home runs in a row received a bonus of $500, plus another $500 if he hit four in a row. Any consecutive home run beyond that total was worth a bonus of $1,000. This accounted for the following win–lose, average number of home runs, and earnings): Hank Aaron 6–1 34 (4.9) $13,500; Mickey Mantle 4–1 44 (8.8) $10,000; Jackie Jensen 2–2 29 (7.3) $8,500.

Mantle...defeated Ernie Banks, 5–3, and Jackie Jensen, 9–2. The rain intensified in the next contest with Jackie Jensen challenging Banks in what was at times a heavy downpour. But not even the elements could dampen what turned out to be the highest scoring and perhaps the show's most thrilling catchup. Jensen returned to the program with a vengeance, belting fourteen home runs, a new record. A total of twenty-five homers, also a new standard, flew out of Wrigley Field. For the second game in a row Banks hit eleven balls over the wall, but on this day they weren't enough.

In a match that bore a resemblance to the previous one only in that it was played in the rain, Jensen defeated Rocky Colavito, 3–2. Jensen's second visit to Home Run Derby was much more successful than his first. Rather than moving on to spring training, however, the former University of California All-American running back voluntarily retired from the game to take care of personal and family problems before returning for one final year in 1961. A career-long fear of flying would have no doubt kept him out of "Home Run Derby" had he not already had roots planted in California.

In the final catchup of the series, Mickey Mantle returned to reclaim the title in an exciting 13–10 win over Jensen. Both sluggers clubbed mammoth home runs, including one of Mantle's which appeared to hit a bird on the roof of a house behind the left center-field wall. It was the type of contest Scott had in mind when he came up with the idea for the program, and his excitement was manifest. Jensen hit five homers in a row (six total) in the fourth inning, picking up a $2,000 bonus and setting a standard no one had come close to. Jensen displayed a huge smile following the inning, causing Mantle to quip, "I don't blame him for smiling. I'd be rolling on the ground laughing up there if I did it!" Then it was his turn. "The Mick," who genuinely seemed to be having fun, answered with four home-run blasts of his own (including three in a row) in the top of the sixth, prompting Scott to exclaim, "I hope we have plenty of baseballs today!" Filled with highlights and sound bites, this program was a fitting conclusion to the program's initial season.

Thanks to its recent revival via cable and satellite, Home Run Derby is more popular today than it was when it originally aired.

APPENDIX D

Chapter written by Jackie Jensen for *There Was Light—Autobiography of a University, Berkeley: 1868–1968*
Edited and with an introduction by Irving Stone, Doubleday and Company, Inc. (Garden City, 1970)

[The following is from the original manuscript with minor corrections.]

My life, unlike that of the many contributors to this book, has been and will probably remain influenced by the world of athletics. If I were to describe myself in capsule form, I would have to say, "I am Jackie Jensen, athlete."

In 1946, I looked upon the Berkeley campus as such a marvelous institution. Its huge gymnasium, the baseball field, the track stadium and Memorial Stadium awed me. The sports complex of the University of California was the important part to me. It took a full year of convincing by professors, assistants and section leaders that I would have to discipline myself to study if I were to succeed in athletics. If I were to live those days again, I would willingly pay 10 times over for what I experienced during the years from 1946 to 1950. But I'm straying ahead of myself.

The Depression years weren't easy for parents, but for youngsters, the playgrounds were active, from morning 'till night. As children, we never owned our own equipment—who did?-but the playground supervision and our attitude made up for the many luxuries our present youngsters seem to disdain. Competition was fierce between the many playgrounds around Oakland, my hometown, since each made up a different neighborhood and class of living. It seems strange now, but I can remember the intense drive I had to beat Crocker Highlands, or Piedmont-playgrounds in the higher-class communities. Even the games of baseball or basketball against Roosevelt, Belle-Vista or McClymonds, lower rent societies, were battles-and all at the ripe ages of 10 or 12 years. Was this when my competitive drives were formed, nurtured and matured for my life ahead? I couldn't really say, but many coaches argue endlessly about that very thing. When and how do outstanding athletes acquire competitiveness; or are they born with it? For me, I would guess that my two wonderful older brothers get the credit. I had to be better than they, especially in sports (of all kinds), and they made it possible by bringing in the extra money to help my mother support 3 sons during some very trying years. Today, Robert, the middle son, is a highly accomplished and noted artist in the Bay Area, and William, the eldest, a successful businessman in Fresno.

Two men pointed the way for me. One, a dedicated person, gave his energies and devotion to many young people just like me who were confused as to their futures and looking for someone to turn to. Ralph Kerchum, now a principal in the Oakland School System, is still inspiring and helping in his way to point young people in the right direction. Ralph was more than a substitute father for me-he was someone to respect and confide in. And strangely enough, when I was 15, he made a recording of all the things I wanted to achieve, and achieve them I did. I wanted to earn a letter in baseball and football all 3 years at Oakland High School; then I wanted to be an All-American football player at the University of California-then play Major League baseball. A pretty tall order for a 15-year-old, but isn't it strange how fate can put a person in the right place at the right time! Those dreams came true, and more. Not that my own efforts weren't instrumental in what success I accomplished. Hours and hours each day were spent perfecting all the aspects of the athletic abilities I needed.

I suppose for any young man with a possible baseball future, impatience can easily set in. I wanted to sign a contract with the Oakland Oaks; but their owner, a most wonderful sportsman named Brick Laws, refused until I had given school a real chance. Between high school and the University of California there was a stint in the Navy, which helped me in a small measure to mature.

The University of California is quite impressive to a freshman, at least it was to me. The beauty of the huge eucalyptus trees, Sather Gate, Wheeler Hall and the other buildings seemed to loom as an unconquerable menace to my athletic career. But the warmth of its faculty reached me that first year when I needed it most. School had never been hard for me, just the idea that I had to apply myself. And the difficulty was that if I devoted most of the time to study, then my sports would suffer. The University nearly won, but baseball gave it too good a fight. Even to this day, I couldn't say how I should have decided to spend the few months that marked the end of study and beginning of my career. Because, even though I spent 4 and a half years at Cal with better than average grades, a switch in majors prevented my receiving a degree. But the memories of those years are filled with events that still hold a special place in my life. Not spectacular events, just University life, as it should be: the late snacks with friends after hours of tough study, the excitement of Big Game week, the proms and double dates, the bull sessions at "Blakes"—and finals!! These were important years and at the same time a sense of carefree life before the challenge of the "Big World." These were years that were peaceful. Everyone had had enough of war and thought it would be the last. No one wanted to fight anything, let alone the "establishment." I mention my feelings about the turmoil that has engulfed California only because it tends to destroy many of the wonderful images that have remained with me for over 20 years-images that I would wish for every freshman entering the University.

I believe that a turning point during my 4 years at California came when I changed majors from physical education to speech. I knew athletics, but the idea of clearly communicating my feelings and knowledge to others became important to me. Speech courses saved me from being a quasi-inarticulate athlete. Through a close and considerate friend, Professor Garff Wilson, I had the thrill of meeting the late Poet Laureate Robert Frost. I couldn't have been more impressed if it had been Babe Ruth! My friendship with the poet continued in later years when I played for the Boston Red Sox. I was never more proud than when he sat in the stands at Fenway Park and rooted avidly for J.J. This friendship opened a way for me that might never have existed; a way to worlds of pleasure apart from sports. Today I'm still an athlete, but interested in politics, conservation, art, wildlife, and history-understanding and respecting the value of education. It's so rewarding to realize how flexible anyone can be if he is receptive to a little encouragement by someone or something. That someone or something in my life was the University of California.

Baseball is a profession in every sense of the word. It is probably as competitive a field as anyone could enter. There is always that young fellow on the bench itching for the moment you relax or slip so that he can take your place. And once he does, [your] ball playing days are numbered. The greatest factor in an active sports career is longevity. When most professional men reach the age when they can begin to reap the harvest of their efforts, the professional ballplayer must make a great transition to a new field of endeavor. A small number stay to coach or manage, but the majority must fall back on their education. Possibly for a few, investments will create a business life to which they can devote their energies.

Others must take up careers completely alien to their backgrounds. My playing days were filled with moments of disappointments and happiness, [as with] any profession. The honors were numerous and rewarding, and I'm quite proud of them. To be judged the best of all your colleagues is the pinnacle of success. In 1958, I was awarded that honor when I won the Most Valuable Player Award while with Boston of the American League. That same year, I was selected as one of the top 10 young men in the State of California for its Junior Chamber of Commerce award. An unusual honor? I would say so, for I was the first professional athlete to ever be included among such other recipients as mayors, lawyers, scientists, explorers, etc. Would I have been considered if I hadn't attended a University? I sincerely doubt it. But, like anyone, I had my share of disappointments. The day in 1952 when Casey Stengel told me I had been traded from the fabulous Yankees to the lowly Washington ball club was perhaps the biggest disappointment I can remember. But the day finally came, 1 year later, that Casey remarked for publication—"The Jensen trade was the worst the New York Yankees ever made." I wish all of life's let-downs could be made good in this fashion. And could a schoolboy baseball player ever imagine in his wildest dreams that one day he would play in the same outfield with his two biggest heroes—Joe DiMaggio and Ted Williams?

So much for the past. Strange as it seems, I've achieved another goal that I recorded when I was 15; a coaching profession and trying to help youngsters in the world of athletics. Trophies and money are empty rewards compared to the satisfaction of contributing to others. Now isn't that an unusual statement from a man who knew success marked by awards—that fame and rewards go together in sports. And I wanted that Most Valuable Player Award so much that I nearly lost it trying too hard.

But changes do occur, either by design or fate, as we advance in years; and these changes must be significant for our own peace of mind. My education and experiences at California built a warehouse in my mind, so that I may choose at my discretion the knowledge I need at a given time. I haven't yet used many of the tools available in that warehouse. But the inventory is there and I feel I'm just starting to reap the rewards.

In our society, there are "givers" and "takers." The University of California gave what it could to me. Now I have my chance to give in return.

APPENDIX E

Eulogy by Cal Baseball Teammate Dick Larner, August 12, 1982

It's with mixed emotion that I stand before you today representing our 1947 National Championship baseball team. While we are all shocked at Jackie's untimely passing, I feel that it is only proper that we pay tribute here today, on this field, where Jackie made so many significant contributions to the success of our university's baseball program.

When Dick Erickson called to invite me to today's function, I sat back reflecting on our days together representing the University of California. I'm sure that each of us who played for Cal on that great team, if called on to discuss our relationship with Jackie, would remember different significant events as each of us saw them during that exciting period in our lives. As most of those who have followed California baseball over the years know, Jackie Jensen played a most important part in leading our team to the national championship. These few games and events stand out in my memory:

1) A must win game with USC played right here on this field. We were behind, 5–0, in the late innings. Jensen came to bat with two men on. Immediately the USC left fielder backed up at least seven to ten steps. Jackie hit the first pitch on a line drive over the left fielder's head that hit the left-field wall on two bounces. We went on to win that particular game.

2) While playing against USC in Los Angeles, Jackie had been heckled throughout the game by a rather loud and boisterous student. Jackie maintained his composure until around the seventh inning. At that time he entered the stands on the gallop-his blond hair flying-looking for the "heckler." Needless to say, the "fan" was halfway to downtown Los Angeles in a few seconds.

3) Or the time Jack and I approached Clint Evans about building up the mound for the upcoming UCLA game. Clint said, "If you two want the mound raised, do it yourselves." You guessed it! Clint came down and almost fainted-we had rakes, hoes, a wheelbarrow, etc.—in fact—we had "redone" the pitcher's mound.

4) We tied USC for the CISA Championship and had to break the tie in a one-game sudden-death playoff. Jack pitched the game with two days' rest and we won 6–3. Bob Peterson, our trainer, rubbed down Jack's arm between innings for almost the entire game. A "gutty" performance!

5) Playing against Yale in the first College World Series game, score tied again in late innings, bases loaded, Jackie sent in to pinch hit-clears the bases, enabling Cal to continue to an 11-run inning. Winning the game 17–4.

There are many more highlights of that season but these five stand out in my memory.

What about Jack, the man-his innermost thoughts, goals and desires? In Jack's freshman year he told me one day that he was going to be an All-American football player. I reminded him only eleven offensive players achieve that lofty goal throughout the whole United States. Jack replied, "Nevertheless, I'll be an All-American." Needless to say, we all know that he not only became an All-American in football but also in baseball.

Later in his collegiate career Jack confided that his athletic dream was twofold. One, to have a successful career in the major leagues and two, after his career was completed to return to the University of California as head baseball coach. As we all know, Jack also achieved those dreams.

I could stand here for the next two hours and tell you stories about Jack the man, the athlete, the human being, the friend; but time doesn't permit. Let me conclude by saying that all of his teammates respected and admired this gifted athlete. I know that I'm speaking for the entire ball club when I say that the university-and all of his many, many friends who have grown to know and love Jack throughout his life-will sorely miss him.

Thank you for including me in this special memorial tribute to Jackie.

APPENDIX F

Eulogy by Cal Football Teammate Frank Brunk

Very few of us on the Rose Bowl teams of '48, '49 or '50 became professional football players. Most of us came back from World War II to complete our education, which in some cases had begun before the War or during the War. Since then most of us have become business executives, doctors, lawyers, educators, coaches, etc. We played football at Cal because it was fun-the fact that we became very good teams was partly due to the chance gathering of some very good athletes and probably mostly due to the fact that we were lucky to have an outstanding staff of coaches like Pappy Waldorf, Bob Tessier, Wes Fry, and Eggs Manske to bring out the talent. So, it was a great thrill for all of us to play alongside a real honest-to-goodness football star-Jack Jensen. He was a classmate, teammate, fraternity brother and friend of mine.

It is my opinion, and I believe it is shared by most people, that Jack Jensen was the greatest athlete to ever play at Cal. His competitiveness, physical coordination, and physical dexterity were unmatched by anyone I ever knew. He could do anything he wanted to because he was such a natural athlete. He could beat the socks off everyone at the fraternity house in ping-pong, he could shoot baskets from almost anywhere on the court, he learned golf, shot in the 100s then one day shot in the 80s, totally skipping the 90s (those of you who play golf can understand the magnitude of that accomplishment).

Jack's football achievements at Cal are many but I will mention only three: second in Cal history in single-season rushing. Tied for first in single-season interceptions with seven. Elected Most Valuable Player by his teammates in 1948.

Those records were accomplished as a freshman through his junior year having given up his senior year to play professional baseball. I am reminded of two plays that demonstrate his fantastic ability and also his unselfish attitude and team play that made him the consummate football player. Against Stanford in 1948, Jack was lined up in punt formation, fourth and 30 yards to go, the ball was snapped, and as Jack was about to kick the ball he saw that someone had broken through the line and was going to block the kick. Literally, in the midst of kicking the ball he stopped, sidestepped the Stanford man, and proceeded to snake his way up the middle, mostly on his own, in one of the most unbelievable runs I've ever seen—31 yards and a first down, a classic run. Cal went on to score and won the game 7–6.

In another game, Jack Swaner was carrying the ball over left tackle with Jensen leading the play. Jensen got through the hole and looked for the linebacker, found him, put his shoulder into him, picked him off the ground and with his own legs still driving deposited the linebacker unceremoniously on the ground, some 5 or 6 yards from the point of impact. I don't recall if Swaner scored on the play but he certainly got a classic block from Jack Jensen.

Further testimony for the greatest athlete are these items: All-American in Football, All-American in baseball, played in the 1946 East-West Game as a freshman, played in the 1949 Rose Bowl game against Northwestern, scored on a 67-yard run, played on the NCAA Baseball Championship team in 1947, played in a World Series game with the New York Yankees, played in an All-Star Baseball Game, American League MVP in 1958

No one in history has ever done all these things.

Jack did not seek the spotlight, especially in his college days. He was reticent about making personal appearances. Basically he was a private person, comfortable with his friends and teammates, allowing his sports to make his statements for him. Some thought he was aloof but that was because they didn't know him. Those who did know him and became his friends stayed friends for life.

Jack worked very hard for perfection. He always reviewed his performances and tried to imagine how he could improve on them. One day after he signed with the Oakland Oaks to play professional baseball, he called me and asked if I would pitch batting practice for him at the Oaks ball park. It was an off day and no one else was there. Jack hauled out two huge bags of balls and we dragged them to the mound. Well I pitched and he hit—hitting the wall—over the wall—whatever was wrong wasn't apparent to me—he pounded my best stuff. If I had ever thought of professional baseball in my life, it was beaten out of me that day.

Jack married Katharine and this single event probably was a major turning point in his life. What a beautiful person, and Jack revered her. She brought out a latent talent in Jack that few people know about. Katharine encouraged him to do some painting and to everyone's surprise, including Jack's, but not Katharine's, he was quite good. They loved the Nevada desert and often went arrowhead hunting, accumulating an excellent collection. Jack enjoyed writing letters and it really showed because he wrote beautifully and expressed himself so well.

Jack finally found peace and serenity and purpose of life on a farm in Virginia with Katharine. It was very much deserved after his years of turmoil, of ups and downs.

I remain unabashed in my admiration of the athlete and my love for the man.

APPENDIX G

WSBX Interview with Jackie Jensen. Aired July 1, 1983

Playing left field here is also unique, and there are fans who can lean right over and give you their venom at a very close range; and there were days that if we didn't have a full house, those sections out there—the two sections closest to the wall would be cleared, and Mr. Yawkey would not allow those seats to be sold upon a request by Ted. [Laughing.] I think only one player in history has been able to do that. There isn't a more manicured ball park in the league to play in. It's a pleasure to play here; it really is. You can dive for the ball and know that you're not going to get hurt because it's too hard; you're not going to break a collarbone or something. Even if the grass around the batting circle or anything started to show a little wear, we'd go on a two-week road trip and by that time they'd had it taken out and new sod put in, and it would be like brand-new grass again. So it always was beautiful. I'm sure that the fans of Fenway, when they look down on this nice green grass, appreciate that, too.

I was talking to Tom Yawkey when Tom was alive a long time ago about Fenway Park and its unique size and shape. There was a lot of talk then: Why don't they make another ball park outside the city limits or something where there was more room? And he said he loved this old place. He said this is the only ball park that was a part of him as far as he was concerned, and that everything that he wanted to do was here and to keep it right in the middle of the city it retains a certain charm, as I mentioned before, and Tom was kind of a voice in the wilderness at the time.

There are a lot of times that we got doubles off this wall that would have been easy outs in other ball parks. There's no doubt about it: It's hard to pitch here. A pitcher makes a mistake on a good right-handed hitter and he's either going to hear something from something tinny [the tin-and-steel left-field wall] or else he's going to hear a big roar from the ball park.

The roof is so low that when the sun starts to get down at that angle in the spring, this time of year, and also in the fall, then the infield is in the shadow and the outfield is in the sun; and you actually can't see the ball going from the pitcher to home plate, so you don't know where the ball is hit.

APPENDIX H

Jensen as University of California Football Statistical Leader

Rushing

YR	ATT	YDS	AVE	TD
1946	51	189	3.7	2
1948	148	1080	7.3	7

Punting

YR	NO	YDS	AVE	TD
1946	9	142	15.8	1

Kickoff Returns

1948	7	158	22.6	0

Interceptions

1947	7	114	16.3	0

Total Offense

YR	PLAYS	RUSHING	PASSING	TOTAL
1946	71	189	105	294
1947	108	434	271	705
1948	176	1080	150	1230

Career Rushing

YR	TCB	YG	YL	NYG	AVE
1946–48	285	1906	203	1703	6.0

Single Season

YR	TCB	YG	YL	NYG	AVE	TD
1948	148	1183	103	1080	7.3	7

Single Game

DATE	YDS	TCB	
9/18/48	192	(12)	vs. Santa Clara

Interceptions–Single Season

DATE	NO	YDS	AVE	TD
1947	7	114	16.3	0

All-Purpose Running

DATE	RUSH	REC	RET	TOTAL
1946–1948	1703	120	601	2424

Cal 100-Yard Rushing Performance

DATE	TCB	TDS	CL	OPPONENT
11/02/46	5	109	Fr.	Washington State
09/18/48	12	192	Jr.	Santa Clara
09/25/48	13	112	Jr.	Navy

10/30/48	27	132	Jr.	Southern Cal
11/13/48	18	122	Jr.	Washington State
11/20/48	19	170	Jr.	Stanford

All-Time Longest Plays
Pass Plays: 80 yards to Paul Keckley vs. Stanford, 11/22/47, for touchdown.
Punts: 67 yards vs. Stanford, 11/20/48.

Cal Football Records When Jackie Jensen Played

	OVERALL			CONFERENCE			FINISH	
Year	W–L–T	PF	PA	W–L–T	PF	PA		Conference
1946	2–7–0	112	169	1–6–0	85	128		9 PCC
1947	9–1–0	275	111	5–1–0	135	84		2 tPCC
1948	10–1–0	291	100	6–0–0	155	40		1 tPCC, 4AP

(When Cal defeated Navy 14–7, an attendance record was set with 83,000.)

APPENDIX I

College Football Awards

- All-American in 7 of 9 major polls plus the most-important All-American Board of Football (leading the other three fullbacks in votes)
- Roos Brothers trophy to the top Cal player with the best average of three kicks (59.2 average with the longest punt 67 yards)
- Bear Backers' trophy for being rated the squads "most outstanding player"
- First Team of the Associated Press' All-Coast Eleven;
- Post-Enquirer Oscar (upsetting a precedent of not awarding more than one a year to the same player-after a game where he added 170 yards to end up with 1,010 for the year)
- Andy Smith Memorial Trophy for the Cal gridder with the most playing time (despite his several injuries)
- Wiley Smith traveling bag by the Examiner's sports cartoonist for the outstanding Bay Area college football performer.
- First Team All-PCC
- Trophy for being the outstanding member of Cal's Rose Bowl team by his teammates (and honored by three hundred people by the Berkeley Breakfast Club at the Shattuck Hotel)
- Northern California's Athlete of the Year.

APPENDIX J

Jensen's Records in Major-League Baseball

YR	TM	G	AB	R	H	2B	3B	HR	RBI	BB	SO	SB	BA
50	NY	45	70	13	12	2	2	1	5	7	8	4	.171
51		56	168	30	50	8	1	8	25	18	18	8	.298
52*	WA	151	589	83	165	30	6	10	82	67	44	18	.280
53		147	552	87	147	32	8	10	84	73	51	18	.280
54	BO	152	580	92	160	25	7	25	117	79	52	22	.276
55		152	574	95	158	27	6	26	116	89	63	16	.315
56		151	578	80	182	23	11	20	97	89	43	11	.275
57		145	544	82	153	29	2	23	103	75	66	8	.281
58		154	548	83	157	31	0	35	122	99	65	9	.286
59		148	535	101	148	31	0	28	112	88	67	20	.277
61		137	498	64	131	21	2	13	66	66	69	9	.279
Totals		1438	5236	810	1463	259	45	199	929	750	546	143	.279

*7 games New York .105; 144 games Washington .286.

APPENDIX K

Trophies, Awards, and Honors
- 1958 American League Most Valuable Player
- 1959 Gold Glove Award for right field, AL (with Hank Aaron, National League)
- Top 100 RBI-per-game lifetime leaders (.65)
- Ted Williams Trophy for Most Valuable Team Player
- Rahnes Award for Outstanding Accomplishments in the field of Athletics
- Berkeley Bear Backers Perpetual Football Trophy awarded to MVP
- 1948 selected by his teammates, All-American Fullback, University of California
- Outstanding Collegiate Back-1948 Touchdown Club of San Francisco
- Andy Smith Memorial Trophy
- L.A. Times Award of Merit
- L.A. National Sports Award
- All-Star Game-Shibe Park, Philadelphia
- Keys to Sacto; Reno; and Somerville, Massachusetts
- Consultant to the President's Council on Physical Fitness and Sports (Reagan administration)

APPENDIX L

Jensen as American League Statistical Leader

YR	RANKING	CATEGORY	NUMBER/PERCENTAGE
1952	first	stolen base average	75
	third	stolen bases	18
1953	first	stolen base average	69
	third	stolen bases	18
1954	first	stolen bases	22
	third	runs batted in	117
	third	stolen base average	75
	fourth	runs produced	84
	fourth	home runs	25
1956	third	total bases	28
	fourth	triples	11
	fifth	hits	182
1957	third	runs batted in	103
1958	first	runs batted in	122
	second	runs produced	170
	second	bases on balls	9
	fourth	total bases	29
	fourth	total average	.980
	fifth	home runs	35
	fifth	on base percentage	.298
1959	first	runs batted in	112
	first	runs produced	185
	third	stolen bases	20
	third	stolen base average	80
	fourth	runs	101
	fifth	total average	.888

ABOUT THE AUTHOR

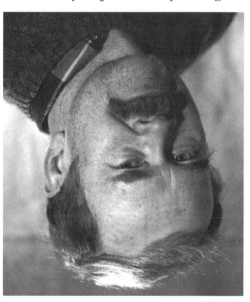

George Martin developed his passion for writing as the result of a fellowship to the Central Virginia Writing Project. He had been an English teacher at Saranac Junior High School in New York, and an English/public speaking instructor and debate coach at Fork Union Military Academy in Virginia. He left teaching to obtain a doctorate in English education from the University of Virginia.

George became a free-lance reporter and columnist for a local newspaper, and had articles accepted for publication by *Cosmopolitan*, *Tae Kwon Do Times*, and *Virginia Writing*. He has taught courses at various colleges and universities and has been published in several educational journals. He has enjoyed writing poetry, vignettes of his life as a young man in the Adirondacks, and, of course *The Golden Boy*, which has taken thirteen years to research, write, edit, and produce.

George got the idea to write Jackie Jensen's biography from his many conversations with Katharine Jensen after the martial arts classes in which Katharine was his student. Initially discouraged when he learned a book had been written about Jack in 1960, George soon realized a lot more needed to be said about Jackie Jensen. The result is this biography.